Essay Index

P9-DTI-844

WITHDRAWN

JUN 27 2024

DAVID O. McKAY LIBRARY

DATE DUE

MAR 20 1997

DEMCO, INC. 38-2931

*Contemporary Movements
in European Literature*

Contemporary Movements in European Literature

Edited by

William Rose, M.A., Ph.D.

and

J. Isaacs, M.A.

Essay Index Reprint Series

Essay Index

BOOKS FOR LIBRARIES PRESS, INC.

FREEPORT, NEW YORK

First published 1929
Reprinted 1968

LIBRARY OF CONGRESS CATALOG NUMBER:

68-16972

PRINTED IN THE UNITED STATES OF AMERICA

The essays contained in the present volume were recently delivered as lectures in the University of London, King's College. They have been revised and, in some cases, rewritten for their issue in book form.

CONTENTS

vii

CONTENTS

PREFACE

This book is the outcome of a series of lectures delivered at King's College, London, during the Lent term of 1927. The lecturers were not asked to conform to any particular viewpoint, and the divergence of their attitudes is the best proof we have of the complexity of the problem to whose description rather than solution this volume is intended to contribute. Almost every attitude with which contemporary literature can be approached is here represented: the descriptive, the analytic, the idealistic, the condescending, the fighting, and the dispassionate.

It would be unwise, even if it were possible, to attempt a synthesis on the basis of the materials here presented, but it may not be out of place to mention some of the problems suggested by the juxtaposition of these varied national and critical positions. There is, first, the problem of a division of the European countries into those basically affected and unaffected by the War, and those in which revolution introduced a further complication. There is the problem of "European Literature" as a concept to be detached from the national records, in which task a clear distinction must be preserved between literary communication and literary unity. There is the problem of the focus of literary activity, of literary capitals, of countries that would appear to be seminal. On this point it would be well not to confuse the eddy of fashion with

ix

the stream of progress. All these are at present doubtfully answerable questions.

Certain things, however, seem to stand out beyond dispute. There has been an important cleavage between generations which explains, though not justifies, misunderstandings reflected in the jealousies of critical judgments. It is clear that processes are more prized than results, and patterns more than subject-matter. It is of interest to note that recognisable and quotable personages have almost disappeared from the modern novel. On the positive side little more has been achieved than a shaking up of feeling and expression that shows itself clearest in the exploration and reconstruction of language. Literary faith has wavered between atheism and agnosticism, and is, perhaps, only just coming round to a primitive idolatry in the New Objectivity which at the moment is the end label of the series: realism—symbolism—anti-intellectualism—futurism—formalism—Neue Sachlichkeit. This faith in the virtue of literature must not be confused with movements of the spirit that in certain countries have expressed themselves in some form of Neo-Catholicism. Politically the hopeful sign is that, whereas in most weakly political countries there is a literary Left and a literary Right, in Russia literary theory and practice appear to have cut across such distinctions and included both political aspects in a covering literary activity. It is also clear that the War and the physical revolutions following it should be regarded as the *result* of the successive waves of æsthetic revolution of immediately pre-War years, and not as the *cause* of movements more obvious in the post-War period. In many cases individuals and groups had already experienced in themselves the changes that were afterwards shared in a public, though perhaps not more painful, manner by the belligerent and adjacent nations.

Whether agreement will be found or not with the views and conclusions contained in the following pages, it is hoped, at least, that the bibliographies, with their lists of available English translations, will render the task of judgment easier to those who are unable or disinclined to struggle with the original languages.

CONTEMPORARY MOVEMENTS IN EUROPEAN LITERATURE

ENGLAND

CONTEMPORARY literature is a serious matter; only half-wits and certain kinds of academic folk regard as matter for laughter the efforts of souls and intelligences to adjust their growth to changing and unpropitious circumstances. Unless we accept this fact of seriousness on the part of those who are creating the literature of to-day, if not of to-morrow, we are wasting our time.

There are in all ages two kinds of literature : that which is of value to contemporaries in helping them to understand the problems of their own time, in helping them to live as contemporaries and not as anachronisms, which is of value to writers in showing them problems and offering them new means of description, of feeling, and of analysis; and there is the literature that is to survive, whether in museums of literature, or textbooks, or in the living consciousness of later readers and writers : two types that we may call the *literature of direction* and the *literature of permanence*. It is difficult, as a living person, to escape the demands made upon one's critical attention by questions of technique and experiment, questions of direction as opposed to achievement. It should be the business of the contemporary critic to deal with direction and intention and sensibility, with the life of

B

literature in the making, and leave to posterity the pronouncement of judgments, the assessment of values, the measuring of greatness, the writing of obituaries, and the chiselling of tombstones.

There should be a clear distinction between those writers, undeniably great, who are of no further significance for the progress of letters, and those whose usefulness, temporary or permanent, consists in providing new ways of seeing, new short-circuits of expression, new systems of inclusion and comprehension. Within our own experience we have all assimilated so much and passed on to so many new problems that our old enthusiasms seem a little distant, strange, and even hobbledehoy. It is a question whether the age must experience this in some collective consciousness, or whether there must always be intellectual martyrs in order that the multitude may sleep more securely. In each age there are literary scapegoats in whom the battles are fought that make intellectual security for the next generation. In the past there have been Donne, Byron, Browning, Wilde, and Henry James; in our own time perhaps James Joyce, T. S. Eliot, and D. H. Lawrence. Over against these literary scapegoats must be set in each age the great monuments, the writers of epics of lost causes, such as Milton. It may be that Byron is a partaker of both elements, suspended between the heaven of Milton and the earth of Joyce.

It is necessary, for the purposes of this present argument, to establish the chronological scope of contemporary literature. The age of any individual investigator will materially bias his arithmetic, but agreement will certainly be found in the view that contemporary literature is fixed, not by those who are now merely alive and writing, but by those who are in touch with present-day feeling, with that mysterious entity that for want of understanding we label provisionally the modern consciousness. Since it is a battle of generations, we may declare war by saying that three generations go to a century, and contemporary literature was born amid the changes of spirit of the mid nineties. Until about 1908 its mind was in the keeping of its parents, who themselves were learning and changing. Between 1910 and 1914 were the years of its adolescence and intellectual turmoil. To the men of this generation the War was a coming-of-age gift. During the War they suffered. Some were silent, some were silenced for ever, some learnt from the older men who shared their agonies, some were frightened out of sanity. Some returned with a trembling balance that was sensitive to every social and intellectual discord, some returned with moral strength, some with weakness. Some, like Edmund Blunden, with a terror still in their dreams, but all changed beyond the power of indifference. To describe this change is difficult, for the generation we are discussing is not yet clear of its toils. Of those who are older, some were equipped with strength to resist the disintegration and do not quite understand, others who did not go to the War live in a world of sentiment that obscures their understanding like a benevolent blanket, but there are honourable exceptions, in literature at least, and those are listened to. Those who are younger, too young to have experienced the War, live for the moment in a great bewilderment, having heard rumours of battle and its glories, but understanding little of its tortures. To them this generation is a horrible example, almost without hope, regarding itself as an entity, and having little of its attention to spare for others. This younger group, that will grow soon into a generation, wishes it had not heard of this war experience, and defends itself by denying its validity as a barrier between generations. This is a sentimental and a gloomy picture, but without it the facts we are discussing remain in darkness.

The French novelist, Stendhal, who died in 1842, predicted that he would not be appreciated till 1880. The Victorian era accordingly and conveniently died between 1880 and 1890. In the nineties Oscar Wilde left his valuable impression on the English spirit; to him and his group modern literary England owes the ease with which it can approach problems of art untrammelled by irrelevant social and moral considerations, owes much of its freedom from cant and much of its emancipation from literary insularity and parochialism. In the nineties Walter Pater died and Hardy wrote the last of his sex novels. In the nineties A. E. Housman published his *Shropshire Lad,* whose strong Teutonic ironies have dwindled into the bucolic complacencies of the modern topographical poets. In the nineties Ibsen came into his own, and the *Yellow Book* waved its æsthetic banner, on which were inscribed the names of such notorious decadents as Henry James, Professor Saintsbury, Miss Victoria Cross, Arnold Bennett, H. G. Wells, John Buchan, and the late Sir Walter Raleigh. The funeral hymn of the nineteenth century was written by Thomas Hardy in his *Darkling Thrush.* The explosion that was to shatter the calm of the future was not caused by the Boer War, but a little after its close by the posthumous publication of Samuel Butler's *The Way of All Flesh* in 1903. It is difficult to describe the processes of its influence, but it is not too much to say that the whole body of English fiction until the publication of James Joyce's *Portrait of the Artist as a Young Man* bore its impress. Certain figures came to the front. Kipling, whose work no longer has relevance to the conflicts of our time, will, nevertheless, be remembered with gratitude for his vigour, his naïve and forceful adjustments to the civilization of his time. Henry James, more difficult to read than many a modern stylistic anarchist, took the novel seriously, and is the one man of his time whose fluctuations of sensibility still bear close relation to our own explorations. Bernard Shaw acted Harlequin with a solemnity that would be comic were it not in retrospect pathetic.

Chronology is somewhat difficult when people born as long ago as 1850 or 1860 still claim to be contemporaries. I do not know that I can admit as a contemporary a man who was writing when my grandparents were quite young people. It would be well to make another classification, in terms of the family, whose conflicts and disintegration accompany or perhaps explain the contemporary world. Kipling wrote most of his work before the end of the last century, yet he may be classed in influence with the rest of the "big five"—Wells, Bennett, Galsworthy, and Conrad. These writers stand in the position of parents to the present generation; they have their being between 1900 and 1914. Wells's *Kipps,* 1905, Galsworthy's *Man of Property,* 1906, and Bennett's *Old Wives' Tale,* 1908, are landmarks in the progress of these authors, and mark a definite incursion of the social elements. After them come the elder brothers and sisters, E. M. Forster, James Stephens, May Sinclair, Gilbert

CONTEMPORARY EUROPEAN LITERATURE

Cannan, J. D. Beresford, Frank Swinnerton, Oliver Onions, Francis Brett Young, W. S. Maugham, and D. H. Lawrence, to pick out but a few who are nearer to us in spirit and have merit of diſtinction and sincerity. The present generation includes Virginia Woolf, Norman Douglas, Stella Benson, Aldous Huxley, Osbert Sitwell, Rebecca Weſt, Wyndham Lewis, Dorothy Richardson, Stephen Hudson, James Joyce, and, though now departed, Katherine Mansfield. There are also a few baby brothers and siſters juſt beginning to prattle, including David Garnett, Margaret Kennedy, W. Gerhardi, William Plomer, and Rhys Davies, about whom one can say nothing as yet. A glimpse at the birth certificates within these groups will show that it is purely mental age that is being considered here.

It would seem from this array of writers that the novel were our chief concern. The order of importance in this present generation I take to be the novel, poetry, and criticism. The drama is mainly parasitical at present, though there is little doubt of a revival in the near future, in which case the experiments in the movement of prose, its tug-of-war, and its fluctuations of rhythm will have contributed largely, if only an adequate framework is found. It does not seem possible for drama and fiction to exiſt prominently together. Drama of the period we are discussing is helpful in showing publicly the same transitional forces as the novel, particularly in the age, the firſt decade of this century, when the problems of society, the changing Edwardian conditions, needed some emphasis. In this display, the drama is a tract, Galsworthy's plays are tracts, and tracts are symptoms, not achievements.

6

ENGLAND

More important than cataloguing the authors we are to discuss is the task of fixing the mental background, and there we have the richest of fields, with, nevertheless, the greatest dangers of error. If our perspective is later judged to be wrong, we must plead that we have been led astray by the statements of those who say they have been influenced. First we have the great influence represented by the intellectual revolt of Samuel Butler, the liberator, for us, and earlier for people like Shaw. Butler is the solvent for the ideas of Darwin into literature, in *Erewhon,* and a queer biology, the struggle for freedom and equality, in *The Way of All Flesh*. Science was becoming a master, its prestige was threatening, and we have Wells in his fantasias exploiting with solemn logic the possibilities of invention. This one must call romance; it certainly gripped. With the new century came the gradual acceptance of the ideas of experimental psychology, meaningless for the general public, except in so far as it provided a new medium of exploration into consciousness, and, above all, the constitution of the mind. The main concern of present-day literature is the enlargement of sensibility, and for the novelist any new information about the constitution of the mind, its background and processes, is of vital importance. There is one danger in this exploration, and it is not without interest that it was pointed out by Bacon, at the threshold of modern science, when he prayed that " from the opening up of the pathways of the senses, and a fuller kindling of the natural light, there may not result in men's souls a weakening of faith, and a blindness to the divine mysteries." We may, of course, translate " faith " and " divine mysteries " as we

7

like, and say that by these processes it is definitely " faith " that is strengthened, that instead of parroting glib formulæ, instead of accepting approximations of processes, we are now in a position to realize the wonder and intricacy of the minds we have hitherto diagrammatized. The increase in reality, not merely realism and likeness, is remarkable, as also the increase of life and intensity, when words are used in accordance with the ascertained nature of thought and imagery.

Philosophers have come and gone; it is not often that they have any direct effect on literature in England, whatever may be their form of embalming in France and other countries. But we have a faculty of misapprehension, or perhaps personal selection, that is very valuable to us. With Bergson's philosophy we established so much contact as to inject an impetus into life which may account for the biographical novel, the novel of biographical duration, whether of one or more generations, that was so popular in the years just before the War. A work of this kind, whose influence was enormous, was Romain Rolland's *Jean Christophe,* translated by Gilbert Cannan, a novelist interesting in his time. I am not sure, as with so many, whether we have any further need of him. This question of " having need " raises many more questions. When do we need an author? Is it when he acts as a channel of communication, when he softens the impact of a philosophy, when he tones it down and translates it into terms of narrative and action into which it disappears as into the sand? I do not know how far this has happened with Croce; certainly it has not yet happened with Einstein, but it is happening with Freud.

The problem of Freud's contact with the novel is one

of the moft fascinating and yet moft difficult with which we have to deal. The War ended with a ftate of unreft, of revolt, of final solution of the problem of the family, and with it, as in no previous war, came a tremendous enlargement of our underftanding of the mechanism of emotion, and also of the mechanism of the imagination, for Freud's *Interpretation of Dreams,* translated and printed in three separate impressions in 1913, deals not only with the body, but with the mind. The dream fantasies were shown to have close affinities with certain processes of literary creation, and particularly with poetry. Certain poets seized upon this, notably Robert Graves, and allowed the queftion of the resolution of conflicts to be the centre point of their conscious doctrine for some while. The conclusions that Freud forced upon the world were ruthless. "Surely we are not so bad as all that," was the protective cry. Many read Freud for the firft time while ftill in the trenches; and juft as it is true that nobody who went through the War was quite the same person again, so nobody who has read carefully in Freud can avoid the complexity and ruthlessness it imposes.

Another work fruitful for the imagination is Frazer's *Golden Bough,* a compendium of legend taken from ftores more deeply rooted in the human unconscious than any other form of creative activity. There are quarrels between the scientifts, but no quarrel can remove the influence of myths connected with birth and death, with the eternal rhythm of the seasons, with tribal taboos of relations within the family; and these things have all become grafted on to the modern consciousness, which desires to become more and more aware of its origins, of its resources, of its possibilities. Certainly the poet jumps at this, and poets of the importance of T. S. Eliot, Robert Graves, and Edgell Rickword, and prose writers of the intensity, albeit a wild and ferocious undergraduate intensity, of Wyndham Lewis, have been deeply affected. This does not by any means exhauſt the mental background, for, in addition to the changing consciousness, the changing forms of the mind, the changing intereſts on a general plane that is shared by writer and non-writer, there is the special influence that the writer as writer muſt undergo, even if the reader is not yet ready to follow, and that is the building of ſtorey upon ſtorey in the edifice of verbal sensibility and atmospheric subtlety.

There is a whole chain of sensibility that the writer muſt be aware of. In the earlier hiſtory of the novel there are landmarks represented by Don Quixote for its bold ſtatuary of character; by John Bunyan with his introspection and soul-griping; Defoe with his world of verbalised allusion; Swift with his intellectual persuasion and passionate, white-hot persuasion in reſtrained form; Richardson with his convolutions of sensibility, the father of all European fictional consciousness; Sterne, acrobat and confidence trickſter—all these are in the more or less conscious education of the noveliſt, but in recent years this process of education has been accelerated to speeds that leave the ordinary reader dizzy. The subtlety, reſtraint, and precision that accompany Stendhal's work, the passionate concentration on triviality and irrelevance of Doſtoevsky, the imperceptible loading of the dice in the seeming plain ſtatement of Chekhov, the serpentine associative logic of Prouſt, all have contributed from abroad to the enrichment of the novel; but these things are idle unless they are recreated in the texture of our own language, and therein lies the interest and the value of the stylistic and technical experiment that so disturbs the reader seeking delight at no cost to himself. The experiments in parody in *Ulysses* give us perhaps our best object-lesson of apprenticeship in action.

It would seem as though what I am describing is the special business of a sect of technicians, that this is the grammar of the literature we can all enjoy without its particular study. This is a misapprehension. The style that arises from these· researches is no angular style, this angularity occurs only *en route* for the standard style of the near future. A remarkable example is to be found in Sacheverell Sitwell's prose fantasy, *All Summer in a Day,* written in English of a purity and simplicity, and yet a flexibility that has not, I think, been often surpassed. And this flexibility—nay, its very texture—is the result of daring innovations that the author has tried out in his poems, where, since poetry cannot explain its short-cuts, they have been much frowned upon and laughed at. Texture and sentiment have both advanced in subtlety, but when we seek for origins we must not mind where chronology leads us. Some of the interesting modernity and exquisite adjustment to modern sensibility in certain poems of T. S. Eliot can be paralleled in the work of Jules Laforgue, who died, aged twenty-seven, in 1887.

We have spoken of intellectual background, of the ancestry of sensibility, both on the normal adult plane, and on what we must call the supersensitive plane (sometimes insulted as the "highbrow"). It remains to speak of some of the waves, now of fashion, now of influence, that have swept enthusiasm into a jaded, though not stupid, world. It is important also to see what has happened in other arts. In many ways the reign of Edward VII. was a marking time, a breathing space in which to recover from the incubus of the Victorian stability. The beginning of the new Georgian reign saw many new influences. In 1910 London was startled by an exhibition of post-impressionist painting, when for the first time in England were seen publicly the paintings of Cézanne, Gaugain, Van Gogh, Matisse, Derain, Vlaminck, Rouault, and Picasso. Derision and keen interest were displayed. Many sensible people were upset and merely vomited, many sensitive people were upset and began to inquire into the new conditions, to ask if the new ways of seeing had any value for literature, and one of the most remarkable indications of direction we have in our period is a comment by Arnold Bennett in December, 1910, after seeing some of these paintings:

> " I have permitted myself to suspect that, supposing some writer were to come along and do in words what these men have done in paint, I might conceivably be disgusted with nearly the whole of modern fiction, and I might have to begin again. This awkward experience will in all probability not happen to me, but it might happen to a writer younger than me; at any rate, it is a fine thought."

This is honesty of feeling, and is very rare until years following. The test was to come with the work of James Joyce.

Among the chief of these waves of fashion was the Russian fever that, from about 1912, with Mrs. Garnett's new translation of Dostoevsky (who was, of course, known and translated in the unready eighties), increased in fury until about 1918 it became the predominant factor in the hectic evolution of young intellect. Its hectic quality is shown clearest in Middleton Murry's biography of Dostoevsky and in parts of his *Evolution of an Intellectual*. The very title of that work gives a consciousness to literary development that was by no means unsymptomatic of the War period. Chekhov, too, was an influence, and it was Arnold Bennett who, in 1909, was, if not the first, one of the very earliest to lavish praise on the new writer, and, most important, to realise the value of his technique:

> " We have no writer, and we have never had one, nor has France, who could mould the material of life without distorting it, into such complex forms to such an end of beauty."

There were the subsidiary influences of Gorki and Artsybashev, but Chekhov and Dostoevsky are the chief. It must not be forgotten that Tolstoy and Turgenev had previously been influential, but not quite in the same manner, nor was the ground quite ripe for this particular fertilisation. The ground had been prepared for some time, of course, by forcible Continental stimulants, and the " Henley Gang," a potent force again in the nineties, has been described as the great " Flaubert-Turgenev-Zola-Maupassant-Goncourt group."

There is still an important group of influences—the ferment that really caused the War, the group of " isms " of the years 1909 to 1914. It was in 1909 that Marinetti issued his Futurist Manifesto, with its machine-borrowed doctrine of speed and efficiency, its hatred of museums and monumental cultures, and its insistence on movement. Then came the cubists, following the primitive researches of Cezanne, seeking for content in the absence of representation. Then in poetry the imagists, who, under the guidance of Ezra Pound, a figure to whom the present generation does not show all the gratitude it owes, suggested a similar abstraction from representation : " Let the poet fill his mind with the finest cadences he can discover, preferably in a foreign language, so that the meaning of the words may be less likely to divert his attention from the movement—*e.g.,* Saxon charms, Hebridean folk-songs, the verse of Dante, and the lyrics of Shakespeare—if he can dissociate the vocabulary from the cadence." It is as the result of discipline of this kind that the writings of T. S. Eliot present us with the most controlled rhythms of contemporary poetry.

With all these " isms " we are in the War, and now at last we are in sight of our problem. There is but one last point, and that is the new habit, taken almost certainly from France, of influence by means of periodicals directed by a group and bent on some definite literary programme or some perceptible standard of judgment. Beginning with the *Yellow Book,* we have a series of stepping-stones, not quite complete; there are some big jumps to be taken. The *Savoy,* under the subtle and sensitive direction of Arthur Symons, brought in the symbolists. The *English Review,* under the guidance of Ford Madox Hueffer, helped into notice so distinguished a band as Norman Douglas, D. H. Lawrence, Ezra Pound, T. S. Eliot, John Masefield, H. M. Tomlinson, Robert Frost, and many others of equal prominence but less significance. Then the *New Age,* under A. R. Orage, which made Nietzsche and Stendhal accessible, and dealt equally with the dignity of eighteenth-century prose and the impudence of twentieth-century arts. Then *Rhythm,* in 1911, edited by Middleton Murry and Katherine Mansfield, the first to publish Picasso and the like, to discuss Van Gogh and Gaugain, and to recommend Croce. The *Egoist,* directed partly by Richard Aldington and T. S. Eliot, published *A Portrait of the Artist as a Young Man,* and portions of *Ulysses. Blast,* by Wyndham Lewis, the last shriek before the catastrophe, brought in the vorticist movement, and taught what afterwards was dimly recognised as Expressionism. After the War, in 1919, came the glory period of the *Athenæum,* most brilliantly edited and contributed of all modern journals, and the *Adelphi,* when a new turn appeared in Middleton Murry's mind. Then two papers, in which standards were rigid almost beyond human endurance, and seriousness was in danger of being swamped in solemnity : the short-lived *Calendar of Modern Letters,* by Edgell Rickword, a critic who has not received all the attention he merits, and the *Criterion,* in its various incarnations, directed by T. S. Eliot.

It is important to remember that the young men who went to the War were these very futurists, cubists, imagists, and vorticists, and that they were the only people who knew what they were fighting for. It was not what they were sent to fight for, because the young men on the other side were fighting for the same things, and the tragedy that killed Wilfred Owen the poet, Gaudier Brzeska the sculptor, and Isaac Rosenberg the poet, on our side, was the tragedy that killed Franz Marc the painter and his poetical comrades of the Sturm group. The War in its poetry may not show its agony clearly enough. Words are always under restraint for Englishmen, but paint is a foreign medium, and an English painter often says more than he knows. In the War Museum and in the Tate Gallery, in the angular drawings and paintings of the young Wyndham Lewis, William Roberts, Edward Wadsworth, David Bomberg,

Paul and John Nash, and even Nevinson, we can realise
something of their temper.

It is difficult to sum up the nature of the War shock,
but it is intimately bound up with the idea of the con-
temporaneous in literature. It is, of course, foolish to
attempt to study the literature of the past if we are unaware of the processes that produce literature in the
present, but, unfortunately, even contemporary literature
has been studied in the recent past with the sole view
of passing judgment, of judgment after the Victorian
standards, by results. The War, by short-circuiting the
normal period of digestion in which contemporary literature, after being revolutionary, is suddenly admitted to
the fraternity of the classics, forced attention upon processes: it was necessary to recognise certain modern
writers before they were dead. Literature was forced into
a closer connection with action than ever before. It was
felt, and sentimentally acknowledged, that young men
suffering in France were externalising their feelings in
verse, not merely in political paraphrase, but in shrieks
of more or less disguised agony. One of the most interesting statements we have is from Isaac Rosenberg, a
poet killed in 1918, whose works, edited by Lawrence
Binyon and Gordon Bottomley, have already an influence
on post-War poetry.

> " I am determined that this war, with all its powers for
> devastation, shall not master my poeting; that is, if I am
> lucky enough to come through all right. I will not leave a
> corner of my consciousness covered up, but saturate myself
> with the strange and extraordinary new conditions of this
> life, and it will all refine itself into poetry later on."

And this is how it refined itself in his " Dead Man's
Dump," one of the greatest poems of the War:

ENGLAND

*   *   *   *   *

" The wheels lurched over sprawled dead
But pained them not, though their bones crunched;
Their shut mouths made no moan.
They lie there huddled, friend and foeman,
Man born of man, and born of woman;
And shells go crying over them
From night till night and now.

Earth has waited for them,
All the time of their growth
Fretting for their decay:
Now she has them at last!
In the strength of their strength
Suspended—stopped and held.

What fierce imaginings their dark souls lit?
Earth! Have they gone into you?
Somewhere they must have gone,
And flung on your hard back
Is their souls' sack,
Emptied of God-ancestralled essences.
Who hurled them out? Who hurled?

None saw their spirits' shadow shake the grass,
Or stood aside for the half-used life to pass
Out of those doomed nostrils and the doomed mouth,
When the swift iron burning bee
Drained the .wild honey of their youth.

*   *   *   *   *

Burnt black by strange decay
Their sinister faces lie,
The lid over each eye;
The grass and coloured clay
More motion have than they,
Joined to the great sunk silences.

That is the War, and there is little more one can say
of it except to record the final changes that were made
upon the people who passed through it. And first the
novel. Of the parents of the present novel, Wells and
Bennett are of importance, since they explored the social

background and function, and saturated themselves in the world of feeling they were employing. In Henry James's parting words in 1914: " The new is an appetite for a closer notation, a sharper specification of the signs of life, of consciousness, of the human scene and the human subject in general, than the three or four generations before us had been at all moved to insist on." The justice of this for the period ending in 1914 is not marred by his objection, which is brought against the present-day novelist as well. " These are the circumstances of the interest, but where is the interest itself?" The new novel came into a world which, continuing till the present day, is marked by new desires for synthesis of knowledge, by new understanding of psychological process, of the main-springs of motive and conduct. Mr. Murry has suggested that the key to style, especially in its modern manifestation, is to be found in Stendhal's definition: " The art of adding to a given idea all the details necessary to produce the effect that idea ought to have," and he quotes from Katherine Mansfield, whose ambition was to tell " the plain truth as only a liar can tell it." It is clear from such prose that there is a closer unity between sensibility and expression than hitherto, that things are not so much described as conjured into existence, not so much alluded to as pointed to. There are many different systems of modern prose, in which a hierarchy and a chronology might be established. In Dorothy Richardson's novels we have what Miriam feels, what floats along her stream of consciousness, made external and seen from the outside in the fulness of its detail and variety. In D. H. Lawrence, whose style varies greatly, we share in the life of man, bird, and beast. It is pantheiftic prose, if one may dare such a label. In Virginia Woolf there is already a mellowness which enables us to live at a slower speed than many other novelifts demand. In *Mrs. Dalloway* occurs this moment, exquisitely rendered:

"Millicent Bruton, whose lunch parties were said to be extraordinarily amusing, had not asked her. No vulgar jealousy could separate her from Richard. But she feared time itself, and read on Lady Bruton's face, as if it had been a dial cut in impassive ftone, the dwindling of life; how year by year her share was sliced; how little the margin that remained was capable any longer of ftretching, of absorbing, as in the youthful years, the colours, salts, tones of exiftence, so that she filled the room she entered, and felt often as she ftood hesitating one moment on the threshold of her drawing-room, an exquisite suspense, such as might ftay a diver before plunging while the sea darkens and brightens beneath him, and the waves which threaten to break, but only gently split their surface, roll and conceal and encruft as they juft turn over the weeds with pearl.

She put the pad on the hall table. She began to go slowly upftairs, with her hand on the banifters, as if she had left a party, where now this friend now that had flashed back her face, her voice; had shut the door and gone out and ftood alone, a single figure againft the appalling night, or rather, to be accurate, againft the ftare of this matter-of-fact June morning; soft with the glow of rose petals for some, she knew, and felt it, as she paused by the open ftaircase window which let in blinds flapping, dogs barking, let in, she thought, feeling herself suddenly shrivelled, aged, breaftless, the grinding, blowing, flowering of the day, out of doors, out of the window, out of her body and brain which now failed, since Lady Bruton, whose lunch parties were said to be extraordinarily amusing,. had not asked her."

Alongside of this and chronologically earlier can be placed a page from Joyce's *Ulysses,* one of his cruder pages, chosen to show a process:

"His heart aftir he pushed in the door of the Burton reftaurant. Stink gripped his trembling breath: pungent meatjuice, slop of greens. See the animals feed.

Men, men, men.

Perched on high stools by the bar, hats shoved back, at the tables calling for more bread no charge, swilling, wolfing gobfuls of sloppy food, their eyes bulging, wiping wetted moustaches. A pallid suetfaced young man polished his tumbler knife fork and spoon with his napkin. New set of microbes. A man with an infant's saucestained napkin tucked round him shovelled gurgling soup down his gullet. A man spitting back on his plate: halfmasticated gristle: no teeth to chewchewchew it. Chump chop from the grill. Bolting to get it over. Sad booser's eyes. Bitten off more than he can chew. Am I like that? See ourselves as others see us. Hungry man is an angry man. Working tooth and jaw. Don't! O! A bone! That last pagan King of Ireland Cormac in the schoolpoem choked himself at Sletty southward of the Boyne. Wonder what he was eating. Something galoptious. St. Patrick converted him to Christianity. Couldn't swallow it all however.

*　　*　　*　　*　　*

Couldn't eat a morsel here. Fellow sharpening knife and fork, to eat all before him, old chap picking his tootles. Slight spasm, full, chewing the cud. Before and after. Grace after meals. Look on this picture then on that. Scoffing up stewgravy with sopping sippets of bread. Lick it off the plate, man! Get out of this.

He gazed round the stooled and tabled eaters, tightening the wings of his nose."

This is not the same thing as saying, "The sight of people eating, and the awful smell of the restaurant, nearly turned his stomach," which merely asks for a polite recognition of the feeling, but is the feeling itself recreated so far as one is sensitive to language. H. G. Wells in 1917 reviewed *A Portrait of the Artist as a Young Man* in these terms: "Its claim to be literature is as good as the claim of the last book of *Gulliver's Travels,* and one conversation in the book . . . I write with all due deliberation that Sterne himself could not have done it better." And on the technique: "Most of the talk flickers blindingly with dashes; one has the same wincing feeling of being flicked at that one used to have in the early cinema shows."

We may understand more of the progress of the novel by noticing the changes in fashionable science, for the nineteenth-century biology, for the early twentieth sociology, which places Bennett, Wells, Galsworthy, and Shaw, and for our own time psychology, which, perhaps, places us. These three together affect the scope of fiction. The incursion of biology, and particularly of evolution, gave us the novel of several generations, because only in such a span can heredity and environment be displayed. The earliest form of it was *The Way of All Flesh,* with its special problems. The incursions of sociology gave us the *Forsyte Saga* and the Five Towns stories. Psychology limits the field and at the same time extends it; it tacked itself on to the older form and gave us the typical auto-biography or life history, *Sinister Street,* or *Of Human Bondage,* and its merit varied with the capacity of the author. Gradually biology is taken for granted, sociology makes fewer demands, and psychology holds the field, and then we get, instead of a slice of life, a plummet into consciousness, and with its use there come new obligations, the most rigid of all being imposed by Joyce on himself in *Ulysses.* There we have the progress of one whole day and night. It is possible to arrange the life of an individual, of a group, to arrange and diagrammatise even the lives of two people in relation to each other, but when the events of one day are recorded ruthlessly their bulk becomes almost unwieldy. In his honesty Joyce was compelled to put down the unconscious as well as the conscious, the hidden as well as the open, the private as well as the public, the forbidden as well as the permitted, the ridiculous as well as the sublime, the incoherence as well as the coherence, the medley as well as the pattern, the obscene as well as the decent, and there came the trouble. Oscar Wilde said justly: "The English public, as a mass, takes no interest in a work of art until it is told that the work in question is immoral." *Ulysses* is the greatest example we have of an attempt to embody and thus clear away the débris of a fading epoch; in this it ranks with, but below, the works of Cervantes, Rabelais, Swift, and Byron. It is in the lineage of the great satirists, Aristophanes, Lucian, Petronius, Sterne, and Dickens, and is a great failure. The failure might be said to lie in its ruthless logic, which demands an inexorable despair. The objection brought against its tone is that it is like using the *cloaca maxima* to cleanse the Augean stables.

D. H. Lawrence brings us to the problem of the sex novel, and of that I can say very little. It is interesting to make a short list of some previous sex novels in European literature. Chaucer's *Troilus and Criseyde,* Shakespeare's *Romeo and Juliet,* Richardson's *Pamela,* Charlotte Brontë's *Jane Eyre,* Hawthorne's *Scarlet Letter,* Flaubert's *Madame Bovary,* Stendhal's *Le Rouge et le Noir,* Hardy's *Jude the Obscure.* After this it seems almost unnecessary to say anything. Women have entered into literature with their descriptions of what has been called the totality of love, and with the new light that psychology has shed upon the processes, and, above all, the mutations and disguises of sex, new obligations are imposed upon the honest artist. As soon as he fulfils these obligations he is attacked. D. H. Lawrence is the one novelist in the history of English writing who has treated sex reverently with full knowledge of its nature, and from it has endeavoured to build up the religion it was in primitive life. And to that end he has continued the reckless exploration of men, begun at the Renaissance, has deepened the naïve explorations of Bunyan, Swift, and Defoe, and the riper researches of Richardson, Proust, and Joyce, and by delving into anthropology, by seeking the basis of emotional existence, frightens the world with the promise of understanding that he holds out to them. Lawrence it is who has most intelligibly expounded the problem of morality. Until the decadent nineties, "moral" was a definite term of praise; since then among many intellectuals it has had a derogatory sense, precluding beauty. May there not be a compromise, in our best English manner, to make "moral ' neither abusive nor laudatory, but merely descriptive of a factor in creative work that uses values as anything verbal must use them? Lawrence urges that morality in the novel is that trembling instability of the balance between the writer and his circumambient universe. When the novelist puts his thumb on the scale, to pull down the balance in his own predilection, that is immorality. In accordance with these terms, *If Winter Comes* is the type of an immoral book.

Poetry must be passed over more quickly, not because it is less important, but because, other than by extensive quotation, it is impatient of explanation. Robert Graves says: "Guess the riddle and you shall have the answer given to you; this is the proper course communication should take between poets." But we are not all poets, yet all of us can make of poetry an experience and not merely a recognition. Now, what is wrong with poetry? It is curious how most discussions of contemporary literature begin with this formula. One of the main objections has been concisely put:

> "The poets in recent times follow a peculiar doctrine. They compose poetry out of words, compose poetry out of learning, and compose poetry out of opinion. They are laborious enough, but theirs is no longer the poetry of the ancients, for they are deficient in the music of joys and sighs."

It is interesting to note, however, that this was written by a Chinese critic of the twelfth century of the poetry of his period. There may be hope for us. The Chinese critic points to many things that are certainly true of our time. The poets do compose poetry out of learning, but with a very special need.

The poet now reads up for his poetry, reads in order to have material for his poem, reads in order that he may come upon something that has served mankind before, and, therefore, may serve him, that will place him in the main stream of mythical creation, for in his reading he may come across some image that may concentrate or crystallise a whole system of thought, may give the focus for many a vague groping that hitherto has had no expressed nucleus, some story that may be a folk-story, bound, by roots of which we are yet ignorant, to the inner strings of creative consciousness. For the poet, the sensitive, alive, modest poet, no longer thinks that he is God's rival in the creation of objects and materials, scenes and people that have already their existence in other material, vegetable, mineral, or animal, but, like the modern artist, realises that he has to recreate in a different medium the feeling of totality the object has, and not the object itself. We are helped much, in all of this literary inquiry, by going to the modern expressions of the arts. It is better to have your apples as Cézanne painted them, with personality, with solidity, with weight, with position in space, than those more usual objects that D. H. Lawrence has referred to as *enamelled rissoles*.

The poet also composes out of words, and very often out of other people's words. "Some words are *childish,* some *feminine,* some *manly,* and of these last some are *sylvan,* others *urban;* of those we call urban we feel that some are *combed out* and *glossy,* some *shaggy* and *rumpled.*" This wild modernism is taken from Dante's treatise on poetical technique, but exactly expresses the view of the nature of words held by Edith Sitwell and displayed in her poetry. The search for assistance has led to a rediscovery of poets, who have themselves struggled with verbal and intellectual material. The influence of John Skelton on Robert Graves, and of John Donne on Isaac Rosenberg, T. S. Eliot and Edgell Rickword is of this nature. Poetry so alimented is not for the readers of newspapers.

They make poetry of learning, and here we have the difficult problem of T. S. Eliot, who has shown signs of poetry most in touch with our present conception of poetry, who has solved problems that have hindered our complete adjustment, who has given expression to certain phases of contemporary sensibility that otherwise would have had to remain concealed. His is frequently the poetry of allusion, often the adventure of a soul among masterpieces; he evokes a mood by alluding to some unforgettable use of it by a major poet in the past; he is learned beyond any other poet now writing; he is rooted in tradition; he calls himself an old-fashioned Tory, and is a contemporary proof of Wordsworth's statement that revolution cannot be successful unless firmly based on tradition. He tries to show what structures can be made out of previous beauties as well as out of the raw materials. His " Waste Land " is the most important poem of the present generation, and, with " Gerontion " and " Prufrock," forms the newest testament of poetic sensibility. In his work is seen most clearly the movement away from rhetoric and towards a nostalgic classicism that is more and more the mark of free poetry to-day.

> " For I have known them all already, known them all :
> Have known the evenings, mornings, afternoons,
> I have measured out my life with coffee spoons;
> I know the voices dying with a dying fall
> Beneath the music from a farther room.
> So how should I presume?"

> " Here I am, an old man in a dry month."

Much of contemporary poetry derives from the imagist school, founded about 1912 by Ezra Pound, Richard Aldington, and F. S. Flint. Its doctrines are concise :

1. Direct treatment of the " thing," whether subjective or objective.
2. To use absolutely no word that does not contribute to the presentation.
3. As regarding rhythm! to compose in the sequence of the musical phrase, not in sequence of a metronome.

This, with the peculiar view of the " image " held by T. E. Hulme (one of our chief losses in the War), is the foundation of the texture of modern verse in so far as it is " austere, direct, free from emotional blather."

ENGLAND

The laſt thing to be discussed is the direction of critical feeling. Much energy has been waſted in the adjourned duel between romanticism and classicism, and those who find these banners without appeal seek the camp of the Baroque as a period of much activity in which a decision is not demanded. This is so much a catchword that many are unaware that while they are shouting Baroque they are using the accents of Rococo, to which properly belong the activities of Lytton Strachey and David Garnett. Criticism and scholarship are in general so divorced that the learning of many of the writers in the *Criterion* comes as an affront to the world of haſty reviewers. There is such a whirlpool of contemporary experiments that unless books are read on the day of publication there is danger of unfairness to a pioneer who is superseded by a smart wielder of his own technique. If the impact of the imitator is received firſt, the pioneer can easily be dismissed as demoded, so delicate is the balance of sensibility, and so unimportant, perhaps, is the unit in this collective development. It is not often that a critic ſtops to link up to-day and yeſterday, to underline the relationship between Katherine Mansfield and Anthony Trollope, to see the unity of technique in Joyce's Mrs. Bloom and Dickens' Mrs. Lirriper, or to find the broader principles of contemporary fictional texture concentrated in the chapter of Doſtoevsky's *Idiot* that describes his epileptic fit. Since conclusions are rare in present-day criticism, we muſt lay the emphasis on method in those few critics who are serious. These are few; they do not extend much beyond T. S. Eliot, Herbert Read, Edgell Rickword, I. A. Richards, H. C. Harwood, Desmond MacCarthy, E. M. Forſter, Virginia Woolf, and they are all academic in varying degree. I use "academic" as a term of praise to mean a methodical examination of all the relevant material, assisted by the power to leap, without error, over intervening laborious stages in the argument. The absence of such elementary qualities in most writers of literary history in academic circles is much to be regretted. Criticism has only recently attempted to establish its own categories for itself, and its most valuable achievement has been to characterise the emotional pattern of that previous generation from which we have so clearly parted company. It is no longer possible for the modern critic to accept the sophisticated mythology of Barrie, for the basis of belief has been so whittled down that the departure of sentiment is dangerously near including that of feeling. This cleavage in individual points is all the more welcome to the present generation since it is part of the general, even European, conflict that in successive decades has become clearer, the conflict of father and son that has given special validity to *The Brothers Karamazov,* to Synge's *Playboy of the Western World,* and Gosse's *Father and Son,* a conflict whose harshest and most conscious movings are to be seen in Germany.

It will be seen from the shape of this survey, by its eddyings and turnings back upon itself, by its unexpected emphasis and neglects, that the period of which it is a mirror is by no means a simple one. Cross rhythms disturb us, there is no simple progress; it is difficult without undue simplification to pick out definite dates for the beginning of definite influences. What is true for one set of writers has to be adjusted for the perspective of another set; many things are taken up by group after group; some catch up what, through ignorance, has been missed; the speed of effect in some cases atones for lateness of contact. One is always tempted to think one's own period more complex than any other, but this at least will be conceded, that our time is more congested than any other of which we have record, and unless we sweep aside everything as merely *Sturm und Drang,* which is only dodging the question again, we must be content for a while to be puzzled, to await the permanent fruits of this time of experiment.

The chief objection to this age, made by those who are awaiting an Aunt Sally, is that we have produced no masterpiece. There has been one brave attempt, *Ulysses,* and that I have suggested is a vast failure, the real reason, I feel, being that it is too solemn. The only masterpiece I can imagine fitting and expressing this age is a monster in the form of a comic synthesis of this confusion, *Hudibras* rather than *Dunciad,* philosophical rather than spiteful, and in the face of this the objectors would shrivel. That Joyce attempted his synthesis in forms of Don Quixote and Sancho Panza is admirable, but the presence of medley within himself, and overmuch information undigested into knowledge, left him without sufficient relevance. This synthesis will be effected by a comparatively simple soul who will perhaps not quite realise what he has done.

When the ground has been ploughed up, when the resources of the spirit have been explored and inventoried, when the tumult has subsided, let your masterpieces come as and when they will. I am not sure that literary history can do much with masterpieces, they teach themselves. For masterpieces there is required faith and holiness, two qualities lacking in the present make up, for the understanding of one's age there is required intelligence, the new war-cry of criticism, and, if a motto is needed, let it be from Blake : "Put off holiness, put on intelligence."

J. ISAACS.

FRANCE

WHEN I attempt to assess the influence of the War on present-day literature in France, my mind goes back to the early days of the War, to try and see how the country received the shock. I remember very well the arrival in my regiment of the mobilised men from the land. Everyone practically was determined to see it through, but under protest. And among those peasants, whose only intellectual life is too often the rampant anti-clericalism of the French southern countryside, the protest took the form of saying: "S'il y avait un Dieu, il ne permettrait pas ces choses là" ("If there were a God, He would not allow this sort of thing to happen"). Of course, this attitude was not allowed to go unchallenged, and a mobilised priest—typical of many others—tried to expound unto us that this was coming upon us through the wrath of God, owing to our sins. I well remember the tempest of indignation aroused by this contention. However wicked we might have been, we had done nothing to deserve this. On our righteous self-consciousness we took a firm stand. The world might go to ruin, but admit that we were wrong we would not. In the citadel of our own selves we were impregnable. A good many country priests had taken up this notion of the punishment of our sins; the protests against them were so bitter that bishops had to circularise their clergy and tell them to water down their Puritanism.

31

Now, these early incidents seem to me typical of the reaction of the people of France to the War; and the States of mind they reveal seem to me to have left their traces on all after-War literature. There has been first a great wave of scepticism, if not pessimism, bringing along with it immorality and anarchy. From these evils, or in the midst of these evils, the refuge is the self: the interests and feelings of the individual remain the one point emerging in the deluge. Each man is still interested in himself, even if he has lost interest in anything else. But all have not lost interest in anything else; and those who have not, against the universal scepticism, fly to dogmatism of one sort or another. As ever in France, they fly to the left or to the right, and a great movement towards Catholicism on one side, and towards Bolshevism on the other, is only too evident in post-War French literature. I am not going to talk politics; but the politics of the nation are the reflection of its moods, and its moods cannot but be reflected also in the literature. This is all the truer if we consider that in fact the new generations that came to intellectual life since the War have given us but little more than promise. The great after-War reputations—Paul Valéry, Marcel Proust, Alain, Brémond Martin du Gard, Pierre Benoît even—go to men who were intellectually formed before the War. It is too early to say whether there will be a difference, and what difference, between the pre-War and the after-War generations. The only thing we can study now is the effect of the War on the men who went through it. So that in many cases the present tendencies are only pre-War tendencies, though exaggerated. The scepticism, the absorbing interest in the self, the dogmatism, the mysticism even, all were there before; but the War has given to each of those tendencies a more powerful expression.

Proust, I suppose, is the greatest reputation that has arisen since the War. And I suppose, looking at the matter from a dispassionate height, that Proust is a good argument for our friend the Puritan. There are enough sins in Proust to justify the gods in sending a second shower of fire over the modern Sodom and Gomorrah. But then obviously the gods failed in their purpose: Proust was not quenched, and he is perched like an ironical and unhealthy flower on the ruins left by the War. What sort of a man was this Proust, to attract the wrath of the gods and then to survive it? Here is the first, and the best, sketch of him to get into literature. It is in Leon Daudet's *Memoirs,* and depicts Proust morally and externally:

"About half-past seven a young man used to drop into the Café Weber in the rue Royale. He was pale, with eyes like a deer, always nibbling or pulling one end of his drooping, brown moustache, and wrapped up in woollens like a Chinese idol. He would ask for a bunch of grapes and a glass of water, declaring that he had just got out of bed, he had the *grippe,* he was going home, and the light hurt his eyes. He would look about, anxiously at first, then mockingly; finally, he ended by breaking out in a delighted laugh, and not leaving after all. Soon he began to talk, and from his lips there flowed, in hesitating, hurried tones, extraordinarily original remarks and diabolically clever comments. His surprising figures played about in the upper regions like a kind of celestial music, such as one might have heard floating above the Globe Tavern, among the companions of the divine Shakespeare. This young man had something of Puck, something of Mercutio about him, and pursued several trains of thought simultaneously. . . . 'I beg your pardon, sir, but don't you think that . . .' Thus the insidious fellow would begin a conversation, and his unsuspecting prey would fall a victim to his powers of analysis, working somewhat in the manner of a thousand ants. For while Proust, with part of his brain, admires and enjoys the sight of something, he criticises it with another part, and with a third stands off watching indifferently what the other two are doing. I am not surprised that Proust is always tired. . . ."

This is not only Proust; it is after-War French literature: " His powers of analysis, working somewhat in the manner of a thousand ants." Proust *à la Recherche du Temps Perdu,* no doubt, but also Paul Valéry with the thousand wriggling, living fragments of his poetry, and Alain with his thirty volumes of two-page essays, Brémond with his hundreds of grubby mystics. All of them, they have the *grippe,* they are going home, and the light hurts their eyes. All of them, they look about, anxiously at first, then mockingly: thus André Maurois at Colonel Bramble. All of them end by not leaving after all: twenty volumes is the least they will give us before they pause. But also in all of them there is a kind of celestial music, and some variety of mysticism is ever ready to shine out through their drifting clouds.

But let us take it in order. I spoke first of scepticism. Now, let me ask you, what is the stock-in-trade of the novelist? With one voice you answer: " Love!" And what worse sort of scepticism can ever befall a novelist than scepticism about love? What greater doubt is there than doubting the virtue of woman? How are you going to write novels if the heroine is no longer faithful to the hero—or the hero to the heroine, if it comes to that? And this worst kind of scepticism has even befallen Proust and the French novelists of to-day. Hence the novel, having by its nature, apparently, to deal with love, necessarily set to work on the theme of jealousy. If the lady is frail, her lover will live in torture. When Proust manages to remember that he is, in a sort of way, writing a novel, and gets away from the dreary and yet fascinating process of spiritually disembowelling himself, when he tries to get on with his tale, what is the tale? *Un Amour de Swann* tells you how Swann fell in love with Odette de Crécy, and how he was perfectly happy for about twenty-four hours, and how he then began to suspect his best friend of wishing to run away with the girl, and the girl of doing more than merely reciprocating the wish. Henceforward, the tale is the telling of the agonies of Swann until he gradually becomes cured of this great malady —not jealousy, but love. Now, he had foreseen his cure, and solemnly promised himself that, once cured, he would devote his tireless energy and his brilliant brain—then temporarily incapacitated by love—to solve the problem : had the girl run away with the friend, morally speaking, or, rather, immorally speaking? But, behold, once Swann is cured of his love, he is also cured of his jealousy, and the problem no longer interests him. So that tale ends.

But watch Proust, or Marcel, as we have to call him, since he gives his hero, in fact, practically no name. After trying his hand—or rather his heart—with various ladies, young or old, high or low, he fixes on Albertine. And why? Because on the railway platform, where he was bidding a bored good-bye, fully intending not to see her again, she inadvertently lets escape a few words which make him think that she has allowed privileges elsewhere. Jealousy flares up—and with it, can we say, love? Anyhow, he jumps into the train, makes up to the girl, and brings her to consent to the extraordinary life depicted in *La Prisonnière:* he puts her under lock and key, and allows her to go out only under escort; and yet every day and every hour he is jealous of her, and even if she as much as pull her blinds up he suspects her of communicating with a rival. Naturally, the girl ends by running away, and no less than a whole volume is necessary to describe the effect produced by her absence and then death. The effect is mainly an agonising passion of discovering whether she had or had not been unfaithful to him.

But why should the traditional frailty of woman have become so much worse in the novels of our time? Please note that I say *in the novels,* for I am no believer in the theory that literature holds a true mirror to life. Literature, and more particularly the novel and the drama, lives in a conventional world of its own. This world is influenced by outside ideas and feelings, but it has little relationship to outside facts. The wave of scepticism that swept the after-War mentality had the effect on the novelists of making them doubt whether woman can ever be virtuous. We who are not novelists, but ordinary men and women, we know better than that. Only why have those gentlemen, whose business it is to try and amuse or instruct us, chosen this line of instruction? Because, in their belief, all higher values were gone. Scepticism attacked love because it had ruined the moral life: no religion was left, no morality, no decency even, no dignity in the inner life. The only thing that could bind a man and a woman was pleasure. And if pleasure offered elsewhere, elsewhere the man or the woman went. Proust has not the faintest inkling of what morality means, nor of the reason why it was invented. In this, and because of this, as a painter of life, he remains inevitably below such men as Balzac and even Flaubert, who had a greater sense of social realities.

Under the assault of this scepticism, the principles which govern the social life break down, and the social fabric begins to disintegrate. Proust pictures a world in decomposition. Here, again, I believe—every common sense person must believe, otherwise we could not live in this world—that he is wrong: he does not see the constructive forces at work. But in his vision of the world, what shall remain? His relationships to others have been made completely insecure. Therefore, he will turn to himself. He will describe to us how he wakes up in the night and does not know where he is, and he will take ten, twenty, thirty pages—admirable pages—to describe it. Here he is on safe ground: he knows how he felt when he woke up in a strange room. Even as he knows how he felt about Albertine, however impossible it may have been for him to know how Albertine felt about him. Hence this monstrous concentration on the self, which in the end destroys its own object. For what does Proust find in himself? That he forgets everything, and then that in another way he remembers everything. But in this everything, what is the thing he wishes to remember? Pleasure. Once in his childhood he dipped a piece of cake into a cup of tea; once in his youth he saw two trees swaying in the wind on the roadside by the sea; once, again, he kissed a certain girl in a peculiar manner. And the taste of the cake, and the vision of the trees, and the kiss of the girl haunt him for ever. What matter the cake, the trees, the girl? All are gone, the girl farthest of all, to other caresses. He does not care for them, or about them. But that peculiar feeling of deep pleasure, that was his life. That he will recapture. And as he grows up the cake appeals to him less, and the trees, but I will not say he concentrates on the girl; no, he disperses on the girls; he is after, not the girls, but the Moment of Pleasure. And this moment becomes a sort of divinity. Through it he has got into touch with one eternal thing: the sense that there is something deeper and more lasting than life itself. And thus, through scepticism, through immorality, through vice, he has reached a sort of mysticism. Listen to him:

"Les maîtresses que j'ai le plus aimées n'ont coïncidé jamais avec mon amour pour elles. . . Elles avaient plutôt la propriété d'éveiller cet amour. . . . Je ne trouvais rien en elles qui ressemblât à mon amour et pût l'expliquer. . . . On aurait dit qu'une vertu n'ayant aucun rapport avec elles leur avait été accessoirement adjointe par la nature, et que cette vertu, ce pouvoir simili-électrique, avait pour effet sur moi d'exciter mon amour. . . . J'incline même à croire que dans ces amours (je mets de côté le plaisir physique, qui les accompagne d'ailleurs habituellement, mais ne suffit pas à les constituer) sous l'apparence de la femme, c'est à ces forces invisibles dont elle est accessoirement accompagnée que nous nous adressons comme à d'invisibles divinités. . . . Avec ces déesses, la femme durant le rendez-vous nous met en rapport et ne fait guère plus. Nous avons, comme des offrandes, promis des bijoux, des voyages, prononcé des formules qui signifient que nous adorons, et des formules contraires . . . pour obtenir un nouveau rendez-vous, mais qui soit accordé sans ennui. Or, est-ce pour la femme elle-même, si elle n'était pas complétée de ces forces occultes, que nous prendrions tant de peine, alors que quand elle est partie nous ne saurions dire comment elle était habillée et que nous nous apercevons que nous ne l'avons même pas regardée?" (*Sodome* II., 3, 231-232.)

This same tragedy in three acts—universal scepticism, concentration on the Self, inklings of mysticism — is enacted in the purer region of poetry by Paul Valéry. Even

as Marcel Prouſt, Paul Valéry has his legend. He did write
something in that forgotten antediluvian pre-War period,
even as Prouſt did. But nobody took any notice. Only
towards the end of the War he published *La Jeune
Parque,* and people began to whisper that a great poet
had been born, but that he was so thoroughly dissatisfied
with the times he had been born into, himself included,
that he would hardly write poetry at all. So it behoved
us to tread very warily if we did not want to frighten him
off again. If we behaved well, he might write another
poem. Few people knew him. Those that did asserted
that he held no high opinion of his own achievements,
and that he had spent twenty years meditating, attempting many things, and scrapping the results, in poverty,
obscurity, and solitude. When you tried to get hold of
something he had written it was out of print. A friend
would lend you a poem he had copied out of an inaccessible volume. Public libraries were no use. Apparently all Valéry's works had been bought up by America.
Then you would receive a circular from a Dutch publisher to the effect that some private copybooks, in which
Valéry had jotted down random thoughts for many
years, would be *privately* printed and sold—at a high
price—only to persons personally acquainted with him—
and you ſtarted wondering which of your friends was
Paul Valéry in disguise. And then he was elected to the
French Academy. At this point the Abbé Brémond and
the periodical, *Les Nouvelles Littéraires,* got hold of him
and dragged him—a singularly passive academician—into
the limelight. But ſtill his books remain out of print,
and it is easier to get a book about him than a book
by him.

Paul Valéry is a disciple of Mallarmé. Which means that beyond everything, art is dear to him. It is a question whether it is worth while to write anything; but if, under certain circumstances, that is excusable, then it is chiefly because of the manner of writing it. The meaning of a poem, or a line, or a sentence, is a secondary thing; the main thing is that the expression should be beautiful; and in order to be beautiful, it must not be immediately understood. It must appeal to the senses, to the ear, to the eye, rather than to the brain. Yet this makes it all the more complicated for the intellect, for the meaning, once reached, must not be a platitude, but a delicate invention. This is called *la poésie pure*. No one understands what it is, since by definition it is not to be understood; it is. And if you don't appreciate it, then you have no sense of poetry, that is all; no one can cure you.

What does all this amount to in practice?

To the fact that Valéry is a philosophical poet who cannot make up his mind either to adopt or to construct a philosophy, and who, therefore, insists more on expression or on detail than on more general ideas. Which means, again, that he is so frightened of committing himself to any statement which might compromise him and prove ever so slightly unsound, that he tries not to come to any statement at all. Note that in this state of hesitation or scepticism he is perfectly happy—or rather perfectly unhappy, since he can hardly be called a happy poet—let us say that, unlike Keats, he is not in the state

"Of being too happy in thy happiness,"

but in that "of being too happy in his unhappiness" to get out of it. If we allow ourselves to be a little frivolous,

FRANCE

we might say of Paul Valéry that he contends, very touchingly:

"I want to be unhappy—but I can't be unhappy—unless I make you unhappy, too."

Now listen to him trying to make us unhappy. This is his most celebrated piece, "Le cimetière marin," and it is very beautiful:

"Ferme, sacré, plein d'un feu sans matière,
Fragment terrestre offert à la lumière,
Ce lieu me plaît, dominé de flambeaux,
Composé d'or, de pierre et d'arbres sombres;
La mer fidèle y dort sur mes tombeaux.

Chienne splendide, écarte l'idolâtre!
Quand solitaire au sourire de pâtre,
Je pais longtemps, moutons mystérieux
Le blanc troupeau de mes tranquilles tombes,
Eloignes-en les prudentes colombes,
Les songes vains, les anges curieux.

Les morts cachés sont bien dans cette terre,
Qui les réchauffe et sèche leur mystère. . . .

Ils ont fondu dans une absence épaisse,
L'argile rouge a bu la blanche espèce,
Le don de vivre a passé dans les fleurs!
Où sont des morts les phrases familières
L'art personnel, les âmes singulières?
La larve file où se formaient les pleurs.

Maigre immortalité noire et dorée,
Consolatrice affreusement laurée,
Qui de la mort fais un sein maternel,
Le beau mensonge et la pieuse ruse!
Qui ne connaît, et qui ne les refuse,
Ce crâne vide et ce rire éternel!

Pères profonds, têtes inhabitées
Qui sous le poids de tant de pelletées,
Etes la terre et confondez nos pas,

41

Le vrai rongeur, le ver irréfutable,
N'est point pour vous qui dormez sous la table,
Il vit de vie, il ne me quitte pas! . . ."

And this is no passing mood evoked by the graves on the seashore. Desolation is the very essence of being. Expression may be beautiful; it is only a shining veil which covers nothing. Nothingness somehow takes upon itself the appearance of Being:

" Cette soif qui te fit géant
Jusqu'à l'Etre exalte l'étrange
Toute Puissance du néant."

The attitude is really the same as in Proust. Even as Marcel suspects Albertine, Valéry suspects God of being unfaithful to him. So that perhaps Life is only a flaw in the pure crystal of Nothingness:

" Soleil! Soleil! . . . Faute éclatante!
Toi qui masques la mort, Soleil,
Sous l'azur et l'or d'une tente
Où les fleurs tiennent leur conseil,
Par d'impénétrables délices
Toi, le plus fier de mes complices (*the serpent is speaking*)
Et de mes pièges le plus haut
Tu gardes les cœurs de connaître
Que l'univers n'est qu'un défaut,
Dans la pureté du non-être!"

This, surely, is pessimism of the deepest dye. Yet here again the Self shall be our saviour. *La Jeune Parque* is represented as winding her obscure way through a perfect puzzle of vegetation, and she asserts:

" Je suivais un serpent qui venait de me mordre."

FRANCE

The serpent, and the forest, are in her soul. The problem is in the soul. The solution may be in the soul:

> " O pour moi seul, à moi seul, en moi-même,
> Auprès d'un cœur, aux sources d'un poème,
> Entre le vide et l'évènement pur,
> J'attends l'écho de ma grandeur interne. . . ."

And what comes? This echo of his own innermost greatness is the echo of the voice of God. Even as Proust, below the turbid pleasures of vice, had found the Eternal Powers, Paul Valéry, behind the rebellion, the doubt and the despair, and the searching of the Self, has found the Everlasting. Read that strange and austere masterpiece of prose, *Eupalinos,* and catch the glimpses of the Eternal Ideas, the echo of the imperishable voices. They are hard to capture; but behind the darkness, in spite of our struggles and our refusals to perceive their presence, they are there, and we cannot deny them. In his desperate need of certainty—in what he calls *la netteté désespérée,* to use one of his most celebrated phrases—Valéry rather understates than exaggerates his feeling of the Presence. But to this minimum we are entitled, even as with Proust, that there is a Presence:

> " Je ne puis te parler que des approches d'une si grande chose . . . les puissances accourent. Tu sais bien que les puissances de l'âme procèdent étrangement de la nuit. . . . Les voici, toutes élargies de clarté et d'erreur. . . . Elles m'écrasent de leurs dons.
>
> Ces faveurs surabondantes et mystérieuses, loin de les accueillir telles quelles, uniquement déduites du grand désir, il faut que je les arrête, et qu'elles attendent mon signal . . . et que je tempère et que j'interrompe la naissance même des idées." (*Eupalinos.*)

I have thus shown, in the two most celebrated writers that France has known since the War, the rhythm of the soul of France in our generation. Scepticism, concentration on the Self, discovery of new gods—or old ones—in the innermoſt recesses of the Self. But not all our writers have discovered new gods. A great many—I dare not say the greater number—have only discovered new devils. France has had no need of Freud. Prouſt has been enough of an eye-opener to those whose eyes needed opening. He discovered by himself a whole swarm of new devils, and let them loose in present-day literature. Even old devils, such as were kept rather behind the scenes by so consummate an artiſt as André Gide, have taken heart again and now ſtrut over the very footlights, undisguised, undismayed. And the very oldeſt devil of all, in *La Garçonne* of Margueritte, has been allowed a rather ugly flight. It is hardly pleasant to dwell on this side of the new myſticism, and it is merely in patriotic self-defence that I remind my British readers that the English Channel is no proteĉtion againſt flying, especially of devils, and that they have also given the world James Joyce.

The line taken by these " discoverers " runs, however, parallel to the nobler lines of our literature, and they only try to follow the advice given long ago by that charming scamp, Alfred de Musset:

" Qu'importe le flacon, pourvu qu'on aie l'ivresse. . . ."

All this has led really to a new conventionalism. We can proteſt that we are not so black as the noveliſts especially paint us. *Sodome et Gomorrhe* are very ſtriking and horrifying places. But our withers are unwrung. We do not live there. In former and more innocent—also, perhaps, more boring—eras of our literature, convention took the form of a well-suſtained assertion that no one ever was really wicked or vicious. Meredith baptised this conventionalism as rose-pink. Our present variety consists in asserting that everybody is as wicked and as vicious as the imagination of the novelist can make them. This Meredith had anticipatingly called dirty drab. It is a convention just as much as rose-pink. It is merely designed to make the work of the literary man easier.

Another convention has been turned upside down also. In novels of the good old sort the heroines were very pretty, invariably very pretty. It seems to me, as far as I can remember, that the present-day heroine is no longer pretty. I am not thinking of shingled or bobbed heads and masculine attire. I have no doubt whatever that there are still a few pretty women about, as there have always been. But—and I compliment them upon it— they keep out of the modern novel. Albertine is not pretty, any more than she is moral. She has—horrid thing—a gross-grained skin. Has there ever been a time before when the heroine had not a perfectly smooth skin? Pierre Benoît's ladies are frequently what old-fashioned males would have called plain, and I refer you to the opening chapters of *Don Carlos*. And there is in Paul Morand's world a Violet who gave me a shock when I read the description of her physical qualities. I found, nevertheless, that although women were no longer beautiful, yet their power of attraction had not diminished. It was obviously not beauty that mankind was looking for. Molière had warned us that love was all-powerful and could make of

" La noire à faire peur une brune adorable."

But the further step was left for the modern novelist

to take, to realise fully that she was *noire à faire peur*
and yet to adore her all the same.

Perhaps, however, the moralists will find some comfort
in the fact that, in this strange world of the novel,
women have become plain at the same time as they
have become immoral. I cannot but feel that on those
grounds the future of virtue is assured.

I will not tire the reader with a catalogue of the conventions that have thus been assailed or brought forward. The
search for new " stunts " has been endless. We have had
Synthetists, Integralists, Impulsionists, Aristocratists, Sin-
cerists, Druidists, Futurists, Intensivists, Simultaneists,
Dynamists, Totalists, Cubists, Dadaists, Surrealists. Why
should we take some more seriously than others? The
recent example of the celebrated Jean Cocteau—sometimes
a delicate and amusing artist—has shown us that they are
all liable to become converted into pure and simple Roman
Catholics. Let us see where their natural evolution will
lead them, and reserve our judgment until their end is
made clear.

The melancholy fate of Cocteau brings us to the escape
from all this welter of "stunts," conventions, and schools.
Dogmatism has appeared with a new strength in our
literature. French literature at the present day is much
more intimately mixed with politics and religion than
English literature. There is a definite group of writers
belonging to the right, and one to the left. The more
striking fact is the formation of the right wing group.
Twenty years ago a French writer could not be a Catholic
and live. To-day, if he wants to take a short-cut to
celebrity and fortune, he becomes a Catholic as ostenta-
tiously as he can. No doubt some mountebanks take

advantage of this. But a band of honest, hard-working writers had to toil under many handicaps to alter the situation to that extent. The pre-War labours of Léon Bloy, Charles Maurras, Léon Daudet, and Péguy were probably the main cause of the change. A fairly large section of French youth, full of high hopes and ambitions, and anxious for leadership, found leadership here and nowhere else. For the radical left has been singularly ineffective intellectually. Curiously enough, the development of the scientific spirit has been a cause of intellectual weakness to the parties of the left. Most scientists and scholars belonged to those parties, and men like Renan, Berthelot, and later Anatole France, played somewhat the part of leaders. But the advance in the critical scientific spirit made it impossible for scientists and scholars to assert any principle or theory with anything like the conviction necessary to make it effective. Real science has reduced every possible assertion to the state of a very fragile hypothesis. Hence the spirit of Anatole France, that plays on the surface or in the depths of things, but never is entirely sure of anything whatsoever. Naturally, youth turned away from such leaders who would not lead. The goddess Reason lost her votaries through being so unreasonably reasonable that she would not commit herself to anything at all. Maurras became a leader of the young—strangely enough, he was not, and is not, a Catholic—but he advised others to become Catholics. He followed the goddess Reason, and she had whispered to him that hers was a vain service. So after Maurras comes Maritain, who once more takes his stand upon Thomas Aquinas, and calls the youth of France back to the old faith. But the great success of Catholic literature

47

has been the Abbé Brémond, now of the French Academy, with his *Histoire littéraire du sentiment religieux en France depuis la fin des guerres de religion jusqu'à nos jours.* The huge volumes began to come out in 1915; they are at present already bulkier than *A la Recherche du Temps Perdu;* and their influence is likely to be as great. Brémond does not try to convince you, any more than Proust does. He reveals in the minutest details the inner spiritual life of hundreds of humble French mystics, from 1590 onwards; details as minute as in Proust; but Brémond's heroes are infinitely more sympathetic than Proust's. He brings the mystic life to us, in all its dreadful familiarity, puerility, convincingness. And he artfully opens his book, for misguided misbelievers, or misguided believers, with a charming tale of how a missionary went to Siam and was kindly received by the head of a Buddhist monastery :

> "Ecoutez, me disait-il, voulez-vous que je vous dise pourquoi vous vous appliquez avec tant de zèle et d'affection à l'étude de la langue et des livres de Siam? C'est qu'anciennement vous avez été Siamois et habile homme dans l'intelligence de tous ces livres, et il est demeuré en vous un petit reste et une certaine réminiscence de ce que vous avez été premièrement."

And in the same manner, says Henri Brémond, the mystics of France are still part and parcel of even the worst unbelievers of to-day, in whom there is *un petit reste et une certaine réminiscence,* which the abbé cunningly fans in our hearts. And we cannot but be grateful to him for his kindliness and charm and persuasive grace —a little as though Renan himself had gone back to the Catholic fold.

He is one of the leaders of a great hoſt, and, as is inevitable in great hoſts, many of the troopers are unpleasant acquaintances. The lateſt scandal is that of Georges Bernanos, *Sous le Soleil de Satan,* a novel hailed by Léon Daudet as a work of genius, and which certainly shows great power. But one of the leading charaĉters is none other than the Prince of Darkness himself; and many people are tempted by God nowadays—via Brémond's myſtics—but few people care to be tempted by the devil.

Which proteſt brings us to the other side. For, naturally, we are gone Bolshevik at the same time as we went Catholic. But our Bolshevism is no more dangerous, I guess, than our Catholicism. We keep *un petit reſte et une certaine réminiscence* of the good old French common sense, and Molière and Voltaire are never far from us. Pierre Hamp, I suppose, is the literary man who belongs—in theory—moſt completely to the left. He has given magnificent literary achievement in his great pictures of the world of labour; he has created a new form of novel : the novel without a hero—or even a heroine— and without a plot or a tale to tell. He will take flax, or fish, or glass as a subjeĉt, and show you how human life is polarised by work; how the peasant lives on the Lys river—and the English traders come to Ghent to buy the flax and drink port; how the faĉtory hand in the North of France loves and toils and makes linen, and how the faĉtory owner loves and toils and makes linen; and he follows it up to the glaring splendour of the big Paris shops and the squalid lives and the rich lives that are built on flax in the capital.

Thus another seĉtion of our youth has fallen in love with the worker as the firſt seĉtion with the faith. Jean

Richard Bloch is perhaps the most ardent spirit on this side; politics do not play any great part in all this, but temperaments. And Bloch has given us the epic of race in work as Hamp gave the epic of work. In *Et Compagnie,* one of the great novels of our time, Bloch tells the tale of relentless Jewish endeavour, and the building up of a big industrial enterprise in a small western town.

But all that side of French literature is dominated by a great figure, too little known in England : the essayist, Alain. André Maurois is well known here, and Colonel Bramble has made the English reader, in the Meredithian phrase, " smart and meditate." Now, André Maurois is, spiritually, the disciple and son of Alain. It is no discredit, but an honour, to him to say that, when he has written a new book, he goes in fear and trembling to the door of the master and awaits judgment. Alain has resumed the great tradition of the French essay. After Montaigne and Pascal and Fénelon and Voltaire and Vauvenargues, the French essay went to rest for a century or so, and then awoke in Alain. Alain is the La Bruyère of our time, as subtle as Proust, as charming and delightfully erudite as Brémond, as open-minded as Voltaire. When people want to know in a hundred years' time how the French of to-day lived and thought, they will not go to Proust (luckily for the French), they will go to Alain. Alain is the man of sense of our time, and the great essayist of a century. He has written the one book on the War that is *the* book on the War—*Mars ou la guerre jugée*—and whether you are pacifist or militarist, Tory or Bolshevik, you must read the book, or remain eternally ignorant of what war is and of what human nature is. But, as I have said already, Alain has written thirty volumes of short essays. He will be a treasure-house open to the plunderings of future generations.

I have mentioned with him André Maurois, who has not given his full measure yet, in spite of his celebrity. The beſt of him is probably as yet the essayiſt, and his humorous knowledge of human nature is more of the essayiſt kind than the noveliſt's. But to my mind he is, perhaps, more of a force for the future than the maſter of an achievement in the paſt.

How numerous the names I should mention here, discussing the promises contained in their present production! When we sent our soldiers home we obviously demobilised a whole army of noveliſts. Had this been known at the time, it might have been counted by recalcitrant critics as an argument for the continuation of the War. But the pacific and omnivorous reader will bless the gods that sent us back Duhamel and Dorgelès to tell the tale after Barbusse; Montherlant to speak of it as *Le Songe,* and then to wander off into Spain in search of sport and bull-fighting with *Les beſtiaires;* Lucien Fabre to explain to us in *Rabevel* how horrible business could be; Roger Martin du Gard to attempt another fifteen-volume epic on the inner life of *détraqués* and semi-supermen in *Les Thibault;* Lacretelle to persuade us in *Silbermann* to be kind to Jews, when they will be kind to us; Mauriac to make us wonder at the ſtrange things that do happen in the countryside in the South of France; and Valéry Larbaud and Paul Giraudoux, *esprits charmants et souples;* and shall we fail to say a good word for Pierre Benoît and Paul Morand? They have entertained us. None of these has produced maſterpieces, perhaps, as yet, but many of them may be expected to do great things at least in the future.

I have not spoken of older men, perhaps of better men, known already before the war : Paul Fort, Jules Romains, Claudel, Gide, Suarès, Eugène Montfort, Edmond Jaloux, Louis Bertrand, Romain Rolland, Rosny, the brothers Tharaud, most of them at the height of their power.

I think it can be said that the literature of France is passing through a fine period. There are innumerable men of talent, many of them young, and the future is rich with promise. Two or three very great men—Proust, Valéry, Alain—stand out evidently; but many of the names I have given may be the names of very great men yet on the way to achievement. It seems to me that, on the whole, prose holds the field, in the novel or the essay, with Proust, Hamp, Brémond, Alain; the drama, in spite of noble efforts by Jules Romains and Jean Richard Bloch, has still to be renovated; in spite of hosts of honourable poets, the only great name is Paul Valéry—and there are those who find him greater as an essayist in *Eupalinos* than as a poet. But on the whole, and whichever way we turn, the present of French literature is worthy of its great past, and justifies the hope that the light of leadership in many enterprises of the mind may still burn there through a long future.

DENIS SAURAT.

GERMANY

WHEN in the eighties of the nineteenth century it became evident that the older writers had shirked the realities of life and drawn over them a veil which gave to ugliness the illusion of beauty, there was a revolt of the younger generation, and modern German literature may be said to have begun. A new theory of Naturalism sprang from sources which have since done more than anything else to change the trend of European thought—the then recent discoveries in the field of science, more especially the theory of Evolution, and the ideas of the early political, socialist writers such as Marx and Lassalle. In addition, there was the cumulative effect of the new tendencies in French, Scandinavian, and Russian literature. The new generation was imbued with the conviction that literature may not dispense with the depiction of life as it is, but, as so frequently in Germany, theory preponderated over practice. In the bustle of activity necessary for the discussion and settlement of weighty questions of style and the relations between science, life, and art, with the consequent important business of setting up programmes and laying down rules, they had little inspiration left for creating works of art in consonance with their theories. The first important naturalist work was Gerhart Hauptmann's drama *Vor Sonnenaufgang,* which was produced in 1889, the year which saw the inauguration of the movement for an emancipated theatre such as was also being founded in France and in England.

The relations between literature and social revolution have always been close. The Storm and Stress of the eighteenth century was really a social struggle fought on the bloodless field of literature, and throughout the nineteenth century there were reflections in literature of discontent with the structure of society. To mention but one of these, Hauptmann's early drama *Die Weber* was particularly appreciated after the Revolution of 1918, and since the naturalist generation the connection in Germany has come more and more in evidence, until in recent years there has been a tendency to mistake the political manifesto for a form of drama.

In attempting to survey the general tendencies in contemporary German literature, it becomes more and more obvious that the aspect which must be emphasised is literature in its attitude to the accepted forms of society.

Naturalism never had undisputed possession of the field, and the most important counter-influence was that of Stefan George and his circle, which, grouped in the early nineties round the periodical *Blätter für die Kunst,* cultivated formal artistry, art for art's sake, than which nothing could be more opposed to the view of the naturalist writers that poetry must approximate as closely as possible to life. The precursors of George, to whom I shall have cause to return later, were the Pre-Raphaelites in England, and Baudelaire, Verlaine, and Mallarmé in France. The pre-War currents in German literature between the two poles of naturalism and the George circle are too numerous to be explained shortly without recourse to artificial groupings, and it is only possible to mention by name those older writers whose influence has survived the War and the younger ones who before 1914 were beginning to show promise.

In the half-dozen years which preceded the War there was a perceptible calmness in literature. Among those whose reputations were already made, and have since endured, were Hauptmann and Wedekind in the field of drama, Dehmel, George, and Rilke in poetry, Thomas Mann and Jakob Wassermann in fiction. Schnitzler and von Hofmannsthal, different yet alike as they are, were the most celebrated of the Viennese writers who had achieved an international reputation. The bubbling of ideas had considerably abated, and literature pursued an even course, troubled only by occasional stirrings of uneasiness at the materialistic tendencies of civilisation and the subordination of spiritual to economic values. The turbulent blood of the writers who had been the hotheads at the turn of the century had now cooled, and the younger generation had not yet found its feet. Hauptmann and Sudermann were still spoken of in one breath, but even before the War the reputation of Hauptmann was on the wane, and to-day it may be said that for the younger generation he has little or no significance, the attempt to put him forward as a sort of official poet of the Republic having met with no success, while Sudermann is now regarded as little more than a master of stage technique.

There were poets at that time who seemed to have an inkling of the coming cataclysm, which is foreshadowed, for example, in the fine poem "Umbra Vitæ" of Georg Heym, who was drowned at the age of twenty-four in 1912:

CONTEMPORARY EUROPEAN LITERATURE

" Die Menschen ſtehen vorwärts in den Strassen
Und sehen auf die grossen Himmelszeichen,
Wo die Kometen mit den Feuernasen
Um die gezackten Türme drohend schleichen."

The humanity and fellow-sympathy for the reſt of creation, which was later to be so ſtrikingly demonſtrated in German literature, is already seen in the poetry of Franz Werfel, the moſt considerable of the younger poets of to-day. This humanity, coupled with a devout searching for God, is expressed in a poem which he published in 1913 at the age of twenty-three:

" O Herr, zerreisse mich!
Was soll das dumpfe, klägliche Geniessen?
Ich bin nicht wert, dass Deine Wunden fliessen.
Begnade mich mit Martern, Stich um Stich!
Ich will den Tod der ganzen Welt einschliessen.
O Herr, zerreisse mich!"

There is something of the humility, the myſtic pantheism, and yet the consciousness of his own individuality, that we find in an older Auſtrian poet who came from the same town of Prague, Rainer Maria Rilke.

In 1913, the year of the centenary celebration of the War of Liberation from the yoke of Napoleon, and the twenty-fifth year of the Kaiser's reign, Gerhart Hauptmann received a commission to produce a *Feſtspiel,* to be ſtaged by Reinhardt, and he wrote a play which lauded the spirit of Peace inſtead of hymning the patriotic fervour of 1813. There was much objeƈtion to the play, and a proteſt from the Crown Prince led to its withdrawal. A year later came the War, and, in common with the writers of all the other belligerent countries, those of Germany felt the thrill of patriotism which inspired them to outpourings of the moſt ephemeral and flatulent type. The poetic resources of the country were, so to speak, adapted to war-work. It has been estimated that the number of patriotic poems published in Germany in the first year of the War amounted to a million and a half. There is no reason to suspect that many of them possessed higher worth or dignity than the majority of those which were produced simultaneously in this country. They could not have possessed less. It is a question whether the verse of this period even reached the level of mediocrity attained by the war poetry of 1870. As in England, where older poets descended to the writing of such pathetic stuff as showed them to be entirely out of touch with the soul and attitude of the men in the trenches, so in Germany the older writers tried their hand at verses which would have suited admirably the bellicose spirit of the wars of a hundred years ago. They were completely foreign to the mentality of the citizen soldier, who realised that the men in the trenches opposite were also human beings, and had little use for the bombastic claptrap produced amid the artificially created atmosphere at home. It is significant that the real soldiers' song was a quaint sentimental medley based on Uhland's famous Volkslied, "Ich hatt' einen Kameraden," which is supposed to have originated before the War and been spread by the Wandervögel; it concludes with the lines:

> " Die Vöglein im Walde,
> Sie sangen all so wunder-wunderschön,
> In der Heimat, in der Heimat,
> Da gibt's ein Wiedersehn."

In this song there is no more of the jingoism of the truculent old gentlemen at the *Stammtisch* than there was in " Tipperary," and the best of the War poetry is in the same Volkslied tradition.

The literature of the War can be divided into two phases, of which the second began in 1917, or slightly earlier. Even in 1914 there were voices raised against war. The group of writers whose mouthpiece was the periodical *Die Aktion,* founded in 1911 and edited by Franz Pfemfert, took their stand against the War from the beginning. A second important expressionist periodical, of a more abstract tendency, was *Der Sturm,* founded in 1910 and edited by Herwarth Walden.

When we come to deal with the second phase, which began with weariness and culminated in despair, it must be borne in mind that whereas in England we speak of " the War " and its effect on the mentality of the younger generation, the Germans speak about " the War and the Revolution," and the difference is vital. The effect of a lost war *and* a revolution was catastrophic. There was in England no upheaval of the national soul as there was in Germany, an upheaval which explains the ecstatic, mystic, even apocalyptic nature of much of the literature produced between 1917 and 1921, the period of chaos.

There was, of course, a very strict censorship, which was afterwards abolished by the Revolution, but the first literary signs of the change of mentality came from the poets at the front, mainly from those of *Die Aktion,* which had been the chief exponent of political poetry, but had been compelled by the outbreak of war to eliminate the political element. After the War it became for a time the literary mouthpiece of the Spartakist movement. One of the most violent of those who raged against the War and its horrors, and at the same time heralded a fraternity which should embrace the world, was the poet Johannes R. Becher.

The new literature appeared under the banner of Expressionism, which, though by no means a new art form, only became popular with the change of spirit about 1917, and reached its climax during the Revolution period. By 1921 it was practically dead. The name "Expressionism" came from the sister art of painting, and was used in the first place to denote the opposite of Impressionism. As Kasimir Edschmid, one of the leaders of the movement, explains:

> "The world is there. It would be absurd to reproduce it. The greatest task of Art is to search out its intrinsic essence and create it anew."

Each object has its profounder aspect, which our eyes are too blinded by experience of its external qualities to see. Everything should be related to eternity. For example, a sick man is not only seen as an individual sufferer, but becomes the symbol of illness itself; his suffering is but a reflection of the suffering of the whole of creation, and when an artist wants to depict a sick man he must depict the very quality of sickness. A house is not seen as a mere construction of brick and mortar, an angular object with qualities of beauty or ugliness, as the case may be, but its actual nature is studied until its profounder aspect is revealed, until it is freed from the restraint of reality and appears as an *expression* of its ultimate character, even if it thereby lose all resemblance to that which generally comes into our mind when we think of a house. Similarly, in expressionistic art, a man ceases to be an individual, he becomes a concrete representation of the abstract conception *Man*. The work of art is the medium by means of which the spectator or reader is enabled to enter into the emotional mood in which the artist created it. Therefore, if the spectator looks only with his physical eye, he may see things which appear to him absurd or grotesque. The Impressionists tried to reproduce the variety of life, and give an optical impression which was momentary. The Expressionists seek to visualise the eternal, and forgo painting pictures of the external world of appearances.

This art is really an attempt to escape from the ugliness and suffering of life by diving beneath the surface, which appears shifting and worthless, in order to find the true basis of the cosmos and something fixed and essential to grasp. The War fostered this tendency, but there is something very similar in Greek philosophy in the theory of Platonic ideas.

In poetry and drama writers tried to obtain their effects primarily by concentration, and to this end they laid violent hands on the language. Articles, prepositions, grammatical inflections, and prefixes were regarded as unnecessary and could be omitted. Substantives could be used to form new and unusual verbs, or verbs to form new substantives. The natural consequence was that each poet tried to create his own language, and since expressionist drama or poetry is not in any case easy to understand, confusion became worse confounded. The tendency to reduce verbal expression to its most primitive form reached its *reductio ad absurdum* in the revolt against intellectualism known as the Dada movement. As one Dadaist poet has said: "We write without taking into account the meaning of words!"

The most celebrated of the anthologies of expressionist

poetry is called *Menschheitsdämmerung,* a title which expresses both the realisation of the twilight of the world which is at the turn and the hope of a new dawn for humanity. The anthology is divided into four sections, headed respectively "Sturz und Schrei," "Erweckung des Herzens," "Aufruf und Empörung," "Liebe den Menschen," titles which explain themselves. It contains not only the work of many of the most celebrated poets of the new school, but also some extraordinarily convulsive efforts.

The following is an example, by no means extreme, of the abstract poetry fostered by the periodical *Der Sturm*. It is by August Stramm, who fell on the Russian front in 1915, and is called "Schwermut":

> " Schreiten Streben
> Leben sehnt
> Schauen Stehen
> Blicke suchen
> Sterben wächst
> Das Kommen
> Schreit!
> Tief
> Stummen
> Wir."

The poet is obviously striving for ultimate concentration and simplicity, using hardly any punctuation except exclamation marks, and we can understand why this particular poem appears in the section "Sturz und Schrei." Stramm is the classic example for this obscure, staccato, stammering kind of verse, to which we cannot attribute much importance, for it is difficult to believe that the emotions or thoughts of these poets were too profound or complicated for expression by the various ordinary media of poetry.

CONTEMPORARY EUROPEAN LITERATURE

There are poets innumerable, but in addition to those who have already been mentioned, or who will be mentioned later, it will suffice to note the group of labourer poets, some of whom achieved considerable celebrity, such as Karl Bröger, Gerrit Engelke, Max Barthel and Heinrich Lersch, the tinsmith, who wrote one of the most popular of the War poems with the refrain, "Deutschland muss leben, und wenn wir sterben müssen."

The endeavour to be original at all costs is perhaps due to a self-consciousness which is characteristic of the majority of minor German poets. They possess too keen a realisation of their poetic nature to be able to produce effortless poetry, or even the appearance of effortlessness. The reader has a continual, uneasy feeling that he is being present during the pangs of creation. In a recent anthology of living poets called *Saat und Ernte,* each poet was asked to choose those of his own poems which he desired to have included, and has prefixed in each case a short autobiographical sketch. To show what I mean by the self-consciousness of these poets, I will quote extracts from two of the autobiographies:

> ". . . an old priestly race bequeathed to me an inclination for the next world. The fighting energy of my ancestors rests in the dreamy veins of their descendant. If these are the elements of my being, they are also the elements of my poetry."

And in another case, after a few words about his lyrical disposition, the poet continues in the following strain:

> " I early felt the superior force of my environment and the incompatibility of my personal, spiritual disposition with the mysterious and dangerous forces of existence."

These quotations are typical of the autobiographies. We may expect such an objective attitude to his own Ego in a Goethe summing up at the end of a long life, but the effect is either pathetic or ridiculous in a young poet at the outset of his career.

Thomas Mann is reported to have said in conversation that the young generation during the War was not revolutionary but loud. That is unjust; but the intense earnestness with which they take themselves would, in a less serious nation than the German, lead one to suspect the profundity of their feelings. It is to be explained by the fact that whereas the older generation looks upon the War as an incident in history, the younger generation regards it as a definite turning-point in civilisation. Their humanitarianism is large; they no longer take for their themes their merely personal emotions and sufferings. Their sympathy is cosmic, and their compassion covers the whole of humanity. That is why their dramatic characters are types, but they are inclined to mistake reformatory enthusiasm, religious fervour, and even political rhetoric for poetry; to consider tempestuous emotion and obsession by ideas a surrogate for a sense of form or beauty.

The fact that characters appear mostly as types, coupled with a strong tendency to allegory, is perhaps the most striking feature of expressionist plays. Walter Hasenclever, in his drama, *Der Sohn,* one of the pre-War expressionist dramas, treats the father-son conflict, which appears again and again in the dramatic literature of this period, and is, of course, of fundamental importance in psycho-analysis, as typical of the father-son conflict which appears anew in every generation. The father represents the principle of authority, againſt which the son, the symbol of the repressed ſection of humanity with its urge for liberty, rebels. Parental love is regarded as selfishness. These young men want themselves to be a beginning, and not heirs to the paſt, with which they want to break more completely than any previous generation had wished to do. It is extraordinary how frequently we find the death-wish againſt the father in the works of this period. As a contraſt we sometimes see the attempt to weave a new myth round the mother, as in Fritz von Unruh's drama, *Ein Geschlecht*. The same attitude towards the father appears in Franz Werfel's *Spiegelmensch*, Arnolt Bronnen's *Vatermord*, Ernſt Toller's *Die Wandlung*, Georg Kaiser's *Die Koralle*, Anton Wildgans's *Dies Iræ*.

Characters are often given mere type-diſtinctions, as in *Ein Geschlecht*, where the characters are The Mother, The Eldeſt Son, The Cowardly Son, The Youngeſt Son, The Daughter, and a Leader of the Soldiers. Reinhard Sorge's *Bettler*, which is the earlieſt of the expressioniſt dramas, having been written in 1910, introduces typical groups such as Newspaper Readers, Proſtitutes, and Aviators, who speak in chorus. Allegorical characters appear in various forms—as a Stranger representing Death in Wildgans's *Armut*, as a Friend representing Rebellion againſt parental authority in Hasenclever's *Sohn*—but this is not particularly novel. In von Unruh's non-expressioniſt play, *Offiziere*, there appears a ſtrange officer among the other officers on board ship who are on their way to fight in South-Weſt Africa, and he represents Death, while as long ago as 1891, Wedekind had introduced a "Vermummter Herr," as a representation of the life impulse, into the last scene of *Frühlings Erwachen*.

The endeavour to create types instead of individuals results often in the creation of a false psychology. Actions do not follow logically from character and environment, and the characters are not drawn in their natural *milieu*, since they are abstract and not dependent, as real people would be, on fortuitous conditions of place and time. Actual scenes alternate with dream scenes, and instead of a dramatic representation we get a lyrical one. The new art, in fact, finds its best expression in the lyric, and between 1910 and 1920 it is the lyrical mood which predominates in literature, even the drama being pervaded with lyricism. The dramatists, in their convulsive search for a new style, often employ an extreme conciseness of phraseology, and their characters speak in jerky sentences which at times remind one forcibly of Mr. Alfred Jingle in *The Pickwick Papers*. The tendency to exaggerated concentration gave rise to a whole group of what are known as *Schreidramen*, where the characters speak either in monosyllables or in incoherent screams. Sometimes the stage directions occupy more space than the text, and here there can, perhaps, be traced the influence of Mr. Bernard Shaw, who in Germany is classed with Shakespeare and Oscar Wilde as one of our three great dramatists.

The logical outcome of expressionist drama, if it had not died an early death, would have been its approximation to the film, for which the frequent change of scene, the gradual elimination of language in favour of action, the complicated lighting, and the alternation of reality with dream scenes seem peculiarly to qualify it. In

Hasenclever's *Sohn,* everything that happens is supposed to be seen from the standpoint of the son himself, as in the film *Dr. Caligari* everything is seen through the eyes of a madman, and the whole action and scenery given the requisite twist.

The majority of expressionist writers are socialists, and the object of their contempt and hostility is the bourgeois, the representative of the existing order, who is regarded as the upholder of an effete economic and ethical system. Frank Wedekind, who with Strindberg is one of the chief founts from which expressionist drama drew its inspiration, had already done pioneer work in the pillorying of the bourgeois, and the two outstanding satirists of to-day, who never tire of holding up the bourgeois, his views and foibles, to ridicule are Heinrich Mann the novelist and Carl Sternheim the writer of comedies, whose ambition is said to be to become the German Molière. Heinrich Mann is celebrated for the trilogy of novels in which he mercilessly lashes German society in the reign of William II., *Der Untertan, Die Armen,* and *Der Kopf. Der Untertan* was first published in 1918, having been prohibited by the censor four years earlier. Mann traces the decadence of the ruling classes in Wilhelmine Germany to the instinct of servility, of deference to the man above. Sternheim has turned out comedy after comedy burlesquing the hypocrisy and other failings of the bourgeois, but his method is purely destructive, and his satire entirely intellectual. The extreme revolutionary attitude is represented by Johannes R. Becher, who appears to confuse the mission of the poet with that of the political orator and leader of the proletariat. The capitalist, as a stockbroker or banker, appears in grotesque guise in Kaiser's *Von Morgens bis Mitternachts* and in Toller's *Masse Mensch*. In Kaiser's *Die Koralle* both the son and daughter of the milliardaire are socialists. Among the poets who actually took part in the Revolution, it is only necessary to mention Kurt Eisner and Ernst Toller, the former of whom was assassinated, while the latter spent five years in prison for his part in the Communist outbreak in Munich.

A striking feature in this rejection of modern civilisation is hostility to the large town. The developing sense of realism in German literature during the nineteenth century, which culminated in the Naturalist movement, had hitherto paid admiring tribute to the mechanical forces invented by man to overcome his natural limitations. Now there came a change of attitude. Mechanical forces came to be regarded as the means by which the workers are kept in subjection in gloomy, smoky towns, where they are unable to obtain a glimpse of green fields or even of the sun. The poets who had sung hymns in praise of machines now switched over to the opposite extreme. The voracious appetite of the towns which destroy everything green and smiling and swallow up the creatures of the countryside, human and animal, is expressed most powerfully by Armin T. Wegner. He sees a vision of towns which reach to the sky and spread over the face of the earth in one vast, endless town:

> " Euch Ebenen, die in das Endlose führen,
> Alle verschlingt unserer Mauern zermalmender Mund.
> Bis wir zum Saume der Meere uns strecken,
> Nie sind wir müde, wir werden nie satt,
> Bis wir zum Haupte der Berge uns recken
> Und die weite, keimende Erde bedecken:
> Eine ewige, eine unendliche Stadt!"

Bound up with this nostalgia for simple forms of existence are disappointment and disillusion at the result of the Revolution, I will not say of the War. The majority of the expressionist poets were highly, if vaguely, idealistic and opposed to the materialism of the age. The abuses against which they had protested disappeared apparently with the Revolution, but too much of the old mentality still remained with those in authority, and the hopes of the young men, who saw the same old world rising like a phœnix from its own ashes, were scattered to dust. A reflection of this disillusionment is to be seen in many of the revolutionary dramas written about the year 1920, in which a character is acclaimed by the masses as a leader, only to be rejected by them since they are incapable of sympathising with his high ideals; he is martyred by the very people he sought to save. Johannes R. Becher had already warned the poets that the masses would swirl over their heads and that they would be the first to be crucified. It may not be out of place in connection with this atmosphere of pessimism to note that the first volume of Spengler's *Untergang des Abendlands* has recently gone into its hundredth edition. Although the title of this book was originally intended as a protest against the optimism of the pre-War mentality, it was seized upon as a catchword after the collapse, when the view was eagerly welcomed that the cultural possibilities of the Western world were exhausted.

It is tempting to draw a parallel with the eighteenth-century Storm and Stress movement, and one thinks involuntarily of Karl Moor's outburst against his ink-spilling century. In the eighteenth century literature provided a substitute for political activity, in the twentieth century literature preceded revolution. The Storm and Stress movement lacked the all-embracing compassion of the twentieth century writers. But the most striking difference between the expressionist movement and all that had gone before is in the attitude to women. Love no longer plays the dominant rôle. The relations between man and woman appear intellectual rather than emotional. Perhaps nothing shows the gulf between Gerhart Hauptmann and the younger generation more than the former's satiric idyll, *Die Insel der Grossen Mutter*. Schnitzler continues to produce psychological and erotic studies of neurotic characters. Stefan George stands at the opposite extreme, and his school appears to be more interested in the friendship of man for man. There is even an apparent lack of sympathy among the Expressionists for the important place given to women by Goethe; and they are, of course, even further out of touch with the smouldering passion of Dehmel. An exception must be made in the case of Fritz von Unruh, in whose work the relation of man and woman is of primary importance. When the sexual element appears in expressionistic work, it is generally in the form of abnormality.

The ideas germinating in the minds of writers at this time can best be seen in four or five typical works. Reinhard Goering's drama, *Seeschlacht,* reproduces the spirit in the navy which culminated in the mutiny of 1917 and the later revolt at Kiel; Fritz von Unruh's War-book, *Opfergang,* is a mirror of the coming change of mind in the army; Clara Viebig's novel, *Töchter der Hekuba,* and its sequel, *Das Rote Meer,* where nearly all the characters are women, describe the terrible conditions at home, and Ernst Toller's *Hinkemann* shows something of the post-War conditions.

Seeschlacht contains seven characters, all sailors, and the scene of action is the armoured turret of a battleship which is steaming towards the Battle of Jutland. The drama reproduces the morbid atmosphere of expectation and the conflicting thoughts in the men's minds. The fifth sailor expresses the awakening sense of revolt against the idea of military duty, and this is perhaps the very first sign, in the works which the censor allowed to be made public, of the coming collapse. But when the battle begins, the incipient mutineer is the bravest fighter. The crew of the turret is wiped out, and the dying words of the fifth sailor are:

> "Ich habe gut geschossen, wie?
> Ich hätte auch gut gemeutert! Wie?
> Aber schiessen lag uns wohl näher? Wie?
> Muss uns wohl näher gelegen haben?"

When it came to the crisis, it was easier to fight than to mutiny, so the drama really ends on a question-mark.

Fritz von Unruh's *Opfergang* was written in the trenches before Verdun in 1916. It describes the preparation for and the actual attack of his company on the fortress; the change from hope to the realisation of failure, and the careless lack of understanding of the people at home when the soldier goes on leave. It crystallises the change in the mentality of von Unruh himself, a regular officer in the Prussian cavalry, whose earlier plays idealised the orthodox sense of duty in the German army, but whose later works are ranked among the finest expressions of that pacific idealism which

sprang from the War. *Opfergang* demonſtrates the ultimate realisation of the tremendous sacrifices which were
made for infinitesimal gain, or even for none at all. It is
beſt compared with Henri Barbusse's *Le Feu*. The French
novel is sober and realiſtic, even cynical, the German book
is full of fire and emotion; together they give a better idea
of what the War on the Weſtern Front was like, both
materially and spiritually, than anything else that has
been written in the field of imaginative literature.

The scene of Clara Viebig's novel, *Töchter der Hekuba,*
is a suburb of Berlin, whence all the men have gone,
and the author pictures the tragic combination of
monotony and fear of what the day may bring for the
women whose husbands, fathers, and sons are at the
War, with the accumulating misery of lengthening
casualty liſts and food queues; the sense of primitive
reality gradually breaking through the old prepossessions
and artificial barriers.

Toller's tragedy, *Hinkemann,* is supposed to take place
about 1921. Hinkemann has returned from the War as
a sexual cripple. The man who could not bear to see an
animal hurt is compelled to earn a living by biting rats
and mice to death at a fair to amuse the spectators. This
cripple is presented to the audience with profound irony
as the "incarnation of German ſtrength." He is seen by
his wife, who feels the deepeſt sympathy for her husband
reawakening, but a man whom he had looked upon as
his friend lies to him that she had laughed. In the ſtreet
he sinks to the ground and people collect round him,
but when military music is heard in the next ſtreet people
rush to see the soldiers. On the way home he purchases
a bronze ſtatue of Priapus, who appears to him to be

71

the god of the present age. His wife tries to bring about a reconciliation, but he no longer has either hope or the will to live. His wife throws herself out of the window, and when her body is brought in Hinkemann prepares a noose with which to commit suicide. "Warum . . . trifft es mich, gerade mich?" he asks. "Wahllos trifft es . . . Was wissen wir? Woher? . . . Wohin?" It is the tragedy, intensified to the extreme limit, of the man returned from the War to find himself estranged from the rest of humanity.

When these works are considered as typical manifestations of the state of mind produced by the events of 1914 to 1923, they are as terrible an accumulation of documents as it would be possible to collect.

The most important dramatic work of this period is to be found in three trilogies by Fritz von Unruh, Franz Werfel, and Georg Kaiser respectively.

The literary career of von Unruh has been rather out of the ordinary. He sprang from an aristocratic family with a long tradition of service to the throne as high officials or army officers, and was, as has already been mentioned, an officer of Uhlans. When he was a cadet, eight years of age, he is said to have been put under arrest for referring to a sunset as "wunderschön," it being argued that expressions in use in girls' boarding schools were not suitable in the mouth of a future officer. His two pre-War plays, *Offiziere* and *Louis Ferdinand,* are in the old tradition. The production of the latter was prohibited in 1913, but in the same year von Unruh was awarded the Kleist Prize. During the War the three works, *Vor der Entscheidung, Opfergang,* and *Ein Ge-*

schlecht, were prohibited by Army General Headquarters. In 1920 von Unruh was nominated by Gerhart Hauptmann, as President of the Schiller Prize Committee, for the Schiller Prize, but the nomination was rejected by the Prussian Minister of Culture. In 1927 the Schiller Prize was divided between Hermann Burte, Fritz von Unruh, and Franz Werfel.

Von Unruh's conception of duty to the monarch, or to military superiors, which is the inspiration of the earlier plays, where it is shown in conflict with the personality of his characters, underwent a fundamental change. It became transformed into the conception of duty to one's fellow-men. The germ of the change is seen in the "dramatic poem" *Vor der Entscheidung,* written as early as the autumn of 1914, and in the trilogy von Unruh attempts to give dramatic form to his inward experience, with his hatred of war and his idea of the new era that is to come. Only the first two parts of the trilogy have so far appeared. The first part, written in the field in 1915 and 1916, is called *Ein Geschlecht;* the second part, finished in 1920, is called *Platz.* In the former, which is regarded as the most powerful war drama in contemporary German literature, the characters are all types; the mother who defends the existing order though she protests against war, the unbalanced daughter, the eldest son, imbued with the life-force and fretting against traditional restrictions, the cowardly son, and the youngest son, who is still immature. This family—the mother, the daughter, and the sons—is a microcosm of the human race.

The scene is at the entrance to a graveyard on the top of a mountain during a war. The whole scene takes place between night and morning. In the valley a battle is raging, while in the cemetery the mother is burying one of her four sons who has been killed in the fight. With her are her daughter and her youngest son. Her two other sons appear under the escort of soldiers. The eldest son has attempted to violate a woman, the cowardly son has refused to fight. They are tied to the cemetery gate, and the youngest son is taken away by the soldiers to be steeled in battle. Between the eldest son and the two women there is a violent scene. The son's nerves have been unstrung by the war, and he manifests a forbidden love towards his own sister, who reciprocates his desire and loosens his bonds. He reproaches their mother, their dead father, religion, law, everything which has hitherto been held sacred. He protests against the setting up of his father as an idol for him to worship, until he hurled the idol down and strode on over its ruins. He despises the mothers who say they wish they had more sons to sacrifice for the Fatherland. "I must go," he says, "where truth prevails, and falsehood no longer like a slug draws its slime over the purest of my impulses." The mother defends the existing order, but also apostrophises all mothers to mobilise against the madness of war. When the morning dawns, the eldest brother tears the cross from his brother's grave and then hurls himself from the wall to his death. Soldiers approach with news of victory; they pay homage to the dead soldiers in the cemetery, but prepare to drag away the corpse of the eldest son. The mother tries to prevent this, and tears his baton, the symbol of authority, from the hands of one of the officers. She announces the coming of a new generation that will make a more worthy use of the staff, and then is killed in a struggle.

The soldiers revolt and, led by the youngest son, rush down into the valley. The cowardly son is freed by one of the officers, because he is not worthy to die, but the other officer, uncertain whether the revolting soldiers can be restrained, begins to doubt the blessings of war. He throws away his red cloak, the symbol of war and its horrors, to be bleached by the sun of a new day.

The youngest son and this second officer foreshadow the new era. The conflict in the poet's soul between his earlier conception of duty and his newly won realisation of man's duty to mankind is solved in favour of the latter. The new humanity of the future is to be held above the narrower conception of nationality. But though von Unruh has a clear consciousness of what he hates and wishes to destroy in the old system, he has no clear view of what he wants to take its place. Yet he does sincerely believe in a better future. The sufferings of the War are only to be justified if a new humanity is to be the result, and in the second part of the trilogy von Unruh tries to come to closer grips with his Utopian ideal. Unfortunately, his creative power is not equal to the passion and enthusiasm which fill him. His characters are too abstract, incorporated ideas, lacking in the flesh and blood necessary for the stage. There is too much declamation, and it is a fault common to most of the expressionist dramatists that they talk glibly of humanity but have not succeeded in creating a plausible human being. The characters of expressionist drama have been compared to the rather wooden medieval drawings, with balloons issuing from their mouths to denote what they say. The dramatists overestimate the intellect, but at the same time they put forth their ideas in an emotional, ecstatic manner which is unsuitable for the presentation of abstract conceptions.

The scene of *Platz* is in a square surrounded by Government buildings. Most of the characters are given names, which are, for the most part, symbolic. The youngest son is Dietrich; the commandant is called Graf Gutundblut; a profiteer, whose opportunism permits him to adapt himself to all changes, is called Christlieb Schleich; and the daughters of the ruler of the State are Irene and Hyazinte. The action is involved and fantastic. The hero of the piece is Dietrich, now no longer the tempestuous revolutionary who seeks his ends by political means. He has undergone an inner transformation, his ideal has moved on to a higher and more abstract plane. He sees in Irene ("peace") a symbol of the future. Humanity is to be regenerated by a new relationship between man and woman. But the action is still insufficiently plastic, the characters still abstract types. In *Ein Geschlecht* the poet's inward experience has obviously been poured hot and glowing into dramatic form, but *Platz* is too much a product of the intellect, and fails to achieve the immediate appeal of the earlier play. Neither is the thought particularly clear, and it is not obvious whether Dietrich rejects the revolution and democracy for Irene's sake or not. When von Unruh is unable to fall back on immediate experience, his inventive talent is too weak to hide the creaking of the mechanism. The work is pervaded with the idea of the regenerating power of love, but this has not prevented von Unruh from inserting incidents where eroticism assumes the form of macabre perversion.

The unpublished, and perhaps unwritten, third part of

the trilogy is called *Dietrich,* and is to solve the problem of the new humanity which has not been solved in the first two parts. It is doubtful, at this stage, whether von Unruh possesses the staying power to round the trilogy off with the third part. He is a visionary, and, as has been shown by his recent tactless book of travel-sketches, *Flügel der Nike,* based on a very short stay in France and a few days in England, he is rather out of touch with reality. The more radical minds in Germany consider that von Unruh's pacifism does not accept the logical consequences; that it is too abstract and lacking in a clear understanding of the facts, a view with which the English reader of *Flügel der Nike* is inclined to agree.

Franz Werfel's trilogy, which was first performed in the autumn of 1921, is called *Spiegelmensch.* It illustrates Werfel's view of the double nature of man, the two conflicting aspects of the Ego upon which much of his poetry is based. In the young Goethe it was the emotion and the reason, in Werfel it is the higher and the lower Self. Thamal, the chief character, retires, wearied with life, to a monastery, where the abbot explains to him that he is not yet ripe to shun the world. He must first experience it. When Thamal is left alone, his glance falls on his reflection in a mirror; he is overcome by a feeling of repulsion and shoots at the reflection, thereby releasing from the smashed mirror Spiegelmensch, his other Ego, the incorporation of his lower instincts. Spiegelmensch becomes his constant companion, his Mephistopheles, and together they set forth into the world. With every new act of guilt committed by Thamal, Spiegelmensch gains more strength. They go to the house of Thamal's father, whom Thamal kills by the mere wish. Eventually Thamal and Spiegelmensch reach the country ruled by Ananthas, the serpent demon, the embodiment of all evil. Ananthas is conquered by Thamal and, at the urging of Spiegelmensch, allows himself to be deified by the people. This is a triumph for Spiegelmensch, that a noble deed should be followed by vanity and the lust for power. Spiegelmensch now thinks that he has turned the tables and can treat Thamal as his servant. In the third part of the trilogy, Thamal separates from his companion and, after various adventures, delivers himself voluntarily for trial. He takes upon himself full responsibility for his misdeeds, and utters his own fatal sentence, in spite of the efforts of Spiegelmensch to entice him again by visions of power, pleasure, and the fear of death. He drinks a cup of poison, which delivers him from his double, who steps back into the mirror. Thamal finds himself back in the monastery, and the mirror he now sees as a window, through which he looks out into a higher life.

There is an obvious resemblance to Goethe's *Faust* and to Ibsen's *Peer Gynt,* to say nothing of Grillparzer's *Der Traum ein Leben.* Thamal has, by his various adventures and experiences, to arrive at a realisation of his higher Self. The piece has many faults; the metaphysical ideas are too much in evidence, the construction is sketchy, but the effect on the stage is nevertheless impressive. Werfel's work is that of a profounder mind and a richer imagination than that of von Unruh, who poses questions but does not succeed in solving them. Werfel's work is more tangible, and he achieves a synthesis of emotion and intellect which in von Unruh appear to work separately.

Werfel calls his play a "magic trilogy." Kaiser's trilogy is of a very different kind. It is a tragedy of capitalism, of the curse of money, a subject which had already been treated in *Von Morgens bis Mitternachts.* The first part is called *Die Koralle* and the other two *Gas,* parts one and two, and Kaiser shows, in the fate of a gigantic gas factory and its workers during successive generations, how the masses prefer to keep their necks to the yoke, and are prepared to crucify their would-be saviour. They prefer to remain slaves to the machines.

The idea which runs through all Kaiser's dramas is the awakening of man from money slavery and drudgery to the realisation of a worthier life. His characters are products of the intellect, incorporated ideas, and, perhaps even more than other expressionist dramatists, he needs a thoroughly expert producer.

Ernst Toller has also tried to express the tragedy of capitalist civilisation in *Masse Mensch* and *Die Maschinenstürmer.* In the former play, it is a woman who leads the people and ultimately sacrifices herself for them. In *Die Maschinenstürmer,* which has as its theme the rising of the Nottingham weavers against the introduction of machinery about a hundred years ago, Toller again presents the idea of humanity and fraternity; but both these plays suffer from overweighting with matter more suited to the political tract than to the stage. He treats men in the mass, but in *Hinkemann* he shows a distinct advance in plastic power, in the ability to create an individual, and he may be classed with Werfel and von Unruh as one of the three hopes of the German stage.

*   *   *   *   *

I have so far been dealing with writers whose outlook on life was moulded or fundamentally changed by the War and its aftermath, and who are still groping their way up the slopes of Parnassus. Among those of an older generation whose influence has survived the War, I will only mention three of outstanding genius—two poets and a novelist. Each of them has the quality of detachment, and in each case it is like coming from the turbulence of a storm in night and chaos to a sanctuary where life flows tranquilly and there is time to think.

The Stefan George group at first sought to preserve detachment from the common herd by printing their works for a select circle in expensive editions, lacking punctuation and capitals, and with an unusual typography. Interest was confined to an æsthetic and esoteric cult, which found nothing suitable for poetry that was not beautiful. Now, however, George tries to influence German culture, but it is significant that none of his disciples has become a creator in any field of artistic production without breaking away from his influence. They have become mostly professors and critics, endeavouring to spread the light as seen by their master, who continues to live in retirement as a sort of prophet.

Though his art is usually regarded as purely intellectual, the emphasis being laid on harmony and form, yet the avoidance of contemplation and the cult of physical beauty are factors of no little importance in judging whether this poetry is of an entirely intellectual nature. George seeks, by strict formalism and elimination of the ephemeral, to create only that which has eternal value. The Expressionists also seek the permanent under the fleeting outward aspect, but by very different methods.

George keeps his distance from the realities of life and imagines that he thereby attains clarity of vision. The Expressionists seek reality on the basis of their War experience, and clarity of vision can only come to them after a Faustian, titanic, spiritual struggle, which is of the very essence of the German nature. And surely it is better that they should reach the harbour of spiritual peace *after* such a coming to grips with their own souls and with life, than that they should follow the example of George and start life without that spiritual conflict which means so much for a man's outlook and artistic development. To begin with the tranquillity of a George would lead, in men of lesser genius, to mental stagnation. Form, style, and thought have infinitely more significance when they are the result of spiritual conflict, and George's work demonstrates the danger of aloofness, for it appears frozen and bloodless, a mere cult of beauty, when compared with post-War literature. We have only to compare the dynamic development of Goethe towards classicism with the static repose of Stefan George to realise the latter's inferiority as a spiritual leader, and it is a spiritual leader whom the Germans always seek in literature. There can be no great art without tragedy, and this is precisely what George has eliminated, so that, instead of creating a world of art after mastering his own soul, his work appears as a flight from environment into a realm of artificial beauty. The Faustian striving is German, and George's art is the antithesis of this.

In contrast to George, the brilliant centre of a select cult, Rainer Maria Rilke has presented himself in his *Stundenbuch* as a lonely brooding monk coming to grips with his conception of God. Man is not for Rilke, as he is for George, the touchstone by which the universe is to be measured. It is in the wretched creatures of the earth that Rilke sees the clearest revelation of God, and it is to them that he addresses his poems, for them he manifests an abounding compassion.

No poet since Novalis has so sung of the longing for Death, and, like Novalis, Rilke finds a projection of the Madonna in the woman he loves, being able to sublimate earthly love into religious emotion. Throughout his poetry breathes a longing for God, whom he feels with mystic pantheism to be present in everything. Rilke was born in Prague, and he began his poetic career by a visit to Tolstoy in Russia, an experience which served to confirm the Slav strain of mysticism in his temperament. Later he became private secretary to Rodin in Paris, another experience which was not without influence on his technique and feeling for form. Rilke's mystic fervour is monastic, of the twilight. It is intensely introspective, and the centre of the poetic world he creates out of his own introspection is God. There is none of the voluptuous appeal of his fellow-Austrian, Hugo von Hofmannsthal. The feeling of humility before God, combined with a paradoxical insistence on God's dependence on man, is best seen in one of the most beautiful poems of the *Stundenbuch*:

> "Was wirst du tun, Gott, wenn ich sterbe?
> Ich bin dein Krug (wenn ich zerscherbe?)
> Ich bin dein Trank (wenn ich verderbe?)
> Bin dein Gewand und dein Gewerbe,
> mit mir verlierst du deinen Sinn.
>
> Nach mir hast du kein Haus, darin
> dich Worte, nah und warm, begrüssen.
> Es fällt von deinen müden Füssen
> die Samtsandale, die ich bin. . . .

GERMANY

Dein Blick. . . .

. . . .

wird kommen, wird mich suchen, lange—
und legt beim Sonnenuntergange
sich fremden Steinen in den Schoss.

Was wirst du tun, Gott? Ich bin bange."

Thomas Mann, whose pre-War masterpiece was the
novel *Buddenbrooks,* and whose *Zauberberg* was one of
the literary sensations after the War, specialises in the
psychology of degeneration, physical and spiritual.
Buddenbrooks possesses the sub-title, "Decay of a
Family," and in this chronicle of the degeneration of
one family Thomas Mann illustrates the decay of bourgeois civilisation which has been preached from a
different point of view by Nietzsche. The Buddenbrooks
were merchants in the old Hansa town of Lübeck. The
earliest generation to which we are introduced is represented by Johann Buddenbrook, a sturdy old business
man, who is succeeded by his son, the consul, the first
in the family to show signs of an un-bourgeois romantic
religiosity. The consul's eldest son, Thomas, who
becomes a senator, betrays signs of weariness and
neuroticism, and the second son is inactive and inclined
to introspection. The fourth generation dies out in
Hanno, the son of the senator, a sickly, dreamy young
musician, who does not live beyond his teens. The mer-
chant family has eventually produced artists and brought
about its own downfall.

The difference between Nietzsche's conception of
degeneration and that of Thomas Mann is that Nietzsche
saw degeneracy in the stereotyped mediocrity of the
bourgeois, whereas for Mann it is the man of action, the

business man, the solid bourgeois who is the healthy type; the intellectual and the artist are abnormal, a deviation from the species, the domination of the intellect or the artistic perceptions being signs of degeneration. All Thomas Mann's works are studies of such decay or of the problem whether the normal man can be an artist or the artist conform to the norm. He is, perhaps, fighting his own spiritual battle. He is tremendously interested in the problem of illness, and his works are full of death-scenes, in the portrayal of which he seems to take a keen artistic and psychological delight.

This predilection for studying people's reaction to illness is seen at its height in *Der Zauberberg*, an enormous novel of some 1,400 pages, full of philosophical meditations and with but little action. The Magic Mountain is Davos, and the scene is a sanatorium for consumptives to which Hans Castorp, a young engineering student, comes on a three weeks' visit to his cousin, Joachim Ziemssen. The doctor discovers that Castorp himself has slight signs of tuberculosis, and he remains at the sanatorium as a patient. His will to recover and return to the normal world, to what is known at Davos as "the flat land," becomes gradually paralysed, and he remains for seven years. His cousin Joachim, whose one consuming desire is to get well and take up the army commission which has been offered him, leaves the sanatorium against the advice of the physician, but is compelled to return and dies. Joachim is drawn in direct contrast to Hans Castorp. He fights against the disease and is conquered physically but not morally. Castorp is demoralised by his illness. One of the physicians, a psychologist, gives a course of lectures, which all the patients are expected to attend, on " Love as a Factor in the Development of Disease." He expounds his theory that repressed love assumes the form of disease, that the symptoms of disease are disguised manifestations of love, and that all disease is, in fact, metamorphosed love. There are various sharply drawn characters who influence Castorp in different ways, including a woman with whom he falls in love. When she leaves the sanatorium, she gives him an X-ray photograph of the upper part of her body, without the face, and he often presses it to his lips.

Castorp is unable to reconcile the conflicting forces, to all of which he reacts, until he eventually ceases to try, and sinks into a state of apathy for which the only parallel I know in European literature is the Russian Oblomov. The thunderbolt which bursts the magic mountain asunder is the War. Castorp awakes from his seven years' sleep, and the last we see of him is in the thick of the fighting in France. It is a touch of supreme irony that it is not Joachim, the soldier, who would not let his illness conquer his spirit, who survives to participate in the War, but Castorp, to whom his illness almost appears to have been welcome as a justification to himself for his apathy and lack of will to face the normal world. There is really no end to the book. The War is employed as a *deus ex machina,* and the author has not succeeded in reconciling the normal and the abnormal in Castorp. It is again the perhaps unsolvable problem of the two aspects of the Ego, of double personality. Goethe, Werfel, and Thomas Mann have each portrayed two opposite aspects of man's many-sided personality, but whether it be the antithesis of reason and emotion, the higher and the lower self, or the bourgeois and the artistic, none of these writers has succeeded in reconciling the two in his works, however successfully he may have done so in his own person. The Expressionists, with their anti-bourgeois intellectualism, were certainly too one-sided to be able to create the synthesis of the old and the new, which is necessary for the establishment of a new social organisation, but they might, perhaps, have learned from Thomas Mann something about the essential nature of the artist.

*　　*　　*　　*　　*

The general impression of expressionist literature is that it was feverish and morbid, intensely impatient, chaotic, but fundamentally idealistic. It was too near the War and the Revolution to be anything but subjective. The War and the subsequent period were treated ecstatically, and the time had not yet come when sufficient distance had been gained for objective, or even satiric, treatment. Expressionist literature reveals the anguish of the German soul, and the only literature with which it can be compared in this respect is that of contemporary Russia, which also tends to treat man in the mass.

The pessimism which appears to darken nearly all the imaginative writing of this time has reference only to the past and the present. With regard to the future it is fundamentally optimistic, even though this optimism is not based on very sound premises. The purpose is vague, and as Germans always need an intellectual purpose and a spiritual leader, the blind groping in an atmosphere of chaos was bound to give place before long to a more tangible aim and a definite direction.

GERMANY

The cry for a New Objectivity is already heard in the land. The post-expressionist painters and writers are tired of types, abstractions, and symbols, and are seeking a New Reality. They are still in the stage of setting up programmes, but it is to be hoped that the inspiration will endure long enough for the production of works of art.

Some writers are turning to historical figures for their subjects; von Unruh has written a drama on Napoleon, and Werfel on the ill-fated Emperor Maximilian of Mexico. At the same time a neo-Catholic group of writers is making headway, the Catholic Church providing a haven for minds which are weary of struggling.

Austria, mainly Vienna and the now Czechoslovak town of Prague, is strongly represented with names like von Hofmannsthal, Schnitzler, Rilke, Werfel, Georg Trakl, Albert Ehrenstein, and Max Brod. The part of the Jews, or those of Jewish descent, is large out of all proportion to their numbers, for the tendencies of modern German literature are more in accordance with the Jewish temperament than were nineteenth-century Realism and Naturalism. I need only mention the names of Schnitzler, von Hofmannsthal, Jakob Wassermann, Franz Werfel, Ernst Toller, Carl Sternheim, Walter Hasenclever, Ludwig Rubiner, Albert Ehrenstein, Max Brod, Ernst Barlach, Else Lasker-Schüler, Ernst Lissauer, Stefan Zweig.

The literature of both France and Germany is overburdened with introspection, but the fundamental difference appears to be this: The German mind has been trying since the War to adapt itself to the changed conditions, to create new forms. The French mind (there

87

are, of course, exceptions) has been less successful in tearing itself sufficiently free from its pre-War grooves to realise that new creation muſt be on a new basis. If anything new and of permanent value to European culture is to issue from the ferment of the laſt decade, the country from which it is moſt likely to come is Germany.

WILLIAM ROSE.

SPAIN

PERHAPS in no country in Europe is the reaction of the twentieth century against the nineteenth century in every aspect of life so marked as in Spain. This conscious opposition is a characteristic feature of all, or nearly all, contemporary Spanish literature.

The great event which affected profoundly the political, social, and literary life of Spain precedes by sixteen years the European War. An event of political, but far greater social and psychological, importance separates two centuries and two generations—the war with the United States of America, which ended with the Treaty of Paris. An increasing number of people gained acute consciousness of the national position and the difficult problems that had to be faced. It was a question of to be or not to be.

The defeat had brought with it a necessary and, as we now see, a highly salutary amputation of the last remains of the greatest empire of modern times. War and peace proved the falseness and emptiness of official pretensions. Slowly the opinion gained ground that the real life of the country was flowing through channels clearly distinct from those which had been created by the political institutions of the nineteenth century, which had been showered upon an indifferent people by a minority of professional politicians. One of the many results of this attitude is the intense dislike the modern Spaniard feels for the professional politician, and the disrepute into which parliamentary rhetoric, the chief weapon of such a politician, has fallen. Responsible people saw the necessity of disciplining public opinion and organising a new policy. At the time the *Union Nacional* began its activities; Joaquin Costa, jurist, historian, and impassioned counsel for the prosecution of the nineteenth century, was the leader. He voiced these aspirations and spoke about the "Europeanisation" of Spain, the necessity of looking after the larder and the school-room, the improvement of agriculture, the development of the natural wealth of the soil, and a radical and urgent school reform. Many, if not most, of the demands of Costa have since become guiding principles in the Ministries of Public Works and Public Instruction.

During this period of severe criticism the younger generation of contemporary writers began to live and to work. It is a period, on the one hand, of profound despondency; on the other, of marvellous hopes and of relief. These young men exalted the moral greatness of their country and denounced its material decadence. But once more these hopes required selection and this reformatory enthusiasm stricter discipline in order to be effective.[1]

The attitude which is common to all these writers is their dislike of the preceding generation. The literature of the nineteenth century in Spain is, according to them, with few exceptions, false, rhetorical, insincere, and either ridiculous or a cesspool of iniquity. One of their more

[1] Some of the daily and weekly newspapers of that period are typical of this national desire for renovation which they express, some of them at least, in its crudest form : *Vida Nueva* (Autumn, 1898), *Revista Nueva* (1899), *Alma Española* (1903), *España* (1903-4). They all were short-lived.

important victims was Don José Echegaray (1832-1916), dramatist, engineer, politician, economist, director of large companies, and official genius, about whom it was said that the engineers excused his mathematical weaknesses by referring to his greatness as a dramatic author, while the critics excused his literary lapses by pointing to his remarkable achievements as an engineer. Be this as it may, his art startled agreeably but did not shock the middle classes, and secured him an immense following and the Nobel Prize.

The younger men trained their taste and judgment by turning in a very different direction. Many of them were under the educational influence of Don Francisco Giner de los Rios, whose personality fills with a luminous glow the Spanish nineties and the first decade of the twentieth century. They wandered over the desolate magnificence of Castile and saw, as it were, Spanish history from the inside. They wanted to be better Spaniards. They visited towns and villages, they founded archæological and historical associations. They rediscovered the great painter of Toledo, El Greco, thanks to the labours of Don Manuel Cossio, who with unequalled generosity has supplied foreign writers on Spain with the fruits, rarely acknowledged, of his researches. They took an interest in popular art and began to understand the history of the Peninsula as an organic growth of immense complexity in quite a new and unexpected way. They turned to the Spanish Classics and studied them in this new spirit. If the nineteenth century was not forgotten it was because a great master of literary history, Marcelimo Menéndez y Pelayo, was the necessary starting-point for all methodical exploration, and, it might be added, because of the spiritual affinity between these moderns and the romantic journalist Larra (1809-1837), a tragic and extremely suggestive figure, who criticised with macabre humour his romantic contemporaries and the vileness of his period.

About this time (1899) Nietzsche was translated by Don José de Caso, a professor at the University of Madrid and a pupil of the great and noble Don Francisco, as everyone called Giner de los Rios. This volume travelled in many a rucksack over the roads of the Spanish provinces and was read in the shadow of many a romanesque or Gothic building. Pio Baroja, about whom I shall speak presently, describes in one of his novels, perhaps his best, *The Way of Perfection,* the first contact with the German poet-philosopher, when, in the scene in which *Zarathustra* is turned into broken Spanish by a German engineer up in the mountains of Peñalara, shortly before sunrise, his Spanish companion thinks, in the presence of the gloriously rising sun, that here may be found a new message of hope and rebirth. We may add that such influences were slight, as the Spanish temper healthily reacted against superman and supermorals.

To this generation belongs Sr. Martinez Ruiz, better known as " Azorin," now of the Spanish Royal Academy.

Azorin's subjects give us a clue to the character of his work. In the endless procession of words, of feelings, personalities and periods, ideas and concepts, he isolates those which seem to him significant; but by saying this we only state that Azorin is an artist. These objects which occupy a prominent place in the field of his vision have been chosen by him because he finds in them a sympathetic response. He sees in them tiny mirrors which reflect his most intimate apprehensions. The artist Azorin finds this response in humble things and humble sentiments, the village and the small town—one of his books is called *The Little Town*—obscure people, amongst them serene and exquisitely cultured personalities which shrink from crude definition, half forgotten writers and artists who are restored to intense life for a moment in a marginal note, ambiguous sentiments, iridescent and contradictory, pain which is sweet joy, intensity in smallness.

His notes—they rarely are more—were printed mostly in the form of newspaper articles, and nearly all his books are anthologies of short essays, such as the early *Confessions of a Little Philosopher* (1904), or the later *Don Juan* (1922), and the recent *Doña Ines* (1925). Perhaps his most typical and therefore interesting period is that of his youth, when he wandered over Spain and wrote *The Route of Don Quixote, Castile,* and *Spain.* Quite recently his play *Old Spain* (with the title in English) was produced in Madrid, and in an even later theatrical experiment he challenges the youngest and most daring exponents of the drama.

The marginal note is his favourite method when his subject is a writer, and one of his books is called *On the Margin of the Classics.* No critic has done more to make Spaniards read and understand the great Spanish writers of the past who seemed beyond hope removed from the spirit of the twentieth century. Azorin is no historian in the ordinary sense. The work of selection, always necessary, is here carried to its utmost limits; of a long work, of a whole period, there remains little more than a sentence, a line from a poem, in which Azorin detects a gesture which speaks to us through the ages or the last pulsations of a life almost extinguished. Sometimes his method is comparative: yesterday—to-day; and then his subject is the passage of time, *real* time, leaving its harmonising and mellowing mark.

Azorin's style has been called un-Spanish. It should be described as very unlike what people in the nineteenth century thought a Spanish style should be. He divests himself deliberately of flowing folds, of ample periods, which please the half-trained ear. His garment is an unassuming grey tunic, poor of ornament but exquisitely and tightly woven. He is geometrical, monotonous, severe, and immeasurably subtle. The grand manner of the preceding generation thundered in rhetorical sentences, but the names of things it had forgotten. Azorin writes short sentences, not syntactically connected, and knows how to call everything by its name. The names of the different instruments used in trades, the classic word long fallen into disuse, the popular expression restored to literary dignity, are the stones he fits into a comparatively simple pattern; but their simplicity is only apparent. A disappearing light, a window, a sentence from some classic become symbols in his hands and every abandoned garden becomes the expression of the secular fatigue of a tired race; the tail light of a train disappearing in the night is turned into a representation of the inexorable passage of time. His subject is the spiritual reality of things, their suggestive value, their poetry. He taught a difficult simplicity and the lesson has been learnt by all in Spain who deserve the name of artist, especially the poets (who had sinned in the past, in Spain, and elsewhere, more than the prose writers). After him come Antonio Machado and Juan Ramon Jimenez.

What vision of Spain does this subtle mind raise before our eyes? Spain is the subject of one of his best books, *Spanish Readings,* and it is the underlying unity of all his work. He says himself: " The coherence of my work lies in a certain curiosity for Spanish atmosphere, landscape, literature, art, towns, domestic interiors, and an anxiety for a future of well-being and justice for Spain." According to him the Spanish spirit consists in a balance of ideal and practice, idea and action, manifest in all literature, even in the writings of the mystics (St. Teresa said: " If you are in the kitchen, understand that the Lord is about among the pots and pans "). The failure of Spain's great historical effort is, according to Azorin, not a discovery of our generation, which not infrequently is sweeping in its judgments and superficial in its generalities. He gives us, for instance, a number of passages from the diplomat Saavedra Fajardo (1584-1648) criticising waste and impolicy, writing that " it is better to govern well than to increase the Empire," and declaring that it is necessary to educate young men abroad ("No youth grows into a success in his own country "). He turns to the first generation which flourished in the sixteenth century and, through his monocle, examines the memorable figure of the philosopher, Juan Luis Vives, professor at Oxford. He gives no account of his views on the education of women or of his logic, but says: " Perhaps he felt more profoundly than anyone the eternal poetry of what is small and belongs to the daily round." Somewhere else he selects a number of very trenchant remarks from the works of the soldier, traveller, and scholar, José Cadalso (1746-1782), who translated Milton, imitated Young, anticipated romantic ideas in literature and life, and was killed during the siege of Gibraltar; and Azorin adds: "The reader will doubtless be surprised by the remarkable modernity of the criticism of this distinguished author." In this quintessential manner he explores the past and not only raises before our eyes writers and thinkers but reinterprets their creatures. It is difficult to forget his vision and reinterpretation of Cervantes' equivocal *Licentiate of Glass*.

In the same selection Azorin, most diffident of men, reveals his own ideals. He does not admire theatrical greatness but spiritual life, which is sometimes more intense and admirable in its minute manifestations than in heroic struggles. In an essay on the obscure Don Diego, the "Knight of the Green Cloak," who met Don Quixote and treated him with courtesy, he says: "Who do you think are more important for the progress and greatness of the nations—solitary, erratic, fantastic minds, always in quest of the ideal, or these prosaic, methodical, law-abiding people who respect tradition, are active, hard-working and honest, merchants, workmen, and labourers?"

Azorin contributed two new qualities to modern Spanish literature; a very personal, unrhetorical style, and a preference for what is small and delicate.

The Basque writer, Pio Baroja, began life as a doctor, then managed his family business, a bakery, and at the same time took to literature with a characteristically

Basque decision and independence, in the same spirit in which his ancestors had, according to the old poem, defeated the hosts of Charlemagne under the leadership of the mythical Bernardo del Carpio. His early work, such as *Sombre Lives,* shows a well-defined trace of his Russian readings, especially of Gorki, and one of his best novels, to which I have already alluded, *The Way of Perfection,* belongs to this early period. It is the story of one of his restless heroes who wander over the face of the earth. Towards the year 1904 he became well known through a trilogy of novels, entitled *The Struggle for Life* (*The Search, Rotten Weeds,* and *Red Sunrise*), acutely realistic in technique and enveloped in an unromantic pessimism, very different from that associated with the first part of the nineteenth century. In these books he depicts the lives of the *Golfos,* the Apaches, of Madrid, of political criminals, beggars, and prostitutes. Shortly before the War he began the vast cycle of stories called *Reminiscences of a Man of Action,* of which he has published so far twelve volumes, amongst them the magnificent *Brigand Squadron.* He narrates episodes in the life of one of his ancestors, his uncle Eugenio Avinareta, conspirator and adventurer, who had fought against the French in 1809, took part in every rising under Ferdinand VII. and the early years of Isabella II., went to Greece to join Lord Byron, embarked for Mexico with General Barradas, and in the year 1830 appeared on the barricades in Paris. This was a man after Baroja's heart, who revenges himself upon his peaceful and sedentary life by re-living the dangerous existence of his pugnacious uncle, who loved action for its own sake, but was devoid of ideals and ideas.

CONTEMPORARY EUROPEAN LITERATURE

This series brings to our mind the longer one—about sixty volumes—of the *National Episodes* by Benito Perez Galdós. It seems to me that although Galdós doubtless shows greater inventive power and creates more profoundly human types, perhaps in a somewhat conventional setting reminiscent of the background of an academic picture with an historical subject, Baroja's deliberately uncouth prose, his absence of artifice, and incredible carelessness, produce—one sometimes doubts if in spite or because of seeming gross errors of composition—an impression of painfully intense life which Galdós rarely, if ever, achieves.

The theme of the vagabond is a classic one in Spanish literature; from Lazarillo de Tormes and Guzmán de Alfarache to Avinareta we have a procession of erratic figures. The great Don Quixote himself, so noble, so human, and so tragic, is he not one of them? But by reference to him the difference between two types becomes clear. He has an ideal, and all his movement is due to his devoted service to this ideal. Lazarillo, Guzmán, and Avinareta have none. Little does it matter if Baroja's hero was a brave soldier and, in his way, a gentleman, while the *pícaros* belong to the lowest of the low. Avinareta, like them, is unsocial and lonely. He is not, as Ortega y Gasset says in his excellent essay on Baroja, a man of organised action, but an adventurer. His political ideals are a pretext. If he differs from the classic little Lazarus, it is because he loves adventure for its own sake, while his ragged predecessor, like some pitiful anti-Faust, asks the moment to stay and is content with a modicum of comfort. . . .

Perhaps Baroja forgets that the healthy man does not

love action, however much he may admire the results of
action—that he is usually lazy. He dreams of an adventurous, varied, cosmopolitan existence in which his Basque
heroes lead an apparently purposeless life, which affords
the writer a pretext for descriptions which are unrivalled
in the contemporary literature of Spain. He excels in the
vision of towns, the large cities through which the
creatures of his imagination pass and repass; the bitter
poetry of the byways of Soho and the dynamic greatness
of the London Docks have been described by him with
great power in *The City of Fog*. The truth is that Baroja
is rheumatic and dyspeptic, and therefore admires the
activities of his heroes, who suffer from no such com-
plaints. This "activism" offers him a safety-valve for his
profound and catholic pessimism. Action is a means of
escape, of escape from oneself, of escape from the
mediocrity of middle-class life; the escape from false pretensions of a man whose greatest anxiety it is not to be
deceived. In the best of his ghastly philosophical novels,
which has acted as a powerful stimulant on every man
of letters in Spain, *The Tree of Knowledge,* he says:
"Life in general, especially his life, seemed to him
something ugly, turbid, painful, and unconquerable."
The only chance is to forget, for what room can there
be for Hamlet-like introspection when our whole being
is in movement? Perhaps it could be said, with some
slight exaggeration, that the belief, so dear to Englishmen,
that exercise and games are a healthy corrective for
those afflicted with a morbid desire to think is here
transferred into a fiercer and more barbarous world.
Those who do not make use of such intoxicants will,
according to Baroja, end like Andrés Hurtado, the hero

of *The Tree of Knowledge,* who poisons himself just when he is about to find salvation in scientific research.

Baroja is a man of unflinching artistic honesty, and in this sincerity, it seems to me, lies the real value of his production. He should be read with care, for no Spanish writer is so unequal. If Azorin as a stylist may be compared to an intaglio-worker, Baroja writes with a complete disregard of all rules of grammar and literary composition. As in the case of Stendhal, the accusation has been brought against him that he wrote badly. Baroja, on a memorable day, threw the grammar of the Spanish Academy out of the window, and followed only his instinct for what is significant and characteristic with a precision and honesty which is, I think, without parallel in modern literature. His very personal idiosyncrasies, his fundamental belief in the stupidity, ugliness, and in-effectualness of the average human life are manifestations of a great and noble temperament. His anxiety is not to be duped, and ferociously he turns on anyone who tries to do so. It speaks highly for the soundness of Spanish literary instincts that the recent inquiry conducted by a Madrid daily paper revealed the preference of the public for this writer, who, less than any other, has ever praised anything or flattered anyone. This great hater, with his irresistible desire to be unpleasant, was declared to be the most popular novelist of the Peninsula.

In the extreme north-west of Spain there is a country which is the lyrical province of the Peninsula. Its capital is the " Rome of the West," St. James of Compostela, to which thousands of pilgrims flocked every year from all over Europe. In landscape and character it differs profoundly from the barrenness and luminous clearness of Castile. The Atlantic cuts deep into the green hills, a gentle, moist air envelops everything, softening hard outlines, and this country is inhabited by a race which, dear to Celtomaniacs of the present, in the Middle Ages supplied the Peninsula with a lyrical dialect which even the poets of Castile had to learn when they abandoned epic poetry for the sweet conceits of semi-popular lyrical song. Not only did the Galician language—not dissimilar from the Portuguese, but lacking its nasal sounds—become the poetic Lingua Franca of the Peninsula, but the feminine, although not effeminate, spirit of this poetry set the fashion in the Middle Ages, when the King of Castile, Alfonso the Learned, wrote his songs to the Blessed Virgin. From this country comes Don Ramón Maria del Valle Inclán, a writer of jewelled prose and of poetry great in technical perfection. Only a Galician could write a pastoral like *Aromas de Leyenda* (1906). In his youth he emigrated to Mexico, and there acquired a treasury of Creole words which seems inexhaustible, as his last sensational novel, *The Tyrant Banderas,* proves. He professed a romantic attachment to the Carlist cause, episodes of which he describes in the trilogy of novels *The Carlist War*. His physical appearance is most striking: one-armed, with a waxen face, a long, now almost white beard, his tortoise-shell spectacles, not reminiscent of America but of the satirist of the seventeenth century, Quevedo. His conversation is a work of art.

If Baroja writes the worst Spanish in which a great talent ever expressed itself, Valle Inclán has written some of the best and the most poetic. His style is marvellously carved, set with precious words, yet never merely precious but always rich in associations and lyrical qualities, charged with emotional significance. His ancestors are Barbey D'Aurevilly (whose *Diaboliques* he imitates in *Femininas*) and Villiers de l'Isle Adam. Like D'Annunzio, he combines chiselled perfection with a preference for scenes of barbaric cruelty. The most favourable approach to this writer leads through the reminiscences of the Marquess of Bradomin, four novels which he calls *Sonatas,* and of which the *Summer Sonata,* a wild Mexican tale, and the *Autumn Sonata,* a Casanovian story which plays in his native Galicia, are perhaps the most perfect literary works of art produced in Spain during the twentieth century. After the year 1908 Valle Inclán began to write dramatic novels in dialogue, after the manner of the great masterpiece— indeed, the greatest before *Don Quixote—La Celestina* (translated by James Mabbe, *Don Diego Puedeser,* into English under the title of *The Spanish Bawd*). I think the most representative of these epic-dramatic compositions is *Voces de Gesta* (1912), a tale of primeval passions which rise up clamorously like natural forces, noble and a-moral like the powers of the gods, from souls which move in the forests of a primitive life. With the subject contrasts the delicate art in which it finds expression. It seems as if this contrast is the essential point on which the æsthetic significance of his work depends, which derives from the eternal pleasure we find in an immaculate human gesture in the face of all the powers of nature and hell. And yet here is no art of cold perfection at all costs, no pseudo-classical architecture, but a skill and knowledge steeped in popular association, local colour, and that Mediterranean worship of the earth which, married to intellect, is at the root of all great art. This applies specially to the later dramatised narratives, *Heráldic Eagle* and *The Romance of the Wolves,* which he called barbaric comedies.

After 1914, but in no connection with the War, we notice the influence of very modern literary forms, and he produces small dialogues, grotesque pieces of witty distortion which he called *Esperpentos (Spooks),* small satirical pieces based on observation of popular types and popular language, far removed from the æsthetic principles of his *Sonatas.* Amongst them are *Divine Words,* a procession of Galician beggars, and *Lights of Bohemia,* a powerful and dreamlike vision of the literary underworld of Madrid.

We have said little about Valle Inclán as a poet, although to find a parallel to such linguistic and metrical mastery we would have to go back to the medieval virtuosos of the *Arte Mayor,* with whom he has a remarkable affinity. His *Pipe of Hashish* is perhaps the best book of nonsense verse ever written, and it is probable that Valle Inclán will survive in history as the spontaneous, incredibly easy metrifier rather than as the artificer of his early years.

> " Mis sentidos tornan á ser infantiles,
> Tiene el mundo una gracia matinal,
> Mis sentidos como gayos tamboriles
> Cantan en la entraña del azul cristal."

And yet he created human types—the exquisite Xavier de Bradomin, who was " ugly, catholic, and sentimental," the terrible Don Juan Manuel Montenegro of the *Comedias Bárbaras*—which will live in history as representatives of the Spanish literature of the early twentieth century;

but I doubt their survival in the heart and imagination of men. Their hold on us—and this is the weakness of this great artist—is violent, but short and precarious. They are products of pure artistry. They lack depth and variety, that convincing appeal which comes from great art, in which all the powers of the human soul have free play, and in which moral fears, doubts, virtue and vice, sin and redemption, are the distant and, of course, unconscious but ever-present accompaniment of the interplay of æsthetic forces. In this sense Valle Inclán occupies a lonely place in the social literature of our time. He far outgrew the sad conceits of "Art for Art's sake." He produced finished and complete work, although his generation finished few things. He left behind a romantic and feudal Spain, and, with his immense talent and the immense knowledge of his craft, he sat for a time uncomfortably wedged between yesterday and to-morrow. And now the gnarled old tree produces fruit, bitter, acid, and refreshing, which far surpasses in subtlety of perfume and unexpectedness of colour that of the youngest and most intensively cultivated trees. Majestically his foliage sways in the wind of 1927.

From Galicia we take the "French Way," the route of the pilgrims of Compostela, back to the Basque Provinces. There was born another of those fierce individualists, of the kind that was never conquered, either by Augustus or by Charlemagne. A Basque can only be conquered by himself, and in this sense St. Ignatius Loyola is the typical Basque. The complement of extreme individualism is found in the rigours of self-imposed extreme discipline. Miguel de Unamuno, Professor of Greek in Salamanca,

and now an exile, is such a man, with aspirations of incredible intensity, and a discipline of his own observance
which is constantly being broken down by his volcanic
temperament.

(Ramiro de Maeztu, who late in life became a passionate adherent to Catholic discipline is also Basque. He
is chiefly known as a journalist, and he lived for many
years in London as correspondent of a Madrid paper.
Under the influence of the Guild Socialists—who, in
their turn, owe much to him—he wrote a book in English
which does not deserve the oblivion into which it has
fallen. Recently he published an interesting book entitled
Don Quixote, Don Juan, and La Celestina, in which he
represents the novel of Cervantes as an expression of
Spanish decadence.)

There is no doubt that Unamuno is one of the most
original thinkers in Spain. He belongs to a generation
that wished to enter the intellectual and political currents
of Europe at any price. Unamuno said that it is better
for Spain to be a first-class African power than a third-
class European one, and that it is necessary to emphasise
national qualities at the expense of that which is superficial importation. His philosophy is intuitive. He was—
perhaps his readings of Plotinus and of Schelling have
something to do with it—a Bergsonian before Bergson,
and a mystic who in *Love and Education* warned the
youth of Spain against the over-estimation of science.
Unamuno is a poet in prose and in metre (*Poems,* 1908).

He is immensely prolific, and his pages are of very
unequal value.[1] In the fierce and lonely atmosphere of
Salamanca he read omnivorously and followed the con-

[1] See his essays, published by *La Residencia de Estudiantes.*

temporary literatures of most European countries. There are few people in the Peninsula who have a knowledge and understanding of English literature comparable to his. To hear him talking to friends and disciples during one of those walks along the River Tormes, with the deep orange-coloured tower of the cathedral in the distance rising up above the bizarre architecture of the ancient city, was an unforgettable experience. He who claimed to be a first-class African did more than any other man in Spain to make foreign writers known in his country.

It can be said that all the work of Unamuno is concerned with one problem—personal immortality. With all the powers of his soul he struggles with the eternal question. He sums up his position in *The Tragic Sentiment of Life* (so ably translated into English by Mr. Crawfurd Flitch), which was followed last year by *The Agony of Christianity* (published in French). For Unamuno Christ reveals Himself as the great warrior against evil, overturning the tables of the money-changers in the Temple, until in *The Christ of Velazquez* He is conceived in a profounder way as the final expression of an eternal mystery. This endecasyllabic poem, difficult and long, contains some of the most intimate aspects of the spiritual life of its author.

A man so intensely absorbed in the spiritual life of Europe had to deal with the one work of art which sums up the Spanish view of the world, the *Don Quixote*. This concern with Cervantes' masterpiece is characteristic of modern Spanish literature, and there is hardly a writer of consequence who has not made some such declaration of Quixotic faith. Ortega y Gasset, Maeztu, and Salvador de Madariaga are examples to the point. The latter's *Guía del Lector del Quixote* is a remarkable study by this distinguished bilingual Hispano-English novelist and journalist, who has collected his essays on Galdás, Pérez de Ayala, Unamuno, Baroja, Valle Inclán, Azorín, and Miró under the title *Semblanzas Literarias Contemporaneas* (1924). Unamuno wrote his *Life of Don Quixote and Sancho Panza* in 1905, and to him must be traced what might be called the "Pirandellian" interpretation of Don Quixote. Don Quixote is here a living personality which incarnates in the realistic brain of Cervantes. It is not Cervantes who invents the Don Quixote to whom the Basque Professor dedicates his commentary of song and prayer. This idea (and we may add that Signor Pirandello agrees that Cervantes suggested to him the idea which is so characteristic of his plays) has been elaborated critically by Professor Américo Castro in his masterly book on *The Thought of Cervantes*.

Ten years after the *Life of Don Quixote,* Unamuno returned to the same interpretation in the story called *Fog* (1914).

It is difficult to give to English readers an accurate idea of the position occupied in Spanish literature by the famous Vicente Blasco Ibañez, familiar to every friend of the cinema, and immensely popular in England and the United States. He comes from the Mediterranean south-east of Spain, and began life as a follower of Zola, although his impulsive temperament differs greatly from that of the French novelist. He possessed great gifts, and his early Valencian novels, such as *La Barraca* (1898), *Cañas y Barro* (1902), are perfect as naturalistic descriptions of the small world of the "Huerta" of Valencia. But he was not content to deal with his rustic provincial characters. He wrote a novel on Bilbao (*The Intruder,* 1904), on Jerez (*The Bodega*), on Madrid (*The Horde,* which Baroja thinks is based on his trilogy), until the notorious *Blood and Sand* (1908) made him a cosmopolitan novelist. Then he wrote *The Four Horsemen of the Apocalypse* (1916) during the War, a book which, for reasons hardly connected with literature, became the most popular American novel of the twentieth century.

He lost his place in Spanish literature, where he ranks as a belated realist of some importance. The success of his impressionistic technique, his prodigious sense of colour, sun, brutality, smells, and sounds, his Mediterranean exuberance, his unbelievable gusto, cannot be denied. But his great talent is evident only in those early novels, which are unknown outside Spain.

The contemporary Spanish theatre is largely due to the work of Jacinto Benavente, who, influenced by French writers like Lavedan and Donnay and to some extent by Shakespeare, upon whose translations he worked all his life, began to write dramas of very simple outline in which conversation takes the place of action, and in which slightly snobbish society people, endowed with great wit, fenced with each other and used language as some elegant foil. The last memory of the melodrama of Echegaray faded into oblivion. It had been dealt its death-blow by Benavente's *Lo Cursi* (1901), an untranslatable title full of suggestive significance.[1]

Benavente explored the possibilities of the symbolic

[1] Pretentious; "refined" and therefore vulgar.

and poetic drama, *The Witches' Sabbath* (1903), *The Fiery Dragon, Princess Baby;* the philosophical comedy, *Los Intereses Creados* ("The world is already old and doddering; Art will not resign itself to grow old, and, in order to appear young, it muſt pretend to babble"); the realiſtic drama, *Señora Ama;* the melodrama, *The Badly Beloved* (1913), one of his maſterpieces which enjoys a great vogue in America. But there is no doubt that he excels in the high comedy of conversation (*As They Are, Autumn Roses,* 1905). The years which coincide with the European War brought him the Nobel Prize, but were unfortunate for his talent. He sank low into moralising and sentimental declamation until, in 1925 and 1926, two works, *Pinpricks* and *The Butterfly which flew over the Sea,* raised him again to the front rank of contemporary dramatiſts.[1]

If Benavente is cosmopolitan in his technique and metropolitan in his subjeᴄts, the brothers Joaquin and Serafin Alvarez Quintero have limited themselves to Andalusia and have produced the Andalusian *Sainete,* a one-aᴄt comedy, which is a delight and an enchantment; *Malasombra* and *The Patio* are winged pieces of poetry. When they attempt ambitious conſtruᴄtions they fail, although there is at leaſt one play in three aᴄts, entitled *Flowers* (1908), which is free from the vulgar and philistine sentimentality which disfigures so many of their longer works. *Flowers,* like the flowers of Seville, is a memory to be cherished.

The generation we have described produced no poets

[1] See Walter Starkie: *Jacinto Benavente* (Humphrey Milford, 1924).

and no poetry besides that of Valle Inclán and Unamuno. The poetry of the Spanish-speaking world was dominated by the genius of the poet of Nicaragua, Rubén Darío, the master and father of all contemporary Spanish poets, the Victor Hugo of Spain. It was a generation, not of poets, but of critics and of scholars. Don Ramon Menéndez Pidal investigates the texts of the Middle Ages and rises to his present rank as leader of the Spanish philologists. He gave rigour and discipline to the Froudian methods of Menéndez y Pelayo, who is so typical of an age and a generation which remembered Michelet too well. Don Adolfo Bonilla y San Martin taught, worked, and produced a great number of historical and critical volumes; Don Rafael Altamira wrote his *History of Spain and Spanish Civilization,* which is in the hands of every scholar.

FIFTEEN YEARS LATER

The rigours of the early struggles are mitigated. Thanks to the " Board for the Extension of Studies," a slowly growing band of scholars have travelled and studied abroad, mostly in Germany. Slowly the opinions of the minority permeate the middle classes. The leader of this generation is Don José Ortega y Gasset, Professor of Metaphysics at the University of Madrid, a lover of baroque prose, a speaker of great power, author of essays which have dealt with almost every urgent problem of contemporary thought. He collected these works in a semi-periodical series which he called *The Spectator.* Steadily he was moving away from the positions taken by the preceding generation. He grew up in the neo-

Kantian discipline of Professor Hermann Cohen in Marburg, but in his later work the mystical Bergsonian vitalism, which is so typical of modern German criticism and philosophy of history, seems to have widened the already loose rational categories of his early speculations, giving a fallacious softness of outline which augurs dangerously for his influence as a teacher and populariser. This influence is considerable and is still growing. Philosophy became through him fashionable in Spain and in South America, and indeed the seduction of his prose at its best is great, as in the sumptuous magnificence of the *Meditations on Don Quixote* or the preface to Moreno Villa's (a graceful poet of much charm) volume, *The Passenger* (1914), one of his least known and most perfect essays, dealing with the nature of metaphor and poetry.

The Catalan, Eugenio d'Ors, who signs his essays and articles *Xenius,* is a philosophical journalist, who, from time to time, collects his articles in volumes which he calls *Glossaries,* in which he attempts to give permanence to anecdote and incident. He is an anti-romanticist, an admirer of classicism, balanced, serene, a fierce hater of those whom Plato called " Detractors of Reason." He has an immense and sincere admiration for the Olympic figure of Goethe. (" It is impossible to speak of Goethe dispassionately. One is prevented by something which it is difficult to confess, but impossible to ignore. It is *envy.*") He wrote some of his more important works in Castilian, such as the *Oceanography of Boredom, The Valley of Jehosephat,* and *The Windmill.*

Without doubt the most significant novelist of this

generation is Ramón Pérez de Ayala, who comes from the Asturias, the legendary little kingdom of the North, flanked by Galicia on the left and Vasconia on the right. His prose brings to mind that of Quevedo (1580-1645); it is hard, solid, rich in idiomatic phrases, ranging over an immense vocabulary; the parallel with the author of *The Dreams* and the *Letter to Lewis XIII*. would be complete if Pérez de Ayala did not possess and express a lyrical and northern sentiment for which we look in vain amongst the metallic reverberations of the great satirist. Of all contemporary writers this Asturian is perhaps the most Spanish in spite of his cosmopolitan life (his wife is North American) and his intimate acquaintance with English literature. He knows the Spanish mystics, and his delicate and precise analysis of souls is more closely allied to the mystic realism of St. Teresa than to the psychological novel of France. St. Teresa's self-analysis is the great point of reference for a more profound historical understanding of the technique of the modern novel. She not only re-discovered vast continents of internal life, but explored them and drew charts, which, apart from their religious value, are important documents for the historian.

Pérez de Ayala shared with Quevedo a youthful delight in obscene subjects, of which his first novel is an example. The same cruel and rather bitter humour is the most noticeable quality of a book, *Troteras y Danzaderas*, entertaining for the reader who has a knowledge of contemporary literary life in Spain, for it contains hardly disguised portraits of Valle Inclán, Azorin, Ortega y Gasset, and of the author, and pictures of life in the capital, amongst them the delicately drawn portrait of a

girl of the streets, to whom the author reads and para-
phrases Shakespeare's *Othello,* chronicling minutely the
intense interest and passionate reactions of the girl. But
Pérez de Ayala is also a poet. Already in 1903 he had
published *La Paz del Sendero,* followed by *El Sendero
Innumerable* and *El Sendero Andante.* The short stories
Prometheus, Sunday Light, and the *Fall of the Lemons*
(which is perhaps his masterpiece and has been translated
into English) have a lyrical quality which, added to the
powerful prose of his earlier books, increases immensely
the range of this writer, who now, in full possession of
his technique, produces the great works of the last ten
years which give him an unrivalled position amongst
contemporary writers. These novels are *Belarmino and
Apolonio, The Labours of Urbano y Simona,* and his
latest book, *Tiger John.* Short poems precede different
sections of these books. These are poetic novels, *Novelas
Poemáticas;* the story of Belarmino, a philosophical
shoemaker, who, inspired by enthusiasm for the last
apostle of Hegelian philosophy in Spain, looks for the
quintessential word which is to express the sum total
of all ideas, and his counterpart Apolonio, also a shoemaker, who wishes to express himself as a dramatic
author. No description of the plot can give an idea of
the wistful and sometimes tender humour which envelops
the most improbable situations. *Tiger John* is a study
of the type of *Don Juan* and of feminine fidelity in the
setting of a small town of the Asturias, in the market-
place of which we meet characters which show, in the
best sense, how local and provincial is the muse of Pérez
de Ayala. Perhaps there is no higher praise, for, by pro-
vincialism in this sense, we mean a rich instinctive life,

a feeling for what is popular and warmly human, which gives to this novel a depth and interest far surpassing the products of intellectual cleverness, unwarmed by these deep fires.

Ayala would be unique if Gabriel Miró did not share his reputation. Like Azorin, he comes from the Spanish Levant, from Alicante. Like Azorin, he contemplates in apparent serenity the silent life of small towns. He narrates intimate tragedies; he loves priests and ecclesiastics and the peace of the bishop's garden in a cathedral city of his native province. His best novels are *The King's Grandfather* (1912), the melancholy *Our Father St. Daniel* (1921), and a continuation of this book, which has created both enthusiasm and hatred, *The Leprous Bishop*, second only in contemporary letters to Pérez de Ayala's most perfect work.

As a poet in prose, a religious poet, he appears in the lyrical evocations of the *Figures of the Passion of Our Lord* (translated into English), which are based on an intense study of texts and of exegetical literature. Even if we deduct the Flaubertian preciosity of some of these pages, there still remain others of pure and luminous beauty, through which move the Figures—the title is not accidental—plastically, almost sculpturally, conceived. He is less subtle than Azorin. They both are Mediterranean. "In my town our eyes are filled from the day we are born by the blueness of the water," says Miró. They both are consummate artists of eclectic observation. But whereas Azorin is an artist of art and is most successful when his subject (or pretext) is a literary work or an historical personality, Miró is a poet of nature, a lover of light, flowers, and scents which, like incense,

envelop his characters—the jovial and elegant Don Magín
from *Our Father St. Daniel,* amateur of the sweets prepared in the nunneries, of every perfume and flower,
parish priest and grand seigneur by divine right, although
he is a humble parson, the Greco-like pale Don Alvaro,
consumed by the fire of his insane loyalty to the exiled
Prince Don Carlos—until in the *Figures of the Passion of
our Lord* the plastic tendency predominates and we find
a quality of sculptural feeling which in some passages is
reminiscent of the art of a Berruguete rather than comparable to that of any other Spanish writer. These plastic
and Mediterranean sensuous qualities are illustrated by
the following passage from *Herodes Antipas* in the
second volume of the *Figures*:

> " Sea of Galilee. The blueness of its waters like the clear-
> ness of the skies. The intense blue and the feeling of cool-
> ness entered amongst all the trees and was married to the
> immaculate marble of the mansion of Herod and the
> golden highways. The blue was enamelled on the whiteness
> of the swans, even on the blueness of the peacocks from
> Ophir poised on the velaria and the cisterns, reflecting on
> the rigid feathers of the ostriches which stretched their
> necks above the box-trees and myrtles. Everything blue :
> the surface of the pool and of the lawn, the shadows of
> the sculptures, the mysteries of the gardens . . . And near
> the end of the lake the cliffs of Gergessa poured the blood-
> red sunset over the shores.
>
> The orange-trees, the pistachios, the sycamores and
> cypresses, that still preserved the afternoon sun, shed a
> fragrance like hot fruit.
>
> An eagle shone in the calmness of the twilight, steady
> and majestic over Tibiriades, resembling the crown of a
> canopy.
>
> Herodias leant out of the peristyle of alabaster and the
> magnificent column of her body rose following the flight."

M. Paul Valéry noted once that the significant
quality of modern literature, even of prose, was a certain

air de confessionel. It is true that intimate self-revelation gives a peculiar colour both to the essay-like prose and the renascent lyrical poetry of contemporary Spain. Two great poets, perhaps artists of genius, take up the succession of Rubén Darío, Antonio Machado and Juan Ramon Jimenez.

Both are Andalusians. Machado is a Sevillian, but, unlike his compatriots, he loves and understands Castile. He is heavy, strong, and dry, a strong-voiced pessimist, and then, again, delicate and tender, never an improviser, always difficult, austere, and slow. His *Campos de Castilla* are majestic in their sadness, like the landscape that inspires them. The *Residencia de Estudiantes,* which, rather than a hostel for students, has become one of the centres of intellectual initiative in Spain, has published his complete works.

Very different is Juan Ramon Jimenez, more feminine, subtle, and delicate, possessor of an ultra-modern sensibility which registers every new impression that reaches him through the padded walls of his noise-proof study, for, like Wagner, he cannot bear noise of any kind. He began by writing elegiac verse, sentimental, simple, and monotonous. After many years of silence he rewrote these youthful experiments after a laborious and carefully thought out work of revision, and since then has passed through periods of great productivity—verse in every imaginable metre, prose (such as the beautiful biography of an ass, called *Platero and I,* written for children), which, read in chronological sequence, are the cleansed, purified, and alembicated diary, horary and minutery, of a naked spirit which constantly changes its temperature and its colour. The Hispanic Society of America published a selection of his poems, and later, in 1922, he himself edited a second anthology.

In Spain lyrical expression has always been the exception, however richly popular song had accompanied every human activity during the Middle Ages. It is interesting to note that the traditional balance in favour of narrative poetry is being altered, and that lyrical poetry (like philosophy in another direction) is occupying an increasing place in modern literary life. Enrique de Mesa, a classicist steeped in the literature of the fourteenth and fifteenth centuries, and Enrique Diez Canedo, a modern humanist and erudite critic of contemporary French literature, are both exquisite poets, and besides them Antonio Machado's brother Manuel, Abril, and the author of *Verbo*, Gabriel Alomar, must be mentioned.

Eduardo Marquina takes poetry on to the stage and writes the three most important poetical dramas of the Spanish twentieth century—*In Flanders the Sun is Set, The Peacock*, and *The Daughters of the Cid*—inspired by a line from the epic poem *The Chanson of My Cid* (about 1150), in which the unknown author breaks through the impersonal style of a narrative poem, raising before our eyes, in an exclamation of poignant intensity, the tremendous vision of the vengeance of the absent Cid for the outrage committed on his daughters.

Twenty-Five Years Later

In the artistic life of Europe, Spanish artists occupy a position which has not been theirs since the seventeenth century. In painting, the representational classicism of the nineteenth century had been reduced *ad absurdum* by the later Impressionists, the would-be scientific "Fauves," and new principles were accepted, based not only on exotic influences (*e.g.,* negro art), but—and this is far more important—on a reinterpretation of the guiding principles of the great masters of the past, more especially Spanish painters, prominent amongst them the Greek of Toledo, El Greco.

The painter Picasso has had a decisive and radical influence on all European artists, and Picasso does not stand alone, for round him are grouped discoverers like Juan Gris, whose recent death we still regret, and younger men like Ismael Gomez de la Serna, who are once more making Spanish painting the centre of interest to those who are sincerely concerned with art as a living, necessary thing, and not as a decorative accomplishment.

The Impressionists loved the psychological novel, which corresponds so closely to the technique of their art. One would look in vain for such books on the shelves of the writers and painters of the present. In Picasso's studio—he is an omnivorous reader—one might find Sherlock Holmes, Nick Carter, and Buffalo Bill, together with Verlaine, Rimbaud, and Mallarmé, but not Paul Bourget or any naturalist. I think it is significant that the literature of the eighteenth century, especially the French eighteenth century, should be much read, and I remember the love of Picasso and his friends for Diderot, Rousseau, and Rétif de la Bretonne. The conclusion is simple. The younger men were sick of a literature and sick of an art which deliberately banished as irrelevant every imaginative expression. Instead of form, shape, architecture—in a word, beauty—we had analysis, study, copies and recopies of the small and miserable life of the nerves and the senses, and if our contemporaries owe a debt of gratitude to those who prepared the way by teaching them such complex analytical methods, it is because in some of the moſt recent literature—James Joyce in Ireland, Prouſt in France—a wider and more complex synthesis has been possible, which makes use of such means, but is juſtified by very different ends. The value of such methods is that of all technique—a means of escape.

The Pontifex Maximus of this new literature is Ramon Gomez de la Serna, a *Madrileño* about forty years of age, small of learning and immense of talent. Ramon is small, fat, pink, and round-faced, incredibly healthy, loud-voiced, and easily carried away by his unbelievable facility for baroque and Góngoriſtic conversation. He is one of the happieſt incarnations of the new spirit of the intellectual youth of Spain. Like Gracián (1601-1658) and the poet Góngora (1561-1627)—whose rise from the contempt into which he had fallen as obscure, affeCted, and "insincere," to his present eſtimation as one of the greateſt poetic geniuses of Spanish literature, is charaCteriſtic of our age—he loves the unexpeCted turn, the ſtrange juxtaposition, the art of the juggler, the brilliance and hardness of outline, the slight quiver and movement of fugitive and elusive feelings and colours. He adores clowns and circus artiſts. He writes as if he was at play. To him writing is like breathing—hours and hours, hundreds of pages. His composition flows without correCtion, without hesition. If Cervantes called the dramatiſt Lope de Vega *Monſtruo de la Naturaleza,* Ramon may be saluted as a little winged monſter of incredible swiftness. The abſtruse spirit of the day has chosen this amiable, natural, and spontaneous young man as the carrier of the new message. Ramon is as well known in France as in Spain, thanks to M. Valéry Larbaud, and is doubtless the most cosmopolitan writer of his generation.

His work, always different and always the same, consists of what he calls *Greguerías,* the name he gives to the initial element which gives unity to all his writings. *Greguería* is a sentence or a few sentences, but never more than two or three lines, in which an ingenious concept finds expression, an image, a strange comparison, a new sensation, or perhaps a pun. Those who are familiar with the literature of the seventeenth century recognise some of the formal qualities of the conceptual writer and philosopher Gracián. His books are strings of *Greguerías* or variations of one *Greguería* carried through volumes. It is incredible how easily these things flow from the pen of this smiling conjurer, who every week, and sometimes once a day, produces a new literary rabbit out of his sleeve or yards and yards of coloured ribbon from his hat. One may acquire some idea of his work by reading the little volume of selected *Greguerías,* or perhaps it may be better to turn to the masterly translation and selection of M. Valéry Larbaud, published under the title of *Échantillons.* Ramon in Spain means to his generation what Apollinaire, Morand, and Giraudoux represent in France.

In Spain, where every artist is a fierce individualist, and, like Adam, feels himself to be the first who wrote, painted, or composed, without tradition, without ancestors, Ramon is sociable and has made his headquarters in the decrepit but picturesque Café de Pombo. Here congregate men of letters, painters, and young philosophers. It is a bizarre and intensely ſtimulating atmosphere; but the members of this group are dispersing, and soon no other memory will remain of these gatherings than the picture by Gutierrez Solarna, a negro and a pupil of Zuloga, in which are to be seen the portraits of its moſt prominent members and the two books which Ramon devoted to the hiſtory and clients of his café.

The production of young Spanish writers at the present moment is considerable. It is difficult to treat individualities, so different from each other and even opposed in their principles, from a common point of view, but I think we may provisionally eſtablish two chief groups which clearly bear the marks of their upbringing.

Firſt, those who are learned, some of them professors in Spanish universities, and all of them erudite, travelled and intellectual. The way was prepared for them by Ortega y Gasset and his philosophy of " concepts," which eſtablished a fruitful link with a *Conceptismo* of the seventeenth century. For Ortega, metaphor is in relation to poetry what the concept *a priori* is to the philosophy of Kant. This intellectual attitude towards the elements of poetry (all poetry is, according to him, conſtruction of metaphors) ends in the highly intellectual verse of Guillermo de Torre, Gerardo Diego, Espina, and Lorca.

These poets have connections with the " Centre of Hiſtorical Studies," presided over by Menéndez y Pidal and the *Residencia de Eſtudiantes*. From there come, directly or indirectly, Federico Garcia Lorca, Gerardo Diego, Alberti, Dámaso Alonso, Jorge Guillén. The majority are professors of hiſtory or philologiſts, and all of them are not only creative writers, but, firſt and foremoſt, reinterpreters of literary hiſtory, prominent amongſt them Dámaso Alonso, a pupil of Professor Américo Caſtro, who has juſt annotated *The Solitudes of Góngora* and translated them into modern prose in an attempt to solve the immense syntaċtical difficulties of these two poems. It is no accident that, before having published this remarkable contribution to Gongoriſtic ſtudies, he should have become known as the translator of Joyce's *A Portrait of the Artiſt as a Young Man.* Gerardo Diego is also a ſtudent of Gongora and a poet of great originality like Jorge Guillén. We should also remember and read Benjamin Jarnés, who is the author of some acute conceptual ſtories such as *The Useless Professor,* published by the *Reviſta de Occidente,* a philosophical and critical magazine edited by Ortega y Gasset.

The critical writers who are moſt clearly allied to this group are Antonio Marichalar, a regular contributor to French, and occasionally English, reviews, author of an important ſtudy on the personality and works of James Joyce, and of a critical essay entitled *Palm,* and the subtle José Bergamin, inventor of aphorisms. He wrote *The Rocket and the Star,* in the preface to which Juan Ramon Jimenez says that Bergamin "has ſtretched out finally and definitely to reach with his hand that rarefied, almoſt colourless region of the air, where dwell the unpublished ideas." And then there is Gimenez Caballero, founder, editor, life and soul of the weekly *Gaceta Literaria* (the Spanish counterpart of the *Nouvelles Littéraires*), who delights us with his critical articles, so new in substance and form, and his knowledge of Madrid-lore in *Three Resuscitations of Spain* (*Bullfights, Caſtanets, The Blessed Virgin*).

SPAIN

The conclusion we draw is that there is a close connection between the scholarly and philological works of these men and the intellectual art of which they are the exponents. The second important group which we have to consider is connected with definitely Andalusian conceptions expressed in the poems of Juan Ramon Jimenez, the music of Manuel de Falla, and perhaps the painting of Picasso. This group is by no means racially confined to Andalusia. Thus, the Castilian, Pedro Salinas, Professor in the University of Seville, the historian of literature who served in the ranks of Pidal, has absorbed some of the flexibility and elements of this Andalusian attitude. A volume of poems entitled *Predictions,* and his perfumed romances dealing with the ancestral history of the Cid (published also in the *Revista de Occidente*), even the economy and agility of his translation of Proust and his stories, so full of novelty, prove that he is one of the most promising of the writers who embody in literature the traditional Andalusian feeling for elegance and distinction. And yet there is a Castilian sturdiness about him. "Here," says Juan Ramon Jimenez in his preface to *Predictions,* "here is Pedro Salinas, all leafy, flowery, and fruity with leaves, fruit, and flowers in vital concentration, his feet still earthy."

Salinas shares his reputation with Claudio de la Torre, who, like Galdos, comes from the semi-tropical seas of the Canary Islands. He made several dramatic experiments, and astonished us with a novel which is certainly one of the most remarkable published in Spanish during the last two years, entitled *From the Life of Mr. Bright,* a story of the sad adventures of an English boy in Seville, a pathetic, tender, and lovable character. To these men, young in years, older ones have to be added, as young as they are in spirit, unprecocious, and slowly matured writers, who now, after years of growth, have produced rich and succulent fruit, prominent amongst them Ramon Maria Tenreiro, a Galician like Valle Inclán, author of *The Slave of the Lord* (1927), a novel which stands alone amongst much that is pretentious in its poetic simplicity and superb beauty of language, and Manuel Azaña, whose *Garden of the Monks* (1927), memories of school life amongst the Augustinians of the Escorial, is the revelation of an exquisitely disciplined and, one side of it at least, infinitely sad and disappointed life, hardened by irony and yet ever ready to slide down sentimental slopes.

The literature of Spain of the last fifteen years, Spanish painting and music, have an influential and vital place in the artistic life of the world. Not for three hundred years have the Iberian contributions to this life been so original and, as far as we can judge, so fruitful.

A. R. PASTOR.

ITALY

ONE of the greatest difficulties with which any person is faced when trying summarily to review contemporary Italian literature is the vastness and diversity of the field he has to cover. This, it may be objected, is no less true of other Continental literatures, with this noticeable difference, however, that a very much smaller proportion of persons in this country are either directly or indirectly acquainted with the works published in Italy during the past twenty-five years. In most cases the writer is but a name; in some he is remembered by the title of his most famous, if not his best, book. Nor is it too much to say, strange though it may seem, that no twentieth-century book—plays excluded—with the exception, perhaps, of Fogazzaro's *Santo* and Papini's *Vita di Cristo,* has ever reached the earlier popularity of *Cuore* and *Pinocchio.* The latter are to be considered almost as classics, while the former owe their fame to reasons largely outside the field of literature as such. No one of the great triumvirate —Carducci, Pascoli, and D'Annunzio—is as well known to English readers as France or Claudel, even in translation. Few have read the first, still fewer the second, while of the third it may be said that his reputation as a person is far greater than that of his novels or plays, and that his claim to a place as a poet in European literature is unknown to most English people. These, however, belong to the past rather than to the present, although the influence of D'Annunzio, and in a lesser degree that of Carducci, is by no means entirely exhausted.

I have raised this point, not in order to compare the relative interest in Italian literature shown by English readers with the admittedly far greater one evinced in other foreign literatures, but rather to point out a fact which is liable to escape attention—namely, that the average cultured Englishman finds it difficult to understand and to appreciate the works produced by Italian writers, and is, indeed, rather out of sympathy with them. Nor is it sufficient to attribute this to the lack of good translations, nor to a widespread ignorance of the language, since it is equally true of many Englishmen who can read Italian. The real explanation may, perhaps, be found in the fact that their idea of Italy—even since the War—is fundamentally romantic and of the past, and that they seem incapable of adjusting themselves to the new conditions. They resent having to cast overboard the accepted, picturesque conception of the Italian, and the necessity for studying seriously his new thoughts and ideals. Perhaps one might even say, paradoxically, that it is easier for an Englishman to get close to a Russian than to an Italian of to-day. That this should be so is largely a question of temperamental difference between the mind of a Northerner and that of a Southerner, mutually complementary, yet mutually antagonistic.

There are, however, to-day two Italian writers who are not only studied, read, and discussed, but who may be said to have exercised some influence in the English-speaking world—Croce and Pirandello. The bracketing of their names, however, should not be taken to imply either a judgment or a parallelism existing between them, but merely the recognition of a fact which anyone can prove, and the interest in which lies in that it shows, to some extent, the directions along which Italian literature of to-day makes an appeal to English readers—that is, criticism and the drama. If Croce, however, has through his work contributed to the intellectual progress of the world, the same cannot be said of Pirandello, to whom attention has been attracted possibly owing to the fact that he comes as a surprise and is unlike what the Italian is supposed to be, far more than on account of any real novelty of idea or stagecraft. As in the case of the futurists, there is some danger that he may come to be looked upon as the literary symbol of present-day Italy, in the place of D'Annunzio, who occupied that position before and during the War. Pirandello, the futurists, and D'Annunzio represent certain phases of development; so, too, does Croce, but while in the latter case the influence exerted is positive, in the former it is largely negative, and to express an opinion on the characteristics of Italian literature based mainly on their works would be as futile and inexact as to judge English literature on the strength of Wilde, Shaw, and the "Blast Group." One point which they all have in common, and which deserves attention, is that they belong to the small number of those, in addition to Papini, whose work has penetrated to England and America, and possesses, therefore, elements of extra-national interest, indirectly connected with the new position attained by Italy in Europe after the Libyan War of 1911-13. Here, however, we are concerned with its effect upon the nation itself, and in this sense it may be said to open a new period in Italian life, which was, at the same time, the outcome of the political and intellectual preparation which had preceded it, and had begun with the completion of Italian unity in 1870.

The later and more complex phase of Italian development, during which the Italians were finding themselves, was largely dominated in poetry and criticism by Carducci, the followers of the historical method, and, in a lesser degree, by De Sanctis (whose rightful position was only recognised at the beginning of the twentieth century), in fiction by Verga, Deledda, and the realistic school, and in philosophy by positivism and materialism. This new period was opened by Pascoli, Fogazzaro, and D'Annunzio, who may be considered as the forerunners. Its tendencies grew more and more antithetic to the ideals of the preceding age. To a narrow and national view of the world it substituted one less national and far wider in interests. Without taking the futurists into consideration, this is fully shown in the work done by the Group of the *Voce* (of which I shall speak later) and by Croce and Gentile in the field of philosophy, æsthetics, and pedagogy.

It would not be a gross exaggeration to say that no Italian writer has exercised upon his generation so widespread or so deep an influence as Croce. It is sufficient to look through a list of Croce's works to see the field covered by him and the extent of his interests. Apart from his *Estetica,* with which everyone claims some acquaintance, at least in theory, it includes valuable contributions to economics, to history, to criticism, and to philosophy proper. It would be a mistake, however, I think, to attribute Croce's influence to the content of his works alone; far more is it due to his method of approaching and solving whatever problem he may have set him-

self, be it of criticism, be it of education. As Renato Serra
—who was by no means favourable to Crocean methods
of criticism—one of the moſt promising young Italian
critics, who was killed in the War, and to whom I shall
have occasion more than once to refer, wrote of him:
" Croce has sailed across the critical sky like an ominous
comet; and people can no longer sleep peacefully in their
beds. It certainly is charaĉteriſtic of Croce that he ſtill
awakens, as he once awakened, violent enthusiasm as
well as opposition." In future years ſtudents will go back
and read with pleasure and profit the discussions pro-
voked by his ſtriĉtures on Pascoli, or Papini's attacks
againſt him, or his polemic with Gentile. But no attack,
however violent, nor misapplication of his theories by
youthful and not entirely competent enthusiaſts, have
been able to touch his position or subſtantially to weaken
it. The fundamental principles upon which his theory of
æſthetics are based remain, on the whole, unchallenged,
however much individuals may quarrel among themselves
as to their application, because his critical method is
sound, of universal application, and equally serviceable
in solving the moſt varied problems of æſthetics.

Throughout Croce's work one is repeatedly impressed
by his determination to find a permanent solution to
each problem, not one that is impressioniſt and temporary, but based upon eternal verities. One may be
reading one of his notes on some hiſtorical, literary, or
economic queſtion, yet one feels all through a unity of
thought in the writer which inspires confidence, even if
one be in disagreement with the conclusions arrived at.
Moreover, the language spoken by him is equally com-
prehensible to a German, a Frenchman, or an English-

man, a quality which few critical writers possess
to-day.

Just as Carducci during the nineteenth century reacted
violently against the uncultured and ill-equipped young
critic of his day who honoured the expressions of his likes,
dislikes, and impressions with the name of criticism, so
Croce, in the present century, reacts against the narrow
pedantry of the historical method in which the work of
art was treated as a chemical substance to be analysed,
as if by this materialistic process the critic would be able
to determine or even fully appreciate the nature and
value of the work. For Croce the function of the critic
is very serious; it demands synthesis as well as analysis,
and the recreation of the work of art in the mind of the
reader. All of which implies and requires intellectual as
well as æsthetic discipline, if one may call it by such a
name, and the destruction of those various categories
which aim at dividing up the activities of the spirit and
pigeon-holing them.

It may not be entirely superfluous here to remind the
reader that his system is based on the identity of art with
lyrical intuition—*i.e.,* intuition animated by feeling. Art,
therefore, is creation, and, therefore, action. Art criticism
(understood in the widest sense, and embracing all forms
of æsthetic activity) consists in ascertaining to what extent
the work of art under consideration represents genuine
intuition. True criticism does neither classify nor moralise;
it is neither hedonistic, intellectualistic, nor psychological,
but *æsthetic,* inasmuch as it expresses a philosophy of
art, and *historic* because it becomes the history of the
work of art. In his final position Croce identifies criticism,
history, and philosophy. From this it logically ensues that

literary history is not to be considered as describing the development and evolution of a work of art; and, since only the essay dealing with a single work of art is permissible, literary history, properly understood, may only be a collection of essays dealing successively with individual æsthetic problems. Croce, therefore, belongs to that third period, following upon the romantics and the positivists, which is idealistic, æsthetic, and neo-romantic inasmuch as it develops and is connected with the criticism of De Sanctis, who is the most important representative of the first of these three.

The resultant widening of the field of criticism, and the fact that the critical faculties are turned equally upon all that represents the art, thought, or history of mankind, is one of the most remarkable characteristics in the Italian literary life of to-day. Critical studies, therefore, abound, and criticism is treated, not as a superior form of journalism, but as possessing an intellectual interest of its own and as an exercise requiring the searching application of all our mental powers. Moreover, this implies, as may easily be seen, a readjustment of values and opinions, the search after a formula which may equally solve cultural and philosophic problems. Italy possesses to-day, to use once more the words of Serra, " a critical ideal, which gives uniformity to analyses and research in literature, music, and art in general, as well as in all fields of erudition and history, which sums up in its novelty much of that which it has inherited from the past."

It is to Croce and Gentile that these young critics owe, in a very large measure, the tools with which they are working and the spirit with which they are carrying out their work. Nowhere more markedly than in Croce's opposition to all forms of rhetoric, and in his constant preaching of the virtues of humility, of hard work, of conscientiousness, and efficiency, has Croce's influence been more valuable to the young Italian. As one critic said of him, if there is one thing he abhors more than any other, it is the reformer and the hawker of some patent panacea instantaneously capable of curing any country, or humanity itself, of all its ills. Croce is no believer in revolutions, but in slow, careful, and constant work, which, incidentally, serves to explain in part his neutral attitude towards the present régime in Italy, no less than to the War. Nor does he tolerate any form of sentimentalism or exaggeration to enter into criticism. He has shown that one may be sound without being pedantic, and that a delicate sensibility is in itself insufficient for the appreciation of the work of art. The effect of teachings such as these for a period of over twenty years, and a constant activity of thought which has never allowed Croce to stagnate, have had incalculable effects upon the whole range of Italian life and literature. Both he and Gentile as Ministers of Education have, with some success, carried their teachings into the curriculum of schools and universities, contributing thereby not a little to the renewal, broadening, and deepening of Italian culture. From what has been said, one might easily be led to conclude that the critics of to-day are all faint echoes of Croce. As everyone knows, his system is based on three fundamental principles:

1. The identity of art and lyrical intuition—*i.e.,* animated by feeling and the conception that *art is creation,* therefore action.

2. That art criticism consists in ascertaining to what extent the work of art which the critic is studying represents genuine intuition. True criticism neither classifies nor moralises, is neither hedonistic, intellectualistic, or psychological, but *æsthetic,* inasmuch as it acts as a philosophy of art, and historic because it becomes the history of the work of art. The final position of Croce identifies criticism, history, and philosophy.

3. Whence it arises logically that literary history should not be considered as development and evolution. Only the *essay* is justifiable, and literary history properly understood can only be a collection of essays dealing successively with individual æsthetic problems. In point of fact, this would not be entirely correct. There are many who are avowedly Crocean, but there are also many who, without being so, in fact, who, though opposed to Croce's views, yet cannot free themselves from the new critical attitude already outlined, and have unconsciously felt his influence. Renato Serra is one of the latter, although a disciple of Carducci.

In one sense Serra might be considered as the Italian counterpart of Rupert Brooke, although his work is critical rather than creative. It would, perhaps, be more correct to say that Serra starts where Brooke left off. In both cases the reader of his works is left wondering in what further directions they would have developed. Just as Brooke's essays in criticism seem to suggest that—had he lived—he might have directed his attention to criticism rather than to poetry, so in Serra's last work, the *Esame di Coscienza di un Letterato,* published after his death, there are unmistakable signs of creative tendencies and a marked lyrical feeling. Not that Serra was not creative in his criticism, as anyone who reads his *Saggi Critici* or his survey of contemporary Italian literature (*Le Lettere*) will see. He is peculiarly happy when dealing with poets, in bringing out their poetic personality, so that the reader feels himself at once in the presence of the poet and is made to listen to him through the interpretative words of the critic. It is this type of criticism which inspired in his followers the conception of " pure criticism "—that is, criticism understood as an art in itself, no less creative than poetry—a view which aroused strong antagonism and was accused of being little more than sensualistic impressionism. As was inevitable, Serra has suffered for the errors of his followers, who after his death tried to turn him into an heroic figure symbolical of the purest aspirations of Italian youth. Here, again, some parallelism with Brooke becomes apparent. But it is in his spiritual autobiography, the *Esame,* that the bond which unites the two writers is most striking. Allowing for the fact that " 1914 " is verse and the *Esame* prose, that Brooke sees the War romantically, while Serra seeks to analyse its effect upon himself and upon the world of art and thought, the one important fact which emerges out of a catastrophe which both consider with horror is the feeling for their native soil, the only positive truth which nothing can change or destroy, the only reality in a world which has gone mad. It is here, apart from the remarkable qualities of the style, that one of the main interests of this book lies, for it voiced the opinions of a great many among the youth of Italy at the outbreak of the War.

Serra starts by asking himself whether, notwithstanding the War, a man may be justified in concerning himself with literature, or whether literature must give place to war. The answer, as might be expected, is in the negative, since there is no point of contact between the two. Out of this springs the second question: What truth is there in the widespread assertion that the War has swept away all the literature of the past, and that it has quickened the birth of a new, heroic, magnificent literature worthy of the great historical moment? To the latter question his answer is that the War will not change anything so far as literature is concerned, and that in itself it has no power to improve or redeem or cancel spiritual values. Neither self-immolation nor death can add anything to a man's life or to his work. What he has accomplished he has accomplished; war reveals soldiers, not poets; it does not change artistic values nor any of the fundamentals of life. After the War there probably may be some changes in political and moral tendencies; that which yesterday was an aspiration, to-morrow may have become an accomplished fact. But the spirit of civilisation will not be changed. If the War can be of any use, it can be so in that it teaches people to suffer, to resist, to be contented with little, to live more worthily, more fraternally, individuals as well as nations, until they have unlearned the lesson learnt at such a cost. Apart from this, it is a blind loss, sorrow, waste, a useless and enormous destruction. I have dwelt upon this volume of Serra at some length because the conclusions which the writer reaches with such lucidity of analysis have had since the War of necessity to be accepted by a large proportion of thinking Italians, and are partly responsible for a considerable part of subsequent events.

If, then, one were to answer the question " What has the result of the War been?" one could safely say that, far from destroying tradition, the War has intensified and strengthened it. It has swept away futurism in literature as in art, and it has marked a return to the classics; yet who could say that the signs of a revulsion of feeling were not already to be found before the War. In effect, the futurist violence, like the violence of men such as Papini, had no real constructive force or programme behind it; it was in the nature of an anti-romantic movement which was trying to clear away the false superstructures which decadents like D'Annunzio had built up, and which were and are contrary to the highest genius of the race. The Italian, unlike the Frenchman, does not naturally indulge in mental gymnastics for their own sake; the mould of his mind and of his language is unsuited to them. However he may try, he cannot break away from the inherited Latin *gravitas* and from an almost devastating sense of logic. That is one of the reasons, I think, why the Italian of to-day is so intensely critical, and why so few are writing verse, and, incidentally, why I have stressed the critical side as much as I have. Indeed, if one thinks back to the early Italian poets and traces the development of poetry through the past seven hundred years, one cannot help being struck by the fact that, whereas English literature possesses a very considerable number of excellent poets, but few really great ones, Italy has had many great, but few excellent ones. To-day it would be difficult to find a dozen writers in verse whose work can compare with the early Masefield, or De La Mare, or Hodgson, or the best productions of the Sitwell family, or of T. S. Eliot. Both Pascoli and D'Annunzio belong to the paſt rather than to the present. It would be false, however, on this account to conclude that the Italian of to-day is incapable of writing poetry. Plenty of poetry is being written, but it is in prose. By this I do not mean that it is poetic prose or any such hybrid, but that the lyricism of these writers uses prose rather than verse, or even free-verse of the futuriſt type, as a medium. Here, again, one may indirectly trace the effect of Croce's teachings, according to which the debate as to the respective character of poetry and prose does not consiſt in an arbitrary diſtinction between prose and verse, underſtood merely as a difference in typographical setting of lines, but in the fact that the function of prose is to explain, discuss, elucidate, and is primarily concerned with the logical and rational activities, whereas that of poetry is imaginative expression. Accordingly, a treatise of philosophy written in verse, in so far as it is philosophy, ceases to be poetry, while, conversely, a simple description of the moſt ordinary occurrence, written in prose, may be the higheſt poetry. In other words, poetry is a work of phantasy and the imagination. Judged by these ſtandards, parts of the *Esame di Coscienza,* many chapters of Papini's autobiography *Un Uomo Finito,* and of the *Cento Pagini di Poesia,* which contain, perhaps, his beſt work, many pages of Soffici's *Giornale di Bordo* and *Lemmonio Boreo,* are poetry. And a ſtill better example is offered by the anthology *I Poeti Italiani d'Oggi,* compiled by Papini and Pietro Pancrazi juſt after the War.

For anyone who is unacquainted with Italian prose since D'Annunzio, the ſtyle of the younger writers comes as a surprise. In the firſt place it has loſt much of its rhetorical emphasis; there is no longer the desire to turn phrases in the manner of this or that model writer. Whether the author happens to be a Lombard or a Sicilian, little or any trace is to be found of dialectal idiosyncrasies in the choice of words or in the turn of the phrase; likewise the style is at once freer and more plastic, yet not so loose. All those who are writing to-day use the same language, with an increased sense of the value of words and greater care in their choice. This improvement is to be found in the daily newspapers, as in the more serious reviews and in books. To a large extent this is due to a finer sense, to a realisation of the dignity and the peculiar genius of the language in itself, and to the spread of culture. Such tendencies were present before the War, especially since 1911, but the War has also noticeably contributed to it by increasing the desire for reading and literary knowledge among all classes and by favouring the multiplication of books and of publishing firms.

Many of the latter sprang up as mushroom growths during and after the War and soon disappeared, but some have remained and are flourishing. Even to-day, when we are told that the publishing business is still in a state of crisis, it is nothing less than astonishing to see the quantity, and still more the quality, of the books which are daily being published throughout Italy. As in other countries, so in Italy, epoch-making books of any kind are rare, but the general level as to matter, manner in which it is produced, presented, and written is very much higher than it has been before. Another point worthy of notice is the type of book. Side by side with the best-seller, of scarce literary value, aiming only at providing amusement, often of an undesirable nature, the bookshops are full of admirable cheap reprints of the classics, of critical ſtudies, of translations, of imaginative works, and of art books. In the latter field alone Italy has made enormous ſtrides since the War. But whereas the older generation before the War was largely dominated by D'Annunzio and his hedoniſtic and sensualiſtic conception of life, the new generation, though no less egocentric, is more idealiſtic, and, above all, it has acquired a greater realisation of its duties. These tendencies have been ſtrengthened by the War, coupled, however, with a vein of pessimism and despondency and a feeling of uncertainty and disquiet. During the intense period of feverish aĉtivity which preceded the Great War there was little time for recolleĉtion or to think out fundamental problems. Italy had ſtarted so late and had so much time to make up. There were a few thinkers, men like Croce and Gentile, but the greater part were content—as in the case of the realiſts—to take life as they found it, without attempting to delve very deep into the why or the wherefore of it all. Their researches did not go very far beyond the analysis of their own feelings and experiences. It is sufficient to glance even superficially at the dramatic produĉtions of the time to see the truth of this. Some of the dramatiſts, such as D'Annunzio, were momentarily affeĉted by pseudo-Ibseniſt or Nietzschean ideas, but for the moſt part the theatre was influenced either by the French or continued in the realiſtic tradition of Verga, or produced hiſtorical dramas in verse modelled on D'Annunzio, such as the tragedies of Sem Benelli. Bracco alone, in this period, ſtands out as possessing an individuality and originality of outlook in his dramas *Piccola*

Fonte and *Piccolo Santo,* and Ercole Luigi Morselli, who, in *Orione* and in *Glauco,* successfully attempted a modern inte. pretation of classical myths in the manner of the satiric drama. To-day we have Pirandello, Rosso di San Secondo, Fausto Maria Martini, and hosts of other lesser writers, whose contributions will probably not stand the test of time, but are none the less interesting as evidences of the trend of contemporary thought. In all these it is easy to detect that spirit of self-analysis and disquiet referred to above, as I shall hope to show more in detail further on. Here I should merely like to suggest that the wave of neo-catholicism which has passed over Italy since the War, and which should be disassociated from seemingly analogous phenomena which appeared during the War, revealed in War diaries and other similar personal documents, is due to this same spirit of pessimism. The so-called religious conversion of Papini, as expressed in his *Storia di Cristo,* is the best example of this attraction towards a faith which is national, historic, and clear-cut. Its very discipline and the part played in it by tradition, which make it so often repugnant to the non-Latin mind, is not, perhaps, the last reason for its hold on many Italians of to-day. Mussolini as well as Gentile has recognised its value as a binding and as an educational force in modern Italy. Yet how far is Papini's neo-catholicism from Fogazzaro's modernism? Who, indeed, to-day thinks any longer of modernism, which represented a moment in the evolution of religious thought almost completely destroyed by the War. Those who, like Pirandello, cannot find comfort in the support of traditional beliefs, turn either towards a non-dogmatic mysticism (such as Giuseppe Manacorda and his group of young mystics) or towards a religion of the State, represented by Fascism. To many (it would be vain to deny it) Fascism honestly is a religion and an ideal. Side by side with these religious tendencies there is yet another, by no means unconnected with them—the feeling for Nature and the return to the soil. These elements, in greater or lesser degree, have always been present in the Italian people and, consequently, in Italian literature; but this is more particularly true of that regionalistic movement, so called, which was very pronounced before the War, and is a phenomenon one cannot overlook.

The regionalism of which I am speaking does not affect the language proper, nor does it coincide with the development of local dialectal expressions in literary forms. Contradictory though it may appear at first sight, it is not a separatist movement, in that it does not aim at supporting the claims of one province or part of Italy at the expense of another. It tends rather to the recognition of the particular spiritual and artistic values traditionally belonging to the region with which the writer feels himself most closely attuned. A good example of this is offered by certain chapters of Prezzolini's recent *Life of Machiavelli*, and a better by Papini's autobiography *Un Uomo Finito*, particularly in the chapter—one of the most beautiful in the whole book, to which he has given the title " La Mia Campagna "—which opens with this significant passage :

"Besides books and the dead, I owe my soul to the trees and the mountains. The countryside educated me as much as the library. A particular and determinate country : all that is poetical, melancholy, grey, and solitary in me I owe to the Tuscan countryside, to the country round Florence."

And, again, elsewhere in the same book, referring to the great Tuscan writers, he adds:

> "In all these men (Dante, Machiavelli, Michelangiolo, Leonardo, Galileo) you feel strength, and a certain plebeian sense of robust realism, sobriety, clearness, greatness without rhetoric, austerity without bigotry or narrow-mindedness. There is a Tuscan genius, which belongs here, with its own characteristics, which is detached from all other Italian geniuses, and with which I feel myself completely in harmony. . . . To find myself, signified, therefore, to find again Tuscany in its countryside and in its tradition."

Here Papini has expressed and defined the essential character of the Italian regionalistic spirit—the search after the *genus loci,* considered as a source of inspiration and not merely from the picturesque or historical point of view. Carducci voiced it in that exquisite sonnet " Traversando la Maremma Toscana," and it is the very heart and pith of the best poetry of Giovanni Pascoli. All of these are Tuscans, yet Italians no less for all that, in the same way as Carlo Linati, who, in his book *Sulle Orme di Renzo,* in which he tries, as it were, to follow up and analyse the spiritual inheritance of Manzoni in the Lombard countryside, is both Lombard and Italian. And in Serra's *Esame* and in the works of Panzini, both Romagnols, one finds the same thing carried out on broader lines, but not varying in spirit.

There is also an intellectual side to this regionalistic movement, which helps to explain certain peculiarities and characteristics of Italian literary development. Italy has never had, so far, a literary centre exercising an influence analogous to that of London or Paris. Hence in the past the literary dictatorship of one city over the rest of the country, such as was the case of Florence from the period of the great triumvirate down to the sixteenth century, and, in a strictly linguistic sense, never really challenged. But Florence was not the centre of Italy, nor had Italy a centre until 1870, and even now Rome may hold that position ideally and politically, but she does not do so actually. If the War has definitely destroyed the last vestiges of provincial separatism, even in the south, it has not changed the character of the several intellectual centres, each of which has well-defined characteristics. As Prezzolini jestingly pointed out in a recent book, in Rome the poet or novelist is a Civil Servant, while at Milan he is more frequently a business man. Thus each city gives its own particular impress to the literary life within it. Naples, for instance, partly on account of Croce, and partly because of its tradition, is philosophic, where Florence is more purely literary. Many of the other cities, such as Genoa, Bologna, or Palermo, have their own small coteries. Almost all have their reviews expressing the tendencies of the several groups, but in a way which differs considerably from what occurs in France, in that the most important of these groups are not provincial, but play, and have played, a part in the literary development of the country as a whole. Indeed, some of these—such as, in Florence, the *Leonardo* and the *Voce,* which followed it—would deserve careful study and much more attention than it is possible to give them here. Of the latter, one may say that there is scarcely a young writer of any importance in Italy who does not owe something to the *Voce*. Founded by Papini and Prezzolini about 1909, its programme included the revaluation of old values, the diffusion of new ideas in literature, art, philosophy, politics, and music. Alongside of it, as an integral part of its activities, a publishing firm—the Libreria della Voce—was started, which has been responsible for publishing some of the most important books that have appeared in Italy in the past twenty years, such as Papini's *Uomo Finito,* Soffici's *Lemmonio Boreo* and *Kobilek,* Slataper's *Il Mio Carso,* and many others. Although the group has now been dispersed, its influence has not been lost or forgotten, and to have belonged to it is still considered an honour not unlike to that of having been one of the contributors to the *Yellow Book,* or to the original *Poetry Review.* In no other city of Italy could such a review have been started, any more than one could conceive another *Critica* (Croce's review) outside Naples or Marinetti's *Poesia* outside Milan. Milan, indeed, ever since the eighteenth century has been the centre of literary controversies. The pugnacious little academy founded by the Verri brothers issued their periodical, the *Caffe,* in Milan; Milan, too, saw the birth of the organ of the Italian romanticists, and in the twentieth century it harboured the headquarters and the head of the futurist movement, Signor Marinetti. As the most modern and " mechanical " city in Italy, it was inevitable that the futurists should choose it. I do not propose to speak about the futurist movement as such—its æsthetic principles are well known to everyone—but merely to refer to the considerable, if negative, effect that it had upon Italian literature, especially through the manifesto of futurist art and that of futurist literature, which were very closely allied. Looked at closely, both these manifestoes tried to destroy the formal and hampering limits imposed by tradition on art and literature by preaching the destruction of all traditional forms and the substitution of a new sensibility, based on speed and the abstract beauty and significance of machinery and words. In neither case was the conception really original, since it was based on an entire misapprehension of the nature of a work of art. "Wireless imagination and words at liberty," far from being as revolutionary as it seemed, was, in effect, the ultimate result of that very decadence which it attacked, carried to its extreme conclusion. The war element of futurism exhausted itself in the War; the rest have disappeared or have been so radically transformed as to be hardly recognisable. Papini and Soffici and Palazzeschi, all of whom had their futuristic moment, have gone to the other extreme, and the same may be said of its best painters, Carrà and De Chirico. Marinetti is forgotten except abroad, where futurism was taken far more seriously than ever in Italy. Yet it would be unfair to say that its influence has been negligible, for its destructive violence acted as an irritant and forced writers and particularly poets to react against sterility and facility, and to face anew the problem of what is poetry. Without "words at liberty" it is conceivable that Croce's influence in this direction, to which I have already referred, would have taken effect more slowly and with greater difficulty, since the futurists cleared away so many trees, so that even the most short-sighted could see the wood.

From what I have been saying, I think it will be fairly evident that if one were to ask what is the characteristic tendency of the present moment in Italian literature, the answer would inevitably be: "Return towards tradition." In few countries does this exercise so powerful an influence as in Italy. Nor can anyone who is acquainted with

Italy's past history—political, literary, and artistic—fail to see the reasons for this. To give but one instance: the Italian language itself, with its Latin structure and weight, tends towards clearness of outline, precise diction, dignity, balance, sense of measure. Whenever any attempt has been made to do violence to these characteristics, it has been followed immediately by a strong reaction. And what is said of the language is no less true of the Italian literary genius, which abhors and recoils from anything nebulous, undefined, or confused. Moreover, the classical world is always present to the Italian; he may, and often tries to, break away from it, like the futurists, but the attempt is bound to fail. The past weighs him down and sets before him exacting standards of achievement, and makes his critical sense acute and often destructive, while at the same time it inspires in him the desire for creation and a certain innate technical facility, which has to be constantly disciplined. Of all languages, there is none easier to acquire a smattering of than Italian, none more difficult to master, even for the Italians themselves, and so the writer of to-day finds himself between the danger of being pedantic or precious, as is so often the case with D'Annunzio, or deliberately familiar and journalistically facile like Papini. These conflicting tendencies are responsible in part for one of the most salient characteristics of recent Italian literature—namely, its fragmentary and personal character. There is no writer to-day in Italy who could or would be able to produce such a work as Proust's great novel, unless it were Croce, and he belongs to an earlier generation, nor anyone who could produce a *Daffodil Fields* or a *Reynard the Fox* (I am merely citing these works as examples, without any implication as to their literary merit).

If one takes a bird's-eye view of the most significant books published within the past twenty years or so, one finds that all of them are fragmentary. Volumes of poems, autobiographical impressions, such as Borgese's *Rubè*, D'Annunzio's scattered notes collected, under the title of *La Leda Senza Cigno* and *Congedo*, or Panzini's *La Lanterna di Diogene*, or volumes of critical essays and studies. It seems as if critics and imaginative writers are collecting material and data, studying one particular aspect of a man's life or work, waiting for the great genius who will come along, gather all this wealth of material and weld it into an organic whole, as Croce and Gentile have done in the field of philosophy. In the theatre alone this characteristic is less acutely felt, and I would suggest that in this field of all the others— apart from that of philosophy and erudition—some Italian playwrights have achieved results incomparably superior to those of poets or novel writers, which are not merely of national and local interest. This is certainly the case with Pirandello, whose work, be it represented by novels, stories, or plays, has a remarkable unity and cohesion.

Pirandello's vision of life, rather than reflecting what is often wrongly considered to be the psychological state of mind of the young Italian intellectual of to-day (although it cannot be denied that it does so in part) in so far as it is universal, is an evidence of the attempt at a limited solution of the problem of life, arrived at by the application of certain easily recognisable philosophical conclusions. It is based on the fact that to live it is not sufficient for man to know that he is alive, but also to feel it. This consciousness of life has for Pirandello become separate from life and is in opposition to it. This separation is the cause of all human unhappiness. On the one side life such as it is in reality, on the other the abstract conception which each individual himself forms of it, and which tends to crystallise it into a definite form according to his ideals, habits, and the traditions and conventions of the society in which he lives. Life, however, is always changing and seeking to destroy these barriers which try to compress it and to dominate it. All goes well till, of a sudden, often without knowing it, these barriers are swept away, and man finds that the artificial construction which he has built himself ceases to possess any significance, and he finds himself, like Rip Van Winkle, a stranger in his own land. Two ways or solutions remain open to him—neither of which can give happiness—either to escape through death or through a feigned death, such as is the case in the novel, *Il Fu Mattia Pascal,* or to consent to build up a new set of illusions, realising that these, in their turn, are liable to be destroyed. Thus Pascal's solution is no solution at all, for in the end he cannot escape from the mask which life imposes upon him without renouncing life itself. According to Pirandello, therefore, the supreme and only wisdom of life is that of accepting life yet never allowing oneself to be tied down by it, and to maintain sufficient freedom of action to permit of changing *with* life instead of attempting to arrest its course which, in practice, is unattainable. Reality being a chimera, nothing remains but illusion; it is useless to attempt to find a definite solution, let us, therefore, continue to build up illusions, knowing them for what they are, and live and suffer although it be all for nothing. Such is Pirandello's ultimate conclusion; one strangely like that which Leopardi reached a century ago, by other ways. In a greater or lesser degree these same pessimistic conclusions are reached by most of the younger dramatic school, such as Chiarelli, and Martini, and Rosso. If one were to attempt to find its causes it would be necessary to go back to the spiritual and intellectual crisis which immediately preceded the War and was rendered more acute by the War. Then, as now, though differently, this state of mind led writers and thinkers to venture into new fields in search of a solution. And this may not unjustifiably be considered as one of the deep-seated reasons responsible for the fragmentariness to which I have referred, as it is of the present tendency to find peace and safety and solidity, from all this welter of contradictions, in a body of tradition, not blindly, of course, and under the stress of emotion, but rather critically and logically, according to the characteristic Latin spirit.

If, then, we look back, in conclusion, at the ground we have covered, and at the various tendencies, it is possible, I think, to draw the following conclusions: First, that the period which opened in the early years of the present century marks a definite though gradual idealistic reaction against positivism and materialism in politics and philosophy, and realism and decadentism in art. Carducci is dead, the aristocraticism of D'Annunzio is waning, and a new and healthier and more universal conception of literary values, not uninfluenced by a closer contact with foreign literatures, is born. Intensity of intellectual activity in all directions, accompanied by the reſtatement of critical values, æsthetic and spiritual, by Croce and Gentile; a general improvement in prose ſtyle, and the development of a new concept of poetry; new intereſt in literary criticism and in philosophical ſtudies, leading to reaction againſt all forms of rhetoric and exaggeration and to a pessimiſtic view of life, which seeks, finally, its solution in myſticism, catholicism, or ſtate worship. These conclusions which I have suggeſted muſt of necessity be approximative and tentative, since it is not yet possible to view the period in its true perspective. For this reason I have only mentioned the names of few writers and works, preferring to summarise tendencies, in an attempt to give a broad picture of the intellectual atmosphere of present-day Italy.

ARUNDELL DEL RE.

RUSSIA

Dr. Rose has pointed out above that in speaking of Germany the term " post-War " is insufficient and, besides the War, a revolution has also to be taken into account. In the case of Russia we may go further. Even the Great War dwindles into comparative insignificance by the side of a greater revolution, and, all comparisons apart, the War passed over Russia almost unnoticed by the Russian mind. Russia did not live the War; she only submitted to it until, weary of submission, she ended by revolting against it. The War, in the case of Russia, is of importance only as the immediate cause of the Revolution. It was neither a national nor a popular war. It was imposed on the nation by an irresponsible minority. The professional soldier, in so far as he survived the first hecatombs, though incompetently led, fought, as he had always fought, heroically, and the mobilised peasant, under the pressure of ancestral traditions of obedience, showed much passive heroism, accepting conscription and the War as an inevitable calamity of the natural order. But the bourgeoisie excelled only in the art of avoiding the front, while a large part of the intellectual élite were conscientious objectors and *défaitistes*. The great poet, Alexander Blok, was a representative figure when he did all in his power to avoid joining the army. He succeeded ultimately in being mobilized as a non-combatant, and deserted his post at the first news of the Revolution. There were, of course, men and boys who joined the army in a spirit of adventure or of self-sacrifice, but they were relatively few. To the long lists of English, French, and German intellectuals who fought and fell in the War, Russia can oppose only one or two names, that of the poet, Nicolas Gumilev, being the most prominent. But Gumilev was a born adventurer, who had already before the War sought danger and romance in Africa, hunting lions and exploring Gallaland.

The Revolution was a very different affair. Its action on literature was profound and many-sided, but before we approach it I must give an account of the starting-point, of the state of Russian letters in the first decade of the present century. In those years Russian literature was divided into two, almost watertight, sections—the inheritors of the intelligentsia traditions of the nineteenth century on the one side, and on the other those who were, loosely and inadequately, called the modernists. This latter movement began in the nineties. It greatly modified and enriched the Russian cultural climate, revived art, metaphysics, and religious thought, daringly questioned the foundations of accepted ethics, cultivating individualism in morals as well as in literary expression. Strongly affected by Dostoevsky, Nietzsche, and the gnostical philosophy of Vladimir Soloviev, it gradually changed the face of Russian intellectual life. By 1910 it was the most vital force in literature, and all subsequent literary developments are conditioned, positively or negatively, by its achievement. There can be no doubt that between 1905 and 1917 the best and most valuable work came from them, and not from their opponents, the realists. The realists, however, were still in the limelight of public attention, and commanded far bigger sales, for they were in closer sympathy with the average majority of the intelligentsia, while their opponents, the symbolists, were pioneers who had to form their public themselves.

The "realist party," in those years, was dominated by a group of writers who may be termed the "nihilists," or the "mortalists," for almost the only theme of all their work was the futility of Life, with Death as the one real reality. The most notable were Andreyev, Artsybashev, Bunin, and Sergeyev-Tsensky.

These writers reflect a very definite phase in the history of the intelligentsia—its moment of disillusionment in all its nineteenth-century humanitarian, utilitarian, social, and revolutionary ideals. The vanity of all human pursuits, of all beliefs and hopes, the vanity, above all, of all civilisation, and an intense awareness of the supreme reality of Death—are the background of all their writings. By the side of Death their favourite themes are that other and even more terrible menace—Madness, and that other indubitable reality—Sex. Suicide, insanity, and sex in its most brutal aspects are the only subjects of their stories. Together, they form the gloomiest episode in a literature whose main characteristic is often supposed to be gloominess. Andreyev (who died in 1919) and Artsybashev (died 1927) were the most widely read Russian authors between 1905 and 1910. Their works are still fairly popular in the United States. Those who have read their books or have seen their plays acted know how unspeakably crude and puerile they are, though Andreyev at least cannot be denied a certain foundation of human (if not of artistic) sincerity. Sergeyev-Tsensky, though much less known abroad, is a finer artist, but the most notable of the whole group is, of course, Ivan Bunin. He is considered by many as the foremost of living Russian authors. This is no doubt a grotesque exaggeration. Bunin has added nothing to the national literary capital that is not implicitly, and sometimes explicitly contained in Turgenev, Goncharov, Saltykov, Tolstoy, or Chekhov, and by the side of the least of these ancestors he is little more than a pygmy. But his best work, *The Village* (1911), and *Sukhodol* (1912), two tremendous and ruthless indictments of the poverty, emptiness, and ugliness of rural Russia, belong to a great tradition, and *Sukhodol,* at least, is a perfectly done masterpiece. Since the Revolution Bunin has written nothing of equal merit. He is to-day the great literary man of the political diehards—a somewhat paradoxical situation for the painter of the ugliest pictures of the Russia that had been swept away by the Revolution. In these two stories the all-pervading feeling of death and nothingness characteristic of this group of writers is given a social and historical foundation. Death in them is not so much an eternal entity as an historical phenomenon—the actual dying of a social order. *The Village* and *Sukhodol* are both symptoms and indictments of the dissolution preceding the death of a whole side of pre-Revolutionary Russia.

All these writers were children of the intelligentsia, a class that was in an advanced state of disintegration and had lost faith in all its ideals. But these ideals were being taken up by the lower, less educated, and less degenerate classes—the so-called semi-intelligentsia, and, eventually, by the proletariat. In literature the spokesman of these new classes was Maxim Gorki. He began in the nineties

with a powerful assertion of biological vitality and a
romantic cult of the ſtrong man, but, early enmeshed in
the nets of degenerate intelligentsiadom, he succumbed to
doubt, and his subsequent career was one of perplexed
and fruitless queſt. Firmly, but, as it were, againſt evidence, he ſtuck to his faith in optimiſtic utilitarianism,
and is to-day the laſt great utilitarian figure in Russian
literature. But he was incapable of the aſtive faith of his
friends, the Bolsheviks, and his support of them was
always half-hearted and hand-washing. In their praſtice,
altruism and revolution—the two mainſtays of the utilitarian creed—appeared to have parted company, and
kindness to have become incompatible with aſtive political
advance. Kindness had had to be sacrificed to progress,
and the revolution in the name of kindness to be performed by means that were the negation of kindness.
This is the source of Gorki's eternal perplexity, though he
has done much to keep it undivulged. But apart from
this order of queſtions, Gorki has given proof in all his
later books (beginning with *Childhood,* 1913) of qualities
that dispense us from asking what he thinks or what he
believes (or disbelieves) in. These qualities are a marvellous eyesight and a power of visual convincingness that
has allowed him, in his autobiographical series, in his
Recolleſtions (especially of Tolſtoy), and in his lateſt
novel, *The Artamonovs' Business* (1926),[1] to produce a
body of work which, for vitality and realism, need fear
comparison with nothing. His fascinated disguſt with the
ugliness, savagery, and meanness of the life around him
gives a particularly pungent taſte to the quality of his
painting, and throws into bolder relief the figures of the

---

[1] English translation, *Decadence.*

great, good, and original men and women he has come against. On the other hand, Gorki the man has acquired a unique position in the literary world owing to his efforts to help his fellow-writers through the worst years of civil war and " war-time communism." We have had within the last fifteen years, and still have, men of greater genius than Gorki, but the sum total of his literary and of his personal achievement makes us recognise in him our foremost living man of letters, the president, as it were, of the republic of Russian letters.

The " modernists " (a word that is both inadequate and exceedingly repulsive, but which is the only one to cover the whole ground of the new movements) were richer in genius than the " realists." The movement found its principal expression in poetry and in what went by the name of " religious philosophy." The greatest of the " religious philosophers " was Rozanov (1856-1919), an isolated figure whose influence, though great, has been singularly elusive and indirect. He carried the negation of reason and the practice of spontaneous intuition farther than anyone before him. He was also a great revolutionary in style—the first to give Russian literary prose the natural movement of spoken language, and a subtlety and flexibility that almost transcend the limitations of articulate speech. Other " religious philosophers " who helped to enlarge and complicate the Russian mind were Leo Shestov, Nicolas Berdyayev, Paul Florensky, and the poet Vyacheslav Ivanov, all of them refined and sophisticated minds whose immediate action was only on small groups of the élite. The great vulgariser of new values and the most widely read author on these subjects was the well-known Merezhkovsky, who, before 1905, was an important transmitting and civilising force, but has since then degenerated into a mere writing apparatus.

From the purely literary point of view, however, the most vital branch of "modernism" was the poetry of the symbolists, no doubt the central literary fact of the whole pre-revolutionary period. The symbolists were united by a mystical and magical attitude to the world, by a highly developed and consciously refined sensibility, and by a will to assimilate poetry to music. The principal poets of the older symbolist generation were Balmont and Bryusov, the pioneers of symbolism, whose verse is rather the worse for wear; the severe and perfect craftsman, Theodore Sologub; the cerebral and subtle poetess, Zinaida Hippius; the enormously influential Vyacheslav Ivanov, the grand master of all the sophistications and complications of symbolist culture; and the most exquisite and refined of all, Innocent Annensky (1856-1909), whose distilled and quintessenced lyrics are among the purest gems of Russian poetry.

The crest of the wave of symbolist poetry is reached in the work of a younger man, Alexander Blok (1880-1921). Unlike most of the symbolists, Blok struck a note that found response in a very wide audience. He has come to be universally recognised as a great national poet. Transcendental and musical, his poetry is akin to that of the great romanticists; his family consists of Lermontov, Heine, Byron, Shelley, Novalis. His main theme is mystical —mystical joy in his union with the "Beautiful Lady" at first; afterwards, mystical despair in being cast out of her presence into the outer darkness of the earth. At first intensely egotistic, Blok's poetry gradually became a social "group-poetry," by a process natural in a symbolist who

discovers in his own mystical experience the "correspondence" and, as it were, the microcosm of the collective
experience of the people and nation. Blok's poetry is
distinctly prophetic, not in any loose metaphorical, but in
the truest psychological, sense: the Revolution, as it were,
played itself in the microcosm of his soul before it was
let loose on a larger scale in the life of the nation. The
feeling of the approaching doom, a thing at the same time
of terror and of hope, the actual breath of a wind from
the future, fills all Blok's poetry of 1907-1916. This prophetic group-poetry culminated in his great poem of the
revolutionary blizzard, written in November, 1917 (*The
Twelve*), after which he became silent, having, it would
seem, exhausted to the dregs all his poetical energy. He
died to himself and to the world several years before his
physical death, which came in 1921.

The poetry of the symbolists was very largely conditioned by foreign influences; and though in its later
stages the national element came into its own, even in
Blok, the most national of the symbolist poets, the foreign
(notably German) element is very apparent. The parallel
development in Russian prose was, on the contrary,
entirely free from foreign influences, and an assertion of
the most Russian aspects of the Russian tradition.
Rozanov's radically new and vernacular treatment of
literary Russian gave the keynote. Gogol, Dostoevsky, and
Leskov became the tutelary geniuses of the new prose.

Of the older symbolist generation, the only one to
achieve much in prose fiction was Theodore Sologub,
whose *Little Denion* (1907), without apparently departing from the canons of nineteenth-century realism,
informed them with a new meaning; the ruthless and

ugly picture of provincial society is a "criticism," not of
Russian life, but of evil life in general. The novelists of
the younger symbolist generation also used the material
of Russian, usually provincial, life, not in order to illus-
trate social issues or to criticise social facts, but to shape
it into new imaginative entities. Abandoning photo-
graphic and journalistic exactness, they revived the "surrealistic" methods of Gogol. They emphasised the
striking, the grotesque, the symbolical. They revolu-
tionised Russian prose by giving it the verbal intensity
and suggestiveness of poetry—another revival of the
tradition of Gogol, of Leskov, and of the early
Dostoevsky. The men who did all this were Andrey
Bely and Alexey Remizov. The former's *Silver Dove* (1909),
and *Petersburg* (1914), and the latter's *Story of Stratilatov*
(1909) were the beginning of a period of Russian prose
which is still continuing. In the years immediately preceding the War a galaxy of new novelists arose, all of
them more or less influenced by Remizov, and utilising
the material of Russian life, not for criticism but for
purely imaginative and non-representational construc-
tions. The most notable were Michael Prishvin, the
author of the best animal and hunting stories in the language, who, though over fifty (born 1873), is still one
of the freshest forces in Russian literature; Eugene
Zamyatin, of whom I shall have more to say presently;
and Alexey Tolstoy. Alexey Tolstoy, a man of abundant
gifts and exiguous brains, has written much that is simply
silly—but at his best he is an admirable story-teller,
whose outstanding quality is a light-hearted, merry spon-
taneity that is very rare among our contemporaries. His
complete absence of ideas and a complete indifference to

all things of the intellect make him one of the first swallows of the great anti-philosophical and anti-intellectual reaction which ended the age of symbolism.

It began about 1912, and found expression in three principal movements: the Petersburg "Guild of Poets," the futurists, and the formalist school of criticism. For all their diversity these movements are united by several common features, the most important being a taboo on ideas in general. Russian nineteenth-century literature had aspired to the expression of social and ethical ideas. The symbolists (and the pessimistic realists) had discovered the futility of social, replacing them by metaphysical, ideas. The new generation put its ban on all ideas, whether social or metaphysical, reducing literature to an art, even to merely a craft, a technique. They rejected the supersophisticated metaphysical culture of the symbolists, but retained and carried still further their technical and formal sophistication and complexity. The symbolists had refined and complicated their technique to give expression to complicated and refined spiritual experiences. The younger generation refined and complicated theirs to construct verbal edifices of pure invention, pure play. The principal external influence traceable in these Russian movements was that of the science of linguistics—an attitude to literature as to a purely linguistic phenomenon being ultimately the main point of their doctrines. They had in this respect already been preceded by some of the symbolists: the works of Andrey Bely on the rhythms of Russian verse, begun in 1910, were an important starting-point for the formalist reaction. In the same year appeared the first poem of Victor Khlebnikov (1885-1922), a poet whose poetry was,

mainly, an attempt to recreate a new language out of the
elements of Russian, shorn of all traditional associations.
The firſt manifeſtoes of the futuriſts and of the (much
more moderate) Guild of Poets appeared in 1912. But
the high-water mark of these movements was reached
during the years that followed the Revolution, when the
futuriſt Mayakovsky sprang into national celebrity, and
when the formaliſt critics brought out the volume *Poetics*
(1919), where their leader, Victor Shklovsky, proclaimed
that a work of art is "equal to the sum of *procédés* employed in it."

The new movements were a definite abdication of
much that had been added to the Russian mind by the
symboliſts—a simplification. The sensibility behind the
work of the moſt characteriſtic of the new poets was
cruder and more rudimentary than that of the symboliſts
had been. (This, however, is true only of the representative men of the movement; by their side and partly in
their ranks there were other poets whose sensibility was
a refinement even on the moſt refined of the symboliſts,
and who annexed new and unexplored provinces of
experience. Such poets were Elena Guro, died 1910;
Count Vasili Komarovsky, died 1914; and, especially,
Tikhon Churilin, whose beſt poetry is directly inspired
by his acquaintance with mental disease.)

The moſt representative men of the new movements
were the two leaders, Nicolas Gumilev and Vladimir
Mayakovsky. The difference between the two, between
the æſtheticism and dandyism of the one and the ſtudied
vulgarity and crudeness of the other, is enormous, and is
further emphasised by the fact of Gumilev having been
a monarchiſt and a victim of the Red Terror (he was

executed in 1921), while Mayakovsky is a Communist from boyhood, and has often lent himself as a mouthpiece of official Soviet propaganda. But both led Russian poetry away from metaphysical dreams and speculations, away from all vagueness and super-sensitiveness, into a more bracing air of action. Their very art they regarded primarily as action, as an act of possession over the brute matter of words. For the first time for many generations they tuned Russian verse to a major instead of a minor key. Gumilev is more traditional: there is much in him that is conventionally poetical, but it is the poetry of manly and active romance. He prided himself on his verse being no relaxing food; old slave-hunters in Abyssinia, he boasted, and political assassins in Russia had found it fit diet for them. Mayakovsky deliberately sought to free himself from all poetical associations. His language and his prosody are those of an open-air orator, and he sums up his programme in these words:

> " We are fed up with heavenly candies:
> Give us plain black bread to feed on.
> We are fed up with cardboard passions:
> Give us a live wife to live with."

The leader of the third movement, the formalist critic, Victor Shklovsky, is an equally representative figure. His best book, *A Sentimental Journey* (1923), is the history of his experiences during the Revolution, which he passed in fighting, organising conspiracies, repairing armoured cars, and teaching young novelists the principles of the craft of fiction.

The February Revolution of 1917, which overthrew the monarchy, was received by everyone with an enthusiasm which, before long, gave place, on the one hand,

to a fierce desire to go on and sweep away all the old
social order, on the other to perplexity, disillusion, and
disguſt in the people. The October Revolution widened
the chasm between the two sides and cleft the nation (or
at leaſt the intelligentsia) in two. For three years Russia
lived in a ſtate of civil war. The ultimate victory of the
Reds, which came in 1920, threw hundreds of thousands
of people, chiefly of the educated classes, out of the
country into Europe, America, and China. Since that date
Russian literature has been divided between the U.S.S.R.
and the emigration. The greater part of the older literary
generation live to-day outside Russia, in conditions of
freedom vouchsafed to them by the democratic polities
of the Weſt. But freedom is evidently not enough to
preserve the vitality of a literature. The work produced
abroad by the older *émigré* writers is diſtinctly inferior
to their earlier achievements, and the younger generation
of *émigrés* have added nothing of any value to Russian
imaginative literature (though they have produced a
vigorous and valuable literature of ideas). Only in the
U.S.S.R. is there a younger generation continuing the
traditions of Russian literary art.

Poſt-revolutionary Russian literature has passed through
two principal phases, corresponding to the political phases
of the Revolution. 1918-1920 were years of civil war,
political terror, and economical chaos. In Moscow and
(especially) in Petersburg they were years of unimaginable
suffering and privation, of life on the brink of ſtarvation,
and of Arctic winters in unheated houses. Still, it muſt be
admitted that authors and artiſts suffered, on the whole,
less than the majority of intellectuals, while those of the
younger generation who were on the Communiſt side

were even in some ways better off than before the Revolution. In Moscow the poets of the literary Left had the time of their lives. Their poetical cafés were the centre of all animation, and they were believed to represent the best in Russian literature. They were full of iconoclastic enthusiasm for a Revolution that was so effectively sweeping away a hated bourgeois world, which, to them, was also a world of Philistines. Their technical, workmanlike attitude to their art was in tune with the doctrines of the new rulers, who worshipped the workman and believed in technique and efficiency. There was then an enormous vogue of the theatre, where the advanced producers were also trying to achieve a purely technical excellency of the *spectacle pur,* of the *show* pure and simple, unadulterated by "literary" irrelevancies. Even the more conservative formalists of Petersburg joined in the general triumph of pure technique. A characteristic feature of these terrible years was the appearance of numerous literary studios, where beginners were taught the elements of poetry and of fiction by masters of the craft. The most notable was the one run in Petersburg by Gumilev and Zamyatin.

The attitude of the older men (and of those of the younger generation who were still full of the symbolist spirit) to the Revolution was different. To some of them it was mainly a hateful and unmitigated calamity, a great crime of the Russian people against God and man. But the most representative symbolists accepted it as a Juggernaut, a purifying catastrophe, the well-deserved doom of a too materialistic civilisation. By its very destruction of all economical values it made possible the advent of a reign of purely spiritual values.

This was the attitude of Blok (*The Twelve*); of Andrey
Bely, who coined the phrase "Culture of Eternity," to
designate the new system of values, and displayed in those
years a feverish activity as writer, preacher, and lecturer;
of the noble old historian and critic, Michael Gershenzon,
who died in 1925. The dialogue of letters on the meaning of culture, which took place between Gershenzon
and Vyacheslav Ivanov in the beginning of 1920, when
the two men were lying convalescent in a nursing home
near Moscow (*A Correspondence between Two Corners*),
is, perhaps, the noblest and most attractive monument of
those years. A more popular expression of similar feelings
will be found in the superficially splendid historical poems
of Maximilian Voloshin on the theme that only now,
after the Revolution has destroyed her material greatness,
may Russia accomplish her mission of becoming a
Kingdom of the Spirit, and in the neat and witty lyrical
epigrams of Vladislav Khodasevich inspired by a yearning after death and freedom from the flesh.

This mystical attitude to the Revolution was essentially
ambivalent—*The Twelve* oscillates between ecstasy and
horror before the revolutionary Juggernaut. A recent and
eminently human expression of this ambivalence is
Remizov's book on the Revolution (*Russia in the
Tornado,* 1927), which shudders at the cruelty and wor-
ships the purifying ruthlessness of the catastrophe that
destroyed the cosy life of the middle classes.

The tide of poetry which had been rising ever since
1905 also reached its high-water mark in 1918-1920. Not
only was the poetical output of those years out of all
proportion greater than that of prose, not only did the
few remaining prose writers reproduce in their writings

the attitude and methods of poetry, but poets were (as they had been increasingly for some time) widely, and what is ſtill more unusual in our age of hiſtory, deservedly popular. Blok, acclaimed as a great national poet; Mayakovsky, recognised as the mouthpiece of the Revolution; the exquisite and dignified Petersburg poetess, Anna Akhmatova, taſted of real popularity and commanded larger audiences than poets had done for generations. The greateſt success of all was that of Sergey Esenin (1895-1925), a young man of peasant extraction, who combined apparent novelty of form and revolutionary sympathies with a quite nineteenth-century sensibility and sentimental wiſtfulness. Less immediately popular but intrinsically more significant is the poetry of Marina Tsvetayeva, the only important figure of the younger generation to have left Russia and become an *émigrée*. Her beſt work is quite recent (1924-1927). She combines an extraordinary freshness of form and inexhauſtible technical inventiveness with equally inexhauſtible vitality, and a simple, hero-worshipping romanticism. For sheer verbal power Tsvetayeva surpasses all her contemporaries, but the really greateſt Russian poet of to-day is Boris Paſternak (born in 1890). His poetry is a perfectly new and unexpected world, a fresh and unprecedented vision of things. For this newness in seeing the world Paſternak may be compared to Rimbaud. He has touched new depths, discovered fresh reaches of unrecorded poetical experience, and created for it a new technique, which, though it sometimes ſtammers and ſtumbles, is an inſtrument of tremendous force and fascination. The very novelty of Paſternak's world makes it difficult to speak of him—criticism has not yet invented for it an adequate vocabulary. In diction he is a futurist preferring, as did Donne, the imagery of ordinary and prosaic life to the orthodox beauties of poetical tradition. His influence on his fellow-craftsmen has been immense. His best work is contained in the lyrical sequence, *My Sister, Life* (written 1917, published 1922). Pasternak's prose, which stands quite apart from the general tendencies of contemporary Russian prose, is also remarkable; he is the only Russian prose writer of to-day to have kept his eye on that neglected and tabooed thing—the human soul. *The Childhood of Lüvers* will, no doubt, be gradually recognised for a work of exceptional significance, and in some distant future become the fountain-head of some new and unsuspected school of fiction.

Of the very youngest poets the most notable are Nicolas Tikhonov and Ilya Selvinsky, the former a disciple mainly of Gumilev, the latter mainly of the futurists, and both inspired by a manly love of action and adventure, and of concentrated expressiveness. In their ballads of the Civil War they have much in common with the novelists, of whom presently.

The Bolsheviks have attempted to create an official "proletarian poetry" by encouraging young workmen to write verse; but all this poetry, though often fairly competent, has failed to produce anything much better than rather conventional rhetoric.

In 1921, with the end of the civil wars, the régime of "War-time Communism" under which Soviet Russia had lived for three years came to an end, and under the Nep (New Economic Policy) conditions became more normal. The horrors of 1918-1920 passed away; but so did uncontrolled Government grants to theatres and studios. The book trade, which had subsisted on official subventions, was revived on the ordinary offer-and-demand basis. Life became less infernal and more humdrum. The régime of terror was mitigated, but, in an atmosphere of general calm, the instrument of suppression was steadily perfected; religion was more actively proscribed; education effectively bolshevised; and the censorship surpassed in rigour anything that had ever been effected by the old régime. The literature of ideas — journalism, philosophy, criticism — was totally prohibited except in so far as the ideas were either perfectly irrelevant to political, social, and religious issues, or conformed to orthodox Marxism and Leninism. Imaginative literature was also called upon to conform with the official orthodoxy. The liberal wing (now in power) of the party, however, gave the notion of conformity a somewhat broad interpretation, and fiction and poetry are no doubt to-day the form of writing that is freest in Soviet Russia—the only one that may give expression to ideas and feelings not necessarily official. But the censorship is very vigilant. Works of outstanding merit by famous authors are known to have been prevented from seeing the light, and still more have to be published in a mutilated form. No allusion to such mutilation being allowed in print, and no trace of it being allowed to be left apparent in the text (in the form of lines of dots or blank spaces), the reader of Soviet literature is under the constant disadvantage of not knowing how far the text he is reading is what the author wrote.

The principal feature of post-Nep literature has been the revival of prose fiction, which has once more asserted its claims as against those of poetry. Among the novelists who are read in Russia we may distinguish four kinds (apart from translations which form, as they have always done, the greater part of the Russian reader's diet): (1) Men of the older generation who were fully formed writers before the War—Gorki, A. Tolstoy, Prishvin, Veresayev, Sergeyev-Tsensky, etc.; (2) writers not above the level of adequate descriptive journalism, who may be (and are) very interesting to the student of life in the Soviet Union, but who do not belong to literature, even though they give their writings the form of fiction; among these one of the most popular is Panteleimon Romanov; (3) writers of what is called in Russian "boulevard" literature, duly adapted to the taste of the average non-literary reader; for instance, Lydia Seifulina; (4) finally, the real literary artists of the young generation to whom I will devote the remainder of the present survey.

The main influences operating on Russian fiction at the moment of its revival in 1921 were those of Bely, Remizov, Zamyatin, and Shklovsky. Bely and Remizov (and their own great masters, Gogol and Leskov) taught the writer of prose to use words and language with the same care as the poet does, and to inform it with every kind of expressive ornament. This kind of prose was called "ornamental prose," and a direct effect of their influence was to draw the writer's attention away from the larger unit of form to the smaller, from the story to the phrase. Bely is himself a master of narrative construction, and his example, together with the great example of Leskov, might have shown the younger writers that it was possible to unite intense verbal wealth with tense narrative interest. But the old Russian tradition of non-narrative fiction prevailed, and was strengthened by Remizov, who had done more than anyone else in the preceding generation to quicken the disintegration of the narrative form, substituting for narrative sequence the surrealistic logic of fairy tales and dreams. The typical Russian story of to-day is devoid of narrative development. When it has a unity (which is often the case), this is not a unity of action, but a static unity of a plastic or pictorial order. This kind of unity had been cultivated by Eugene Zamyatin, who gave his stories a kind of skeleton by reducing the theme to geometrical expression, as the cubists do. Zamyatin, who in real life is a shipbuilding engineer and Professor of Shipbuilding at the Polytechnicum of Leningrad, and the formalist critic, Victor Shklovsky, taught the younger generation to regard the art of fiction as a pure technique devoid of all " human " and psychological significance whatever. Shklovsky also attempted to oppose the non-narrative tendencies of the old Russian tradition, of Remizov and Zamyatin, and advocated the Western novel of pure narrative action. He invoked the example of Dumas and R. L. Stevenson, but he was mainly attracted, not so much by the normal development of the narrative, as by its freaks and sports. He introduced the notion of "playing with the plot" in order to destroy or emphasise the " narrative illusion," and ultimately, instead of Dumas, succeeded in drawing general attention to Sterne. *Tristram Shandy* became, rather unexpectedly, a major influence in Russian literature; it was hardly calculated to strengthen the narrative tendency in it. So even Shklovsky helped to advance the disintegration of the narrative form.

The subject-matter of the younger novelists is more

often than not taken from the civil war or the Revolution. But their attitude to these events is mainly æsthetic. They appreciate in their material the elemental grandness of the historical process, the fascinating poetry of horror and cruelty, the thrill of heroism and adventure. Some of the main characteristics of their art may be ascribed to the influence of their subject-matter. The predilection apparent in Bely and Remizov (as in Gogol and Leskov) for the grotesque, the unusual, the extreme, and the improbable was reinforced in the younger novelists by the spectacle of the Revolution, when all that was customary and familiar was washed away, and history seemed to revel in an orgy of unexpectedness. The grotesque, the horrid, and the cruel are emphasised in their stories by their studiedly cool and casual way of relating it. One of the aspects of the unusual and out of the way is the heroical, and an heroical spirit (not individual hero-worship, but a leaning towards heroism in general) is prominent in the stories of many young authors. It goes hand in hand with a complete absence of all sense of the individual; there are practically no personalities in modern Russian fiction. The hero is the group, a whole nation, a district, a regiment, an army. The crowd, whether gathered in one place or diffused in space, is the principal agent—a crowd, as it were, spear-topped with heroes that are not in any psychological sense individuals, but only protagonists well rooted in the chorus. It must not, however, be supposed that the absence of the individual entails an absence of the concrete. The men-mass of the Russian novelists is not the abstract mass-man of the German dramatists arrived at by the elimination of all individual features, but a perfectly concrete and individual crowd, as different from another crowd as any man may be from another man.

The most characteristic novels displaying these features are *The Bare Year,* by Boris Pilnyak, the first in time (1921); the Siberian stories of the civil war of Vsevolod Ivanov; and the masterpiece of the genre, *My Native Land,* by Artem Vesely (1926). This latter novel is in every way characteristic; it is the story of a whole district during the civil war. There is little narrative development, but it is full of the spirit of a great struggle. The style, very intense, is racy and vibrates with life. The author's sympathy is kept in balance between the Reds and their enemies, the insurgent peasants. What, however, gives the book a place apart and makes it better than representative is Vesely's sense of humour, which rises at times to genuine comedy—a virtue very rare in modern Russian literature.

Of the other "ornamental" novelists, I will only mention Leonid Leonov, a man of obviously brilliant gifts, a true disciple of Remizov, and a master of his native tongue, but who has not yet produced work of undoubted significance; and especially Isaac Babel, whose stories of the Polish campaign of 1920 (*Konarmia*) are the most *perfect* work by any Russian prose writer since the Revolution. Babel has a narrative gift, though only in the limits of the very short story, an extraordinary command of dialect, and the very personal art of permeating the horror and squalor of war with the thrill and poetry of heroism, while never for a moment letting one forget the horror and squalor.

The absence of narrative and even of character interest and the excessive elaboration of style (admirable in

Leonov, Babel, and Vesely, but intolerable in inferior writers) makes all this literature an unfit staple diet for the general reader. A reading public cannot subsist without plain narrative to go on, and the necessity of supplying it with this commodity is realised by everyone. The novelist who sells best to-day in Soviet Russia is Ilya Erenburg, the author of that remarkable satire of the bourgeois world, *Julio Jurenito* (1922), but in his latest books the manufacturer of mere thrilling and meretricious melodrama. Nor does he suffice for the market, and foreign novels are translated in immense numbers: *Tarzan,* the novels of Pierre Benoît, and the detective stories of Mr. G. K. Chesterton are among the most universal favourites. Apart from this, a serious effort has been made to react against the ruling school of fiction, against excessive elaboration of style and neglect of narrative, against the absence of all distinct moral judgment. The first swallow of the reaction was the work of Leo Lunts (1901-1924), a dramatist of singular promise, whose early death was a severe loss to Russian letters. At present the most notable figure of the reaction is Constantine Fedin. His novel *Cities and Years* (1924) is an admirably told story full of admirably drawn, strongly individual characters that stand out quite distinct from the crowd. It is also a serious and significant criticism of the character of a typical Russian intellectual, a considered judgment on the ineffective man who wants to preserve his moral purity by not committing himself to action, and of the man of action who sacrifices all his values to one supreme value and to action in the good cause. Fedin leaves us in no doubt as to which of the two is right. *Cities and Years* is the only post-revolu-

tionary novel that contains creations of character worthy
to be mentioned by the side of those of the great nineteenth-century novelists (especially the wonderful figure
of the peasant Fedor Lependin), and the only one
embodying a distinct and active attitude of moral *choice*
in the presence of the great realities of war and revolution. Fedin is not a prolific writer. Among the few
shorter stories he has published since *Cities and Years,*
there is one which marks an even further advance in the
creation of character (*Transvaal,* 1927), and confirms his
position as the most prominent hope of the Russian novel.

In the drama the immature but vigorous and promising
tragedies of pure action of Leo Lunts stand alone; he is
the only modern Russian dramatist whom it is possible
to mention. Since the death of Chekhov the Russian
drama has been (as Mr. Isaacs has remarked of the contemporary English drama) a purely parasitic growth, and
has produced nothing of any value at all (the plays of
Blok are pure poetry, and the plays of Mayakovsky first-
class propaganda rather than drama). This is all the more
curious, as the Russian *theatre* has been all this time
singularly vigorous and fertile. But the new producers
have worked without the aid of dramatic literature, and
this lack of dramatists has helped to emphasise one of
the main tendencies of the modern theatre—to emanci-
pate the stage from literary influence.

The literature of ideas has ceased to exist in Soviet
Russia. It is quite alive among the *émigrés,* where the
young generation, though failing to produce any important poetry or fiction, have given birth to the only
significant post-revolutionary movement of ideas—the
" Eurasian " movement. It may be defined as a com-

bination of cultural and religious traditionalism with a practically complete acceptance of the social and political results of the Revolution. But nowhere does the new generation show any trace of the metaphysical fertility and complexity of the preceding generations. The Russian mind seems to be tired of the sophistications of Dostoevsky, Soloviev, Rozanov, of the symbolists and religious philosophers. It craves for doctrine and dogma imposed from the outside rather than for any liberty of speculation. This is why Marxism, with its rigid insistence on orthodoxy as announced by Marx and defined by Lenin, is so congenial a philosophy to the Soviet intellectual of to-day. Those who are not satisfied by it, as the Eurasians are not, tend more and more to submit to the unquestioned guidance of the Orthodox Church. This need for dogma and conformity seems to be a natural result of the anti-metaphysical reaction, for all intellectual activity and curiosity are being directed towards technical and practical ends—the techniques of art, of literature, of politics, of economics, or of engineering. First principles are no longer investigated, but accepted. We may expect an age when the Russian mind, technical and practical in its practice, will submit its techniques and practices to one ultimate dogma placed above all questioning.

D. S. MIRSKY.

SCANDINAVIA

I⊤ is, I understand, the plan of the present volume to express the contemporary standpoint as it appears to the younger generation; not what is generally regarded as the function of the university teacher—to attempt to place the literary movement of the day in its historical perspective. Historical perspectives are usually depressing things, and I have much sympathy with the view that the critic and elucidator of contemporary phenomena is better without them. It is surely time enough for later generations to try to see a literary movement *sub specie æternitatis;* let us who are of the living present see that present with the warm appreciation of the contemporary who is heart and soul, as our French neighbours say, " in the movement." Now, it is just a little difficult for us of the older generation to fulfil this function satisfactorily. We have too much disillusionment to be ashamed of. We have seen too many men of letters who, in our early days filled us with enthusiasm and high hopes, pass out into the twilight of comparative oblivion, or settled down into the comfortable mediocrity which commands boundless circulations on both sides of the ocean. Or, on the other hand, we have to confess, to our humiliation, that in our youth we looked askance at, or failed to recognise at all, poets who have since proved themselves to be real builders of literary empire. Thus we have grown wary and chary of joining in the chorus of immediate con-

temporary appreciation; perhaps, indeed, we are inclined
to be carping in our judgments. I think this is a disadvantage, an unfortunate limitation in us, for the sympathetic appreciation that is born of the emotion of the
moment is a precious thing; it is positive and conſtruc-
tive—and in the world of the imagination it is the con-
ſtructive alone that matters—whereas the critic who
wraps himself in the chilly robe of the literary hiſtorian
is apt merely to discourage young effort and aspiration.
To tell a young poet or noveliſt that his work is worthy
to ſtand with the beſt of the paſt, even if it is patent
flattery, is a more helpful thing than to say: "This will
never do!" Thus I think that this invasion of the university into what is usually regarded as the province of
the journaliſt is to be welcomed.

I am confronted with a difficult task. I do not
think the promoters of this scheme quite realised how
difficult when they asked me to contribute to it. They
have invited me to write on Scandinavian literature.
There might have been some juſtification for such an
invitation a generation and more ago, when there were
Pan-Scandinavian dreamers—in Scandinavia and outside
it—who cherished high hopes of a spiritual unity among
the peoples of the North, of a single great Scandinavian
literature. But there is no Scandinavian literature to-day;
there are national literatures of Denmark, of Sweden, of
Norway, and in the twentieth century these literatures
have each been pursuing paths which with every year
diverge more and more; they are further apart to-day than
at any moment of their paſt hiſtory. Thus it would have
been quite as reasonable if in this volume a single contributor had been entruſted with all the Latin literatures

of Europe. Nor, indeed, when I have mentioned these three literatures have I exhausted the field I might be expected to cover; something ought to be said, were I competent to say it, on the present literary aspiration of that marvellously interesting island, the first home of Scandinavian poetry, Iceland; and an exhaustive survey would also require that consideration should be given to the Swedish literature of Finland.

To attempt to do all this is, of course, impossible. I have not had the time in a busy life, in which these literatures have been only a side-issue—if a dearly loved side-issue—to familiarise myself with them with a fulness which would entitle me to sit in judgment of them. And much of what I have to say in this cursory survey has—I frankly confess it—been acquired by a quite inadequate and, from our academic standpoint, deplorable process of browsing and sampling. I take, however, some consolation from the fact that, when I look back on what I wrote on the literature of Scandinavia thirty years ago, it has justified itself better before the tribunal of literary history than what I wrote then on my own particular field, the German movement. And thus I venture to hope that, even without undue encroachment of the historical perspective, my survey may have some validity.

It is now fifteen years since the last of the great European Scandinavians in the field of creative literature passed away, August Strindberg. To speak of him thus lies outside my present task. But the stimulus and influence of this mighty tragic genius, who drew so deep a furrow across the literature of Europe, are far from exhausted. For his own people the sixty odd volumes of his collected writings are one of their most precious possessions. There may be much in his work of disputable value, but no one denies that he endowed Swedish prose—and I would remind you that the Swedish tongue is one of the most musical and beautiful of all modern tongues—with a flexibility, delicacy, and force which give it a place with the best. Opinion about Strindberg is gradually crystallising, and I think two aspects of his work—for us outside Sweden, at least—are standing out more and more significantly as his life recedes into the historic past. The first of these is his spiritual wrestling with the dark powers, that woe unutterable which filled so large a space of his mature life. Here is a man who, like the great Florentine, had veritably sojourned in hell, one of those unhappy mortals who, as the great Danish thinker Kierkegaard said, are, by the inscrutable designs of Providence, chosen in every age to suffer, that the world may move forwards. It has always been one of the particular missions of the literature of the North to depict for us the relations and wrestlings of the soul with the dread unseen; no note is more persistent in Northern folk-lore. The other aspect of Strindberg's work which seems to me of especial importance is that he has given us a new technique of the drama. The drama has never been more than an episodic phenomenon in the Scandinavian literatures; there are lacking in the North those great centres of population and literary centralisation which have always been necessary for the steady development of the drama; but this defect has its compensations. There is no clogging dramatic tradition in Scandinavia, and the individual dramatist has, in consequence, always had a freer hand than elsewhere; he has not been obliged to show consideration for ingrained conventions. Holberg, Ibsen,

Strindberg, have thus all been pioneers and innovators in the domain of the theatre. If the cinema and wireless broadcasting do not succeed in killing the theatre altogether, I believe that Strindberg's art—not merely that of the naturalistic plays, which have already, I dare say, spent their force in the European theatre, but of the great and far too little known historical dramas of his later years—will be a very real factor in the theatre of the future.

We are not unfamiliar in England with living Swedish writers. We know something of Heidenstam; we have felt the spell of Sweden's greatest woman-writer, Selma Lagerlöf—of that marvellous plasticity and Goethe-like balance, which are so refreshing in this age of nervous restlessness; qualities which, I would add, seem to me to come to finer expression in the work of her later life than in the famous *Gösta Berlings saga* which gave her her European reputation. But although these writers are still happily with us, I do not feel that they belong to my present survey. There is a moment when every writer is of and in the movement; it may come early; it may not come until he himself has long crumbled to dust and ashes; but to few writers—even the greatest—is it given to occupy the vanguard of progress for more than a very brief period of their career. In the case of both Verner von Heidenstam and Selma Lagerlöf this period lies back behind my present survey.

What we have not recognised in this country is that to Sweden Europe owes the richest lyric poetry of our time. Here, again, Sweden has had, as in her drama, the advantage of freedom from a too burdensome tradition. Her young poets have not the same reason to be oppressed

by the thought which lay so heavy on the German singers
of the later nineteenth century, and which has lain on
our own, that all the songs have been already sung; that
there is no room for new ones. I do believe that the lyric
revival in Swedish literature at the end of the nineteenth century was the moſt important happening in
the European literature of that age; certainly it was
the moſt hopeful and wholesome at a time when
fin de siècle-ism and poetic bankruptcy were rampant in all the greater lands. No other literature, not
even that of Germany, so uniformly rich in lyric expression, could boaſt of men of such indubitable genius as
Guſtav Fröding, Verner von Heidenſtam, and—perhaps
the moſt delicate and gifted of them all—Erik Axel
Karlfeldt. But in all ages when lyric inspiration is
vigorous it is never a matter of isolated phenomena; and
the leading Swedish critic of the turn of the century,
Oskar Levertin, himself a poet of rare, pre-Raphaelite
delicacy, could write:

> " I wonder whether the Swedish public really knows what
> a poetic age it has the advantage of living in. I wonder if
> it is really aware of how completely Swedish poetry has
> renewed itself in the laſt fifteen years. . . . One might
> have expeċted that a pause would ensue after the outburſt
> of poetic ſtrength in the nineties. But behold! after that
> generation there rise up on every side others; and not
> merely the names are new, but also the temperaments and
> the modes of expression."

That was written a good many years ago; but I think it
is ſtill true. To us, living in a land where poetry can so
often only be printed by the grace of an altruiſtic publisher, the quantity of verse which issues from the press
in Sweden is something of a marvel. And one is ſtruck
by its suſtained freshness, originality, and power. There

seem to be always new lyric poets in Sweden worth listen-
ing to. To characterise the individual singers who ought
to be discussed in a survey like the present, would be impossible; and even to enumerate them might, by its
inevitable omissions, appear invidious; after all, the appreciation of any contemporary lyric is apt to be a very personal matter. I have, I should like to say, had particular
pleasure from the fresh breath of the sea in the poetry of
Gustav Ullman and of Sigfrid Siwertz—the more so as
this element is so sparingly represented in the older lyric;
Sweden's poets have found more inspiration in her
great mystic lakes, Wener and Wetter, than in the wide
horizons of the open sea. I would emphasise the concentrated force in Bo Bergman's finest verse; the lurid pas-
sionateness of Sven Lidman's; the pellucid beauty of the
poetry of Anders Österling, whose warm appreciation of
the most intimately national in our own poetry—even of
Wordsworth, who is usually a book with seven seals to
the non-English mind—gives him an especial claim on
our sympathy. To me personally the strongest and at the
same time subtlest of comparatively recent poets is
Vilhelm Ekelund. But Ekelund also illustrates what I
think is an element of weakness in the newer lyric: its
increasing amenableness to foreign influence; the note
of imitation is more insistent in the new century than it
was in the last decade of the nineteenth; the new generation is less independent, less peculiarly national than men
like Fröding, Heidenstam, and Karlfeldt before them.
It is a pity to my mind that Ekelund, with his splendid
lyric power, should have fallen under the spell of German
Hellenism; for in the rarefied air of an æsthetic idealism
his muse has ultimately lost her voice altogether. And he

does not stand alone in this respect. Nietzsche and the latest phase of the French lyric have had a marked and undue influence in Sweden; and even expressionism is beginning to draw its grey, bloodless veil over Swedish poetry. In these days, too, the Swedish lyric has grown pessimistic in tone; and there is a tendency in even the most gifted talents to abandon verse for prose. But the foreign element which is most seriously menacing the purity of Swedish literature is neither French nor German, but the influence of America. Americanisation is, I venture to think, a real danger to Sweden as an independent literary power in Europe. Too many of her ablest writers have been lured to transpose incongruously into Swedish terms the unpoetic phenomena of trans-atlantic hustle and commercialism. The fine spirit of the older generation, Per Hallström, may have escaped evil consequences from his residence in America; but it is not the case with some of the younger men, even if they have never crossed the Atlantic. The Anglo-Saxon element in the flamboyant verse of Karl Gustav Ossiannilsson seems to me rather American than English; and in the domain of the novel, to mention only one conspicuous example, that fine talent, Henning Berger, might have done greater things had he been less obsessed by admiration of the American attitude to life. And America has returned the compliment by industriously translating Swedish books, with the result, alas! that we in England are condemned to read much of the modern literature of Sweden in what is certainly not English pure and un-defiled; even Strindberg himself speaks to us in some of his masterpieces with an unpleasant American accent. There is, however, I am glad to think, some hope of this

being remedied, thanks to the splendid generosity of Mr.
Bernard Shaw in placing his Nobel Prize at the disposal
of an Anglo-Swedish Foundation.

I have a difficulty in speaking of contemporary
Swedish prose in such positive terms as of the verse; it
is hardly in the same sense a phenomenon of European
significance. But my reading is perhaps not extensive
enough to juſtify me in expressing a definite opinion.
The clear-cut, brilliant talent of Hjalmar Söderberg—if
ever there was a transplantation of the genius of France
to the north, it is surely exemplified here—has made an
impression beyond the Swedish frontier, and might well
have made a deeper one. For readers who turn to
Swedish literature to find something peculiarly Swedish
which they cannot find elsewhere, the prose of Sven
Lidman is perhaps the moſt intereſting: his cycle of
novels, *Silfverſtååhlarna,* is never, in spite of inequalities
and a sometimes oppressive religious atmosphere, without
diſtinction and subtle poetic beauty. I believe the Swedes
themselves regard Sigfrid Siwertz as one of their moſt
prominent contemporary noveliſts; and his beſt book,
Selambs (of which there is an English translation) is not
easily forgotten; it opens up with its ruthless depiction
of devaſtating egotism, new and unexpected glimpses
into the modern soul. Yet it seems to me to fall short of
that diſtinction which imperatively demands the attention of the great world outside the author's own land. It
is a pity that Siwertz does not possess, I will not say the
" art to blot," but its modern equivalent—so necessary
in these days of endless, superfluous writing in all literatures—the art of writing little. Thus I doubt whether
Geijerſtam—even if his talent is not wearing very well

—has yet a worthy successor in the modern Swedish fiction of the kind in which he excelled.

I turn now to Denmark. And I cannot begin to speak of Danish literature without expressing our English sympathy with the Danes in the loss of their very great critic, Georg Brandes. Brandes was, if ever there was one, what Nietzsche called a "good European," and unquestionably the most potent critical force on the Continent of the last fifty years. It is true what is called the Brandesian epoch in Danish literature has long passed into history; but to Brandes belongs the honour of having piloted his little country out into the main stream of European poetry and ideas, of having revealed to the world the vital forces in the Dano-Norwegian literature of his time; nay, more, of having helped the greater nations of Europe to appreciate their own men of genius.

We have always been more familiar with Danish literature in this country than with Swedish, thanks largely to the sympathetic interpretations a generation ago of Sir Edmund Gosse, which did so much to open up to us the treasure-house of modern Northern literature. If I had to characterise the literary temper of the Danish people in a word, I should compare it with delicate Chinese porcelain; Danish poetry is an extraordinarily sensitive and fragile thing, a thing of fleeting iridescence, of tones almost beyond the range of ordinary ears. I will not repeat the old tag that the Danes are the most French of the nations of the North. For it is misleading, and not even justified. As a matter of fact, Sweden has always, since the seventeenth century, shown herself more amenable to French literary influence than Denmark. The delicacy, the restraint, the subtle irony of Danish literature are quite different from the similar qualities in French literature. Only Denmark could have given us that lonely and exquisite masterpiece of prose fiction— one of the great novels of the nineteenth century, whose influence has not yet spent itself—Jacobsen's *Niels Lyhne,* or the silver filigree, the exquisite lace-work, of a writer like Herman Bang. Neither of these men has a mentality which could be called in any degree French—not as, for instance, Söderberg's is in contemporary Sweden— and neither has made any particular appeal to the French reading public. But both Jacobsen and Bang belong to a past with which I am not here concerned.

To the English reader who is interested in Danish lyric poetry the last great name is that of Holger Drachmann. We are unreasonably ignorant of its later developments, more ignorant, I dare say, than we are of those in Sweden. It is strange that so richly gifted a lyric genius as Viggo Stuckenberg should be hardly even a name to us; nor do we know the verse, fascinating in its exotic colouring, of Sophus Claussen or Johannes Jörgensen. The fresh, intimate realism of that fine poet of the Danish " mother earth," Jeppe Aakjær, is a closed book to us, and we might be surprised to learn that the last phase of Danish lyricism numbers one poet of very great gifts indeed, Valdemar Rördam. This lyric has not made so deep an impression on the mind of Europe as that of the Swedes, and perhaps just for the reason which I have already indicated—the over-sensitiveness, illusiveness, and apartness of the Danish poetic mentality. It is difficult for us other Europeans to attune our ear to the Danish soul in its finest manifestations, to hear at all its most intimate pulsations. But we would do well to remember that the Danish lyric by no means came to an end with Holger Drachmann; indeed, I for one have never been so impressed by Drachmann's genius—he certainly overtaxed it—as many of his countrymen, and I see a great hope in the generation that has followed him.

Still, for us outside Denmark it is her novel that matters most. I have already mentioned Herman Bang, and some years ago I broke a lance in one of our reviews for one of the most eminent of Danish present-day novelists, Henrik Pontoppidan, who, with a fine spiritual realism, has given us a wonderful composite picture of the Denmark of our time. But Bang and Pontoppidan do not, in the sense which I must keep before me, belong to the immediate present. I dare say I should here give the place of honour to Johannes V. Jensen, who looms largest in the present literary world of Denmark. He is a writer of wide imaginative sweep, and, when he can hold his talent in check, of very real power; moreover, he has at his command a persuasive and arresting prose style. After a literary apprenticeship—I ought rather to say literary "wander years"—which took him all over the globe, he made the essential discovery that literary cosmopolitanism is a vain mirage, and that the first duty of a national writer is to be national. He has given us a splendid series of books which penetrate to the bed-rock of the Northern soul, much as Hamsun's do, but without that fantastic and often parochial note of the Norwegian writer. I should like to lay emphasis on the true and beautiful literature of the province, and especially of the province of Jutland, which seems to me a very precious asset in contemporary Danish work. I mention only the names of Jakob Knudsen of the older generation, and, again, of Jeppe Aakjær in the more immediate present. But there is also a new fiction in Denmark which is concerned with big ideas. Martin Andersen Nexö reflects the great social changes which are coming over the post-War world, although his literary workmanship is inferior to that of some of his less conspicuous contemporaries. Future generations will, I think, show more interest in those adventurous journeyings out into the spiritual unknown of men like Knud Hjörtö, Harald Kidde, who died, unfortunately, before his talent had reached its full maturity, and Jens Anker Larsen. Here Danish fiction is courageously attempting to find ingress to new worlds of spiritual experience. That is what Jacobsen achieved for the literature of Europe with his *Niels Lyhne* in 1880; and with this example and heritage, which has placed in Danish hands a more delicate instrument for probing the human soul than any other people possesses, it may again be given to Denmark to lead us into new worlds.

And now to turn to the literature of Norway. I am again faced with embarrassments, and this time quite peculiar embarrassments. There is no more significant happening in the recent history of Europe than the forging of Norwegian nationality. With the help of her railways—triumphs of engineering skill—north and south, east and west, are being brought together; the idea of nationality, of national community, is invading the isolation of Norway's lonely valleys; and one common aspiration is gradually emerging and binding her people together. Now it is this process, if I have judged aright, which is reflected in the Norwegian literature of to-day. To us in this country that literature has hitherto meant pre-eminently the giant figures of Ibsen and Björnson; but Ibsen and Björnson belong in a sense no longer true of any Norwegian writer to-day, to Denmark as well as to Norway; the language they wrote was not very different from that of Copenhagen. They belong quite to the past, a past that the War seems to have made enormously distant. We have thus to focus our eyes afresh to appreciate the Norwegian literature of the present. This is not altogether easy, for, if I understand her literary production rightly, Norway does not very much care whether we outsiders interest ourselves or not in what she is doing. None of the Scandinavian peoples is, to all appearance, so indifferent to finding an audience for her books outside her tiny population, which, I would remind you, is a mere fraction of that of London. The truth is, Norway is so intent on the great task of welding her people into one, finding her own soul, that she has little time to think of the world outside. She is determined that her new national literature shall not be of the old Dano-Norwegian stamp which brought her worldwide fame some fifty years ago; or she will at least transmute the Dano-Norwegian tradition into an unmistakable expression of her national independence.

I do not, of course, wish to say that this indifference permeates all or, consciously, perhaps any of her individual writers; but it is the general impression which her books leave upon us. To begin with, her writers employ many tongues; even when they adopt definitely " riksmaal " or " landsmaal," their speech is liberally tinged with dialect colouring. This is an initial difficulty to us when we try to penetrate into her most intimate books. Even the best of dictionaries leave us in the lurch. But this obstacle is well worth trying to overcome in order to gain access to a literature which, in a higher degree than any other of our time, is a literature born of the soil. It is what the Germans call "Heimatkunst," "home art," but a "Heimatkunst" far more fundamental than that Germany has achieved or even dreamt of. Norwegian literature to-day is pre-eminently a literature in prose. I would not say that the lyric awakening of the North, which is to be observed in the sister countries, has entirely passed Norway by; we must not forget the imposing figure of Arne Garborg; and there are singers, like Herman Wildenvey, who have given voice to new and fascinating notes in lyric poetry. But the towering figure of Wergeland seems almost still too near the present to give young poets sufficient confidence to launch out on new courses. The particular glory of present-day Norwegian literature is the novel. Again, we are not ignorant of that novel in England. But the authors whom it has been found worth while to translate are not the most specifically Norwegian authors, but those, like Johan Bojer, who have adopted something of the Anglo-Saxon idiom to which we are accustomed. But one does not in Norway itself reckon such writers among the more vital national forces. An exception might be claimed for Knut Hamsun, whose work is widely familiar to us; but I am doubtful if the intimately national in Hamsun's work appeals to us. Possibly, indeed, Norway estimates his somewhat redundant and undisciplined talent too highly; it is a question whether he has had enough to say to justify the many volumes he has filled. I would rather lay weight on the work of that extraordinarily interesting writer, Hans E. Kinck, whose death not very long ago

Norway had to deplore. Kinck has not made it easy for us to approach him; he is not concerned with conciliating our Anglo-Saxon taste in fiction; but he is perhaps on that account all the more worthy of our attention. When Olav Duun was awarded the Nobel Prize a year ago, it was generally attributed by our journalists to a concession on the part of the Swedish Academy to northern particularism; but if there may have been a difference of opinion as to who in Norway should have been selected for the honour, no one who has frankly faced the decline of the novel in the greater literatures will question the wisdom of the Academy in thus honouring Norway. The number of fresh original writers who in that land live out obscure lives behind their dialect palisade is astonishing, and no one who ventures to make raids into their territory will come back empty-handed. Let me only mention, without discriminating between " riksmaal " and " landsmaal," the names of Jens Tvedt, Tryggve Andersen, Kristoffer Uppdal, Johan Falkberget, that fine woman-writer, Ragnhild Jölsen, cut off in her prime before she had found harmony with herself, and Hans Aanrud, whose exquisite little book, *Sidsel Sidsærk* is a pure delight. One figure, however, stands out from this vigorous literature of the Norwegian soil, who, it seems to me, claims imperatively the attention of Europe— Sigrid Undset. Her novel, *Kristin Lavransdatter,* which is now available in English translation, is—I say it without hesitation—the finest historical novel our twentieth century has yet produced; indeed, it dwarfs most of the fiction of any kind that Europe has produced in the last twenty years. I will not dwell on its power as a vivid picture of a remote historical past, for that, it seems to

me, is beside the mark; the Waverley Novels do not live
in our hearts for their historical truth. I dare say, too,
the consistent realist will find much to question in Fru
Undset's realism; it may well be objected that those men
and women whom she has set in a dim Norwegian past
are really modern souls, with a delicacy of emotional life
and a sensitiveness to the beauty of the world which are
not of the fourteenth century. But that surely is a virtue,
not a defect. The greatness of this book—and it is the
only criterion that matters—is that it is imaginative
creation of a high order, and that its men and women
live. It unrolls—unrolls ruthlessly—the history of a
woman's soul, as it has been laid bare in no other
book of our time. Of Fru Undset's other work I have not
room to speak: her delicate cameos of the modern life of
the Norwegian capital, and her second historical novel,
Olav Audunssön i Hestviken, which may be inferior to its
predecessor in structural unity, but hardly in the beauty
of its individual parts. It is enough to say that with Sigrid
Undset Norway has once more produced a writer of
European significance.

In concluding this necessarily brief survey of the state
of letters in the North, I must try to draw my threads
together, and say what it seems to me these literatures
mean or may mean to us outsiders. I was asked to discuss
particularly the influence of the War on them. I have not
done so, mainly because my reading has not been extensive or intimate enough to allow me to envisage them from
this point of view. I might, it is true, have dwelt on
the reflection of the War in individual works; but
such an enumeration of immaterial facts is hardly, I
think, what the editors of this volume had in view. I

ought to have dwelt on the significance of the War in intensifying, for instance, the idea of nationality in Norway, who owes her existence as an independent national entity to the great European War of a hundred years ago; and it would have been particularly valuable had I been able to distil from these Northern literatures the effect of the internecine degradation of Europe on their general outlook on life; shown how far the vein of pessimism in recent Swedish and Danish books is attributable to this cause. It is not, perhaps, altogether fancy that has led a recent critic to see a reflection of the European tragedy in the terrible Ragnarók of the Black Death with which *Kristin Lavransdatter* closes. But I have not felt equal to this task. I would only say that from the kind of precipitate which the War has left in the literatures of the peoples more particularly involved in it, those of the North have been singularly free. They show less of that degeneration into superficiality and anæmic brilliance, that dallying with words and æsthetic vagaries, which have been the unexpected and unfortunate heritage of the War to the greater literatures of Europe. Literature in Scandinavia has remained a sound and living thing, a national thing. It is often deplored that the reading public in the North is so amply supplied with translations of English, French, and German books that their own writers are severely handicapped. But this does not seem to be the case. Scandinavian writers are able to produce books of conscientious integrity and sincerity of artistic purpose, such as with ourselves or in France would mostly spell bankruptcy to the publisher. Perhaps the wholesale importation of foreign popular literature is really a kind of blessing in disguise, which makes it unnecessary for the native writer to write detective stories, "shilling shockers," and the like; while the Scandinavian "highbrow"—if he exists, which I am optimistic enough to doubt—can satisfy his fastidious appetite on the imported literature that caters for this class. But it certainly is true: the Scandinavian writers of to-day who inspire our respect neither stoop to flatter the multitude by giving them sentimental or sensational books, nor the "highbrow" who demands the attenuated fare he calls "clever." They write out of their own hearts; they seek to reflect faithfully, and to recreate plastically, the people and the land they know; to be national writers in the old noble sense. Their best literature is soil of the soil, and that, it seems to me, is the greatest virtue which any national literature can possess. And if I were asked what might be the mission of these literatures in the community of peoples, I should say that it is to point out the way to health, to show how the ravages that have come in the train of the Great War may be repaired. These Northern writers on whom I have laid emphasis show us the way back to sincerity, reality, truth; they hold the mirror up not to their own ego, but to the national life of their people. Thus they may help us to free literature from the clogging vice which marks all impoverished epochs, the vice of being a mere literary affair of clever literary folk.

J. G. ROBERTSON.

CZECHOSLOVAKIA

I

IN a recent message to the newly established Institute of Czechoslovak Studies at Columbia University, Karel Čapek suggested that the most remarkable achievement of the Czechs is their mere existence. And he went on to point out that a hundred years ago the Czechs had practically no literature. This is a circumstance which must, of course, affect the method of treatment when modern Czech literature is being discussed. I mention this in extenuation of any departure which I may make from the general scheme of this volume. The need for such a divergency is further prompted by the fact that Czech literature is comparatively unknown in this country. The approach to it cannot, therefore, be quite the same as to a literature which is already familiar here, and it may be necessary for me to be more didactic in tone than would otherwise be the case. There is one other point which I should here emphasise—namely, that I shall devote more space to poetry than to prose. This is not because there is a lack of good Czech prose. But the Czech temperament is fundamentally a lyrical one, and its most noteworthy expression hitherto has been through the medium of lyric poetry. And if we trace the development of Czech literature during the nineteenth century from the revival onwards, we shall find that its poetry made more rapid progress than its prose.

With regard to the revival itself, I will here only say that historically it has been attributed to the influence of the ideas of the French encyclopædists. P. J. Šafařík, who was one of its chief figures, and whose evidence is therefore of particular value, described it in 1825 as being due primarily to what he describes as the electrical effects of two works, one by Franz Count Kinský (*On the Necessity and Advantages of a Knowledge of the Bohemian Language*), which appeared in 1774, and the other by Balbin (*In Defence of the Bohemian Language*), published a year later. At a very early stage of the Czech revival we find such a work as Kollár's *Daughter of Sláva,* which, though very unequal in quality, shows a certain greatness of conception, and has by no means lost its interest to-day. It comprises a series of several hundred sonnets, which form a curious medley of history, philology, and fantasy, expressing Kollár's romantic conceptions of an ideal Slavonic brotherhood. Many of the sonnets have a genuine lyrical charm, and even to-day the stately rhetoric of the " Prologue " (1824) has lost little of its old appeal. It opens as follows:

" Here lies the country, alas, before my tear-laden glances,
 Once 'twas the cradle, but now—now 'tis the tomb of my race;
Check thou thy steps, for the places are sacred, wherever thou turnest.
Son of the Tatra, arise, cast to the heavens thy gaze,
 Or to the mighty old oak, that stands there yonder, incline thee,
 Holding its own against treacherous time, till to-day.
Ah, but more evil than time is the man, who a sceptre of iron,
 Slavia, on thy neck, here in these lands has imposed;
Worse than savage encounters and fiercer than fire and than thunder—

CZECHOSLOVAKIA

He who in frenzy blind covers his kindred with shame.
O ye years of the past that as night are lying around me,
O my country, thou art image of glory and shame;
From the treacherous Elbe o'er the plain to the Vistula faithless,
From the Danube until Baltic's insatiate foam,
Where the mellifluous tongue of the sturdy Slavs once resounded,
Now it, alas! is still, silenced by onslaughts of hate."

The other literary results of this highly interesting movement consisted mostly of linguistic and antiquarian works, or translations, with which such honoured names as Josef Jungmann and Josef Dobrovský are associated. Josef Dobrovský (1753-1829), an ex-Jesuit, accomplished an enormous amount of work in purely linguistic matters, and the scope of his studies extended over the whole domain of Slavonic philology. His endeavours were supplemented by Josef Jungmann (1773-1847), who not only compiled a detailed Czech dictionary, but dealt also with prosody and literary history, besides translating Chateaubriand's *Atala* and Milton's *Paradise Lost*. Reference has already been made to P. J. Šafařík (1795-1861), whose most important contribution to the progress of the movement was a treatise on Slavonic antiquities. Here, too, the name of Fr. Palacký (1798-1876), the author of the famous *History of the Czech Nation,* must be mentioned.

The labours of these pioneer scholars were modest enough in their initial stages, but it was not long before their effects began to spread in a manner which even they themselves had hardly expected. By the middle of the nineteenth century Czech literature had penetrated far beyond the restricted circle of poets and scholars, by whom it had at first been cultivated. There was already a general reading public, and various European influences were leaving their traces in the works of Czech authors.

Thus, the Byronic movement, which had such stimulating effects upon the Russian and Polish writers of that period, resulted in one noteworthy poem. This was *Máj*, by K. H. Mácha, which appeared in an unfinished state in 1836, and was not duly appreciated until after Mácha's death in the same year. The romantic interest in folk-songs, which produced Percy's *Reliques* in this country, had analogous effects in Czech literature. As early as 1825, F. L. Čelakovský, who translated Scott's *Lady of the Lake* into Czech, had begun to collect Slavonic folk-songs, and in 1829 appeared his *Echoes of Russian Songs,* which was followed ten years later by an analogous collection of Czech songs. Then, in 1853, K. J. Erben issued his famous *Garland,* which contained a number of folk-legends retold in ballad form. Erben also collected the prose folk-tales of all the Slavonic nations. This tendency of the Czechs to occupy themselves with the other Slavonic literatures has persisted to the present day. Another typically Czech tendency in literature, to which I shall have occasion to refer later, is satire, social and political, and that also found a talented exponent at this early period in the person of Karel Havlíček, who translated Gogol and Voltaire, wrote an anti-romantic account of his travels in Russia, and composed a number of witty and disrespectful epigrams about priests and the Austrian Government. He was the first Czech journalist of any distinction, editing in particular such historically important papers as *The National News* and *The Slav.* This enabled him to contribute to the political advancement of the Czechs, especially as he himself took an active part in political life as a parliamentary deputy. It would, perhaps, have been better for him if he had confined himself to literature pure and simple, for as a result of his outspoken views he came into conflict with the Austrian Government. In 1851 he was forcibly removed from his home and interned at Brixen in Tirol, where he remained for three years. He did not long survive his release, and died in 1856, a victim of the absolutism which arose after the revolution of 1848 and for some time hampered the progress of Czech literature.

II

It was not until about 1860 that the Austrian absolutism, which had lasted for a decade under the régime of the minister Bach, was relaxed in favour of more tolerable conditions. The Czech generation of authors which now arose was anti-romantic in tendency, although the members of it issued their first joint collection under the title of *Máj*, as an indication of their homage to Mácha. Of these authors, the most important was Jan Neruda (1834-1891), who excelled both in prose and poetry. His most famous prose-works are the *Old Town Stories,* in which he depicted with pathos and humour the lower middle-class life in Prague, as he had known it in his childhood and youth. He also wrote innumerable newspaper feuilletons and travel sketches, which are still greatly admired. This side of his work rather suggests the manner of Dickens. His poetry has been compared with that of Heine, and there is a slight resemblance. But here I find it necessary, in reference to Czech writers, to distinguish between what may be called their internal and their external significance respectively. Neruda occupies an important position in the history of Czech literature, and his internal significance is justifiably great. I doubt, however, whether his external significance, by which I mean his stature when compared to the great European writers, is at all proportionate to it. His poems, such as those in *Songs of the Cosmos, Simple Themes,* and *Ballads and Romances,* are spontaneous and sincere, but I hesitate to describe them as great poetry, in any acceptable meaning of that term.

The Czech literature of this period, both in prose and verse, is rich in popular elements. This popular tradition has been followed ever since by those writers who, in general, are opposed to international influences. Their poetry tends either towards idyllic themes, derived from peasant life and treated in the manner of the folk-song, or the national subject-matter is dealt with in its social aspect. For my present purpose it will suffice if I select only Svatopluk Čech (1846-1908) as a typical representative of this movement. Like Neruda, he is famous both as a prose-writer and a poet, and, as far as Western Europe is concerned, his prose tales and sketches, which are often extremely effective, would probably be more interesting than his poetry. Here, again, the principle of internal significance operates, and Čech's *Songs of a Slave,* containing rhetorical protests against national grievances, which are here identified with social rather than political injustice, although one of the most famous and popular volumes of Czech poetry, could hardly be expected to meet with as high an appreciation from the foreign reader.

CZECHOSLOVAKIA

III

As I have juſt mentioned, one of the outſtanding features of Czech literature is the cleavage between the national or Slavonic movement and the international tendencies. The conflict, which in a somewhat modified form ſtill exiſts, is really the result of two political mentalities, one conservative and the other progressive, and especially from 1880 onwards it was the cause of much acrimonious discussion between the opposing camps. The adherents of the international or cosmopolitan tendency were associated with a literary periodical called *Lumír*. What they really aimed at was not a submission to foreign influences, as their opponents alleged, but, on the contrary, an emancipation from the dependence upon German sources of intellectual progress. Accordingly, they planned, among other things, to supply the Czech nation with translations from the world's great writers in their own language. A large part of this project was carried out by the induſtry of one man, Jaroslav Vrchlický (1853-1912), who, all things considered, muſt be accounted the greateſt name in the whole of Czech literature. His firſt volume of poems, *From the Depths,* appeared in 1875, and from then onwards Vrchlický displayed a remarkable fertility in the production of lyric and epic poetry. There have been writers who were extremely prolific in the domain of drama or prose fiction, but Vrchlický's seventy volumes of poetical output are probably unique in the hiſtory of literature. I mention this only in passing, and this quantitative factor has, of course, little bearing upon his poetical merits. With such a mass of work there is bound to be inequality and a certain quota of definitely inferior material. Nevertheless, if we make all allowances for this, Vrchlický's poetical achievement is astonishing. It is, therefore, unjust to dispose of him merely as a wholesale versifier. He was much more than that. His poems, at their best, reveal him as a master of style and form. He enriched the Czech language and introduced every variety of metrical form into Czech literature. But, in addition to his original poems, Vrchlický produced a regular library of poetical translations, which include the whole of Dante, Ariosto, Tasso, together with much from Shelley, Victor Hugo (perhaps his favourite), Camoens, Goethe (especially *Faust*), Whitman, Calderon, Mickiewicz, and numerous other English, French, Italian, German, Spanish, Portuguese, Scandinavian, and Slavonic authors. His translations enlarged the scope of Czech culture, and contributed greatly towards emancipating it from its dependence upon German sources. The importance of this achievement was not realised by a number of Czech critics, who, in the name of nationalism, reproached Vrchlický for his cosmopolitan tendencies, and failed to do justice to his artistic powers.

There are two aspects of his activity which must be taken into account: the stimulating effect which he produced upon the progress of Czech literature, and the intrinsic merits of his best work. Critics have praised one or the other of these two functions, but rarely both. He died, in 1912, a tired and broken man, leaving clear traces of his creative influence even upon those poets who had no great sympathy for the spirit of his creative methods. His last volume, *The Sword of Damocles,* contains some of his best poems, which, as the title suggests, were written

with a foreboding of the calamity which befell him. Here
is an example of Vrchlický's early lyrical manner:

THE GRAVE-YARD IN THE SONG

" Nightingale, on whom in nights of splendour Hafiz was intent,
  Where sing'st thou now?
Rose, o'er whom full often Dante, plunged in meditation, bent,
  Where bloom'st thou now?
Star of sweetness, unto whose dream-laden brightness from his
  cell,
Tasso's woeful plaint was lifted and his thronging sighs were
  sent,
  Where gleam'st thou now?
Heart, that out of flames wast woven, out of roses and of wine,
Heart of Sappho, whence by Eros lyric melodies were blent,
  Where beat'st thou now?
Happy billow, that didst ripple tenderly round Hero's foot,
When Leander, faint from swimming, by the stormy waves
  was rent,
  Where flow'st thou now?
Cast into the song your gaze, for there a mighty grave-yard lies,
'Neath whose surface all the bodies of the gods by man are
  pent,
  There weeps he now!"

Music in the Soul (1886).

And this illustrates a somewhat different phase of his
work:

MARCO POLO

" I, Marco Polo, Christian and Venetian,
  Acknowledge God the Trinity and cherish
  Hope of salvation in eternity
  For my sin-laden soul : in this my faith,
  In this my trust is set. What of my love,
  Ye ask? And I give answer tranquilly :
  My love is long and distant journeys, ever
  New-found horizons, new-found peoples, fresh
  Exploits on ocean and dry land, and ever
  Fresh enterprises. (This, my forebears' blood).
  Much have I seen, to much have given ear;
  I reached the land, whereof ye scarce have inkling,

205

Where amber grows like golden foliage,
Where salamanders (that ye dub asbestos)
Blossom and blaze like lilies petrified,
Where glowing naphtha gushes from the earth,
Where there is equal wealth of rubies, as
Of holly here in winter; where across
Their back and on their shoulders they tattoo
The image of an eagle; where the women
Alone rule, and the men are given up
From birth to heavy service till they die.
I gazed upon the realm whose ruler is
Khan of Cathay; and I have sat at meat
With those who feed on men: I was a wave
Amid the surf: the mighty emerald
(Pre-destined for the Vizier of Bagdad)
Beneath my tongue I carried through the desert.
For thirty days and nights I came not down
Out of my saddle. I have seen great deserts
Like ruffled raiment billowing afar;
The ocean sleeping underneath the moon
Like a stiff winding-sheet; strange stars ablaze
Beneath strange zones. I visited the realms
Of Prester John, where goodness, virtue, and
Righteousness ruled, as in a legend,—yea,
Now meseems almost that I even reached
The wondrous nook of earth, where Alexander
Once lighted on the wilderness of Ind,
And came no farther on his way, because
Of mighty downpours that abated not.
(Perchance upon the faery realm he there
Set foot, or e'en upon the town celestial,
And shrank away in dread, when at the gate
An angel put a skull into his hand,
Saying: 'A few more years, and this shall be
Thy portion,—this, and not a tittle more!')
And I beheld that land of mystery
Where lay the paradise of earth, where flowed
The spring of youth, concealed within the grass
Amid a thousand others, whence I drank
From many, and, 'tis very like, from youth:
And therefore all endured I with acclaim,
And therefore all, as in a mirror, I
Perceive within my soul, and now portray it.
The world is changed of aspect: I shall die

CZECHOSLOVAKIA

Like others, but my heritage remains.
The lust for seeing all and learning all,
To ransack all for the delight of man;
Legion shall be my sons : they shall proceed
Farther than I, but scarcely shall see more,
For earth sheds wonders as a snake its skin.
Old age I know, with many dreams and secrets,
And that suffices me. And they who come
After me, let them take, as it may chance,
Of what remains to them, as best they can,
As I did. I sit foremost at the feast
Of distant journeys, and it likes me well,
All prospers me, and I fare well with all.
To make all life a vigil over books,
To rack one's brain 'mid piles of yellow parchments,
Seeking the truth of writing and of thought,
Is much, in sooth; to live an age in camps
'Mid rolls of drums and trumpets in assaults,
O'er ramparts in a rain of missiles, in
Ruins of towns, amid laments of women,
Weeping of children, groaning of the fallen,
Is much, in sooth; to be a holy bishop,
Legions of spirits to escort to heaven
(The which he knoweth not) by solace of
The faith alone, and by the word of God,
In marble and in gold to hearken to
The cadence and the dreamy grief of psalms,
Is much, in sooth; but to behold and know
With one's own eyes the distant, ample lands,
And oceans, plains and star-tracks of the skies,
And divers folk, their habit, usage, gods,
This, too, availeth somewhat, and hath charm
By special token of its newness, that
Doth ever change. And I have lived it through,
I, Marco Polo, Christian and Venetian."

New Fragments of an Epic (1894).

Vrchlický was, of course, the chief personality connected with the periodical *Lumír,* to which I have already referred as being the official organ of the cosmopolitan tendencies in Czech literature. Two other members of

207

this circle should here be mentioned. One is Julius Zeyer (1841-1901), who was aloof, isolated, and exclusive. His poetry, chiefly epic in character, was sumptuously decorative in style, and its exotic subject-matter was derived from Scandinavian, Celtic, Spanish, and Oriental legends, from the Charlemagne cycle, and from the early history of his native country. Zeyer travelled widely, and the manifold impressions which he thus obtained were not without influence upon his poetry. At home he felt himself neglected or slighted, and, indeed, it was not till after his death that his literary work was adequately appreciated. In *Jan Maria Plojhar,* a semi-autobiographical novel, Zeyer has left a striking account of the vicissitudes which moulded his strange personality. Then there was J. V. Sládek (1845-1912), whose original poetry is much more popular in tone than that of Vrchlický or Zeyer. Sládek lived for many years in America, and, on his return to Prague, he devoted himself largely to a new Czech translation of Shakespeare. Before he died he had completed thirty-two plays, and his work has since been completed by Antonín Klášterský (b. 1866), also a follower of Vrchlický.

IV

The conflict between the cosmopolitan and nationalistic tendencies in Czech poetry continued from 1880 for several years, and it was marked by numerous interesting exchanges of opinion, into which I cannot here enter. The dispute came to a head in 1894, when J. S. Machar, a writer of whom more will be said presently, wrote an article attacking one of the poets of the previous generation named Hálek. Vrchlický himself, who had hitherto been sympathetic towards Machar, now turned away from him, not because he disagreed with his views, but because he thought the manner in which they were expressed was lacking in respect for Hálek. The result of this was that several of the young poets formed themselves into a new group, which they called the modernists, and in 1895 they issued their manifesto, which, in effect, was a plea for the rights of individual expression in art. Of the numerous writers who signed this manifesto, three —J. S. Machar, Antonín Sova, and Otakar Březina— must now be considered.

First, let us take Machar, whose article on Hálek had started this literary revolution, as it has been called. At this time he was thirty years old, having been born in 1864. His early poems, such as the volume entitled *Confiteor,* had been elegiac and sentimental lyrics, influenced by Heine, de Musset, Byron, and Lermontov. His real kinship, however, is with Havlíček and Neruda, and later he turned to political and religious satire. Then, gradually becoming more and more objective in manner, he began a series of historical poems, mostly in blank verse, under the general title of *Consciousness of the Ages,* which owe something of their general plan to Vrchlický's *Fragments of the Epopée,* and, hence, also to Hugo's *Légende des Siècles.* The period covered by these poems extends from the earliest times to the present day, the last volumes, the eighth and ninth, having been published only a few months ago. In a work of these dimensions there is bound to be inequality, and some of its contents, especially in the later volumes, are marred by hasty composition with its attendant faults. But there is much to admire in this cycle of poems, which reveals

Machar's keen insight into character, and his ability to
seize upon the dramatic possibilities of a situation. His
attitude is undisguisedly anti-clerical, and altogether his
respect for tradition is of the slightest. In this respect his
" Tractate on Patriotism " is significant :

" That nook of earth wherein I grew and lived
   Through childhood, boyhood, and my years of youth
   With all sweet folly of first love, with all
   First pangs, deceit and misery of it;
   That one white township in the vale of Elbe
   With dusky forests on the far horizon,
   With its old castle, with its wild-grown park,
   Its placid market-square, its church, that, shaped
   Outlandishly, peers forth with huddled tower
   Across the countryside; billowy fields;
   Avenued paths; the agony of God
   Where cross-roads meet; the meadowlands that flank
   Calm streams; our cherished hamlets round about;—
   That nook of earth is all for which I crave
   In the shrill streets of this afflicting city.
   Yet rather is it craving for the years
   Of youth I lived there. . . . Since the soul portrays
   Fondly unto itself those places, craves
   Piningly for them, while—fond thing—it harbours
   A trembling hope that by returning thither
   It may turn back its years of youth . . . I know
   That I would likewise love another place
   If I had passed elsewhere my years of youth. . . .

   This is my native land. Naught else. I lack
   Aptness to worship that terrestrial
   Concept, which diplomats have glibly framed
   In their bureaus; which pedagogues to us
   Imparted out of atlases; the which
   Must needs, as each and all terrestrial
   Concepts, to-morrow, maybe, shrivel or expand,
   According as upon some battlefield,
   In dreadful strife which is not our affair,
   More striplings fall on that side or on this.

   I have not found my pride in history,
   That temple of idolaters, wherein

CZECHOSLOVAKIA

Dreamers devoutly cast themselves to earth,
And in a frenzy beat their breasts because
They too are Czechs: nay, even as elsewhere,
Our annals are a file of dreadful deeds
(By us accomplished and by us endured)
Of recreant men, of surging passion-throes,
Betrayals, dominations and enslavements;
And these, befalling openly, became
Clear-ringing currency of daily catchwords
For tricksters of to-day, here as elsewhere.
Nor do I vaunt me of our own days. We
Than others are no whit the better. . . .
We are but palterers and caitiffs; where
Power is, there do we bend our necks to it
In slavish wise; wherefore are we abased
By evil lords. Time-serving braggarts we,
Testy and witless, laughing-stocks amid
Our pride, and palsied in vain peevishness.
Felons we have, dotards and pillagers
And hucksters dealing in pure love of country,
And a mere handful of the men who are
Ever untainted and downright,—but these
All nations have elsewhere,—ye gods, is this
To be, perchance, our fountain-head of pride?

I am no patriot, nor do I love
My country, for I have none, know none, nor
See cause for loving one. . . .
I am a Czech, even as I might be
A German, Turk, Gypsy, or negro, if
I had been born elsewhere. My Czechdom is
The portion of my life which I do feel
Not as delight and bliss, but as a solemn
And inborn fealty. My native land
Is within me alone; and this will I
Trim round at no man's beck, nor give it tinge
To match with fashion's daily whim; nor shall
They rob me of it; when above my tomb
The grass has grown, it shall go living on
In other souls—and if, some day to be,
In them it wither, then and only then
Shall it be lifeless, as old Kollár sang.

And if I toil for it, then that is toil
For Czechdom as I feel it in myself.

And if I ever pride me on it, then
I pride me only on my life. . . ."

Golgotha (1902).

The same tendencies are displayed in his prose works, especially in the highly unconventional *Rome, The Confession of a Literary Man,* and *The Jail,* the latter being a graphic account of the events connected with Machar's imprisonment by the Austrian Government during the War. Machar's lack of respect for authority brought him into frequent conflict with the Austrian censor, and among the Czechs themselves he made many enemies by his unorthodox interpretation of patriotism. The following is an extract from *The Consciousness of the Ages,* which occurs in the fifth volume of the series, entitled *The Apostles,* published in 1911:

CROMWELL AT THE CORPSE OF CHARLES I.

" The strength and soundness of this body promised
Long course of life. . . . Even as on King Saul,
The Lord bestowed all gifts on him, and him,
Even as Saul, He sentenced with His sentence. . . .
We were the voice of Him, the sword of Him.
He doth but lend authority to kings,
But gives the people power to judge a king;
For kingly power thrives only from the people.
And since this Stuart was a murderer,
A traitor, tyrant, foe unto his people,
The spirit of the Lord departed from him,
And him His wrath delivered to our judgment.
Thus, after the exemplar of old times,
And as exemplar to all coming ages
Hath been this body's fate. . . . The people are
E'en as the apple of God's eye, and most
When the Lord yields a king unto their judgment.
Falsehood, deceit, and feigning were his weapons
And they are broken as a reed doth break;
And all his men-at-arms and servitors

Bowed them like sheaves before our smiting swords. . . .
Now staunchly onward, ever in God's counsel,
And from the earth blot we out all amongst us
Who in base pride run counter to the people—
And God thereof shall have His glory, and
A godly benison this land of ours.
Cherish we glowing trust upon the Lord,
And keep the powder in our muskets dry!"

The Apostles (1911).

The personality of Sova, who was also born in 1864, is an almost complete contrast to that of Machar. He is a sensitive dreamer, a lyric poet, the subtlety of whose diction is admirably adapted to the impressionism and allegory which he handles with such consummate art. Sova has passed through a complex development, and much of his poetry bears witness to the intense emotional stress which produced it. Yet, in spite of his leanings towards subjective and introspective verse, he possesses the typical Czech social and racial consciousness, by which some of his most effective poems were prompted. He has also written novels and short stories, in which his bent for psychological analysis is very pronounced. Sova's earliest volumes, which appeared at the beginning of the nineties, consist of descriptive verse, the subject-matter of which was derived from the streets of Prague and from Sova's home in Southern Bohemia. But this preliminary phase has little in common with the main body of Sova's work, which is copious and varied. His artistic development has been complex, but it may be regarded as comprising three aspects—the poet in relation to himself, his fellow-countrymen, and mankind respectively. Sova's introspective poems include some of the finest lyrical poems in the Czech language. The sufferings of a sensitive and passionate soul are here recorded in the most subtle and melodious of cadences. The disillusionments caused by the poet's contact with the realities of life drove him to seek escape in a dream-world of his own. This theme was treated in a series of beautiful visionary poems, in which Sova's gift of symbolic utterance is strikingly exhibited. In these poems, too, he elaborated a type of free verse which harmonises completely with the subject-matter of the poems themselves. In course of time Sova's inner discontents yielded to a mood of reconciliation, which is expressed at its maturest in the volume *Harvests,* published in 1913. It was thought at first that this volume, suffused by an autumnal warmth and calm, comprised the zenith of Sova's poetical achievement, but the succeeding decade stimulated him to an unusual fecundity. The volumes which followed contain poems written with the crystalline purity and simplicity of folk-songs, ballads, and, above all, verses which exhibit Sova as one of the most enlightened spokesmen of Czech aspirations. In his earlier books he had distinguished himself by his uncompromising criticism of Czech conditions, but where national injustice coincided with social wrong he could fierily vindicate the cause of his race. Sova, though deeply rooted in his native soil, and thoroughly modern in outlook, has also faced those problems of human destiny which are not circumscribed by frontiers nor restricted to any one epoch.

The two following poems form typical examples of Sova's lyrical manner. The first, " Yellow Flowers," is from a collection published in 1897:

> " Fields of death grow sere in gloom,
> Throbs the land with lute of doom.

CZECHOSLOVAKIA

Someone comes, a flower he strips,
Pressing it to feverish lips.

The agèd folk are on the brink,
And in sips their wine they drink.
On their locks the moonlight rests,
On withered skin and drooping breasts.

They will tarry yet a span,
Something yet their gaze will scan,—
Still to the fields they will not go,
Yellow blossoms rustle low.

They will not die. They answer ' No.' "

And the other was published in 1900. The title of the
original is " A Mood " :

" Never so eerily yet
Soughed my native wood;
I should weep, I should weep
If I but could.

There is mockery in the twilight
Beneath each heavy bough.
The evening seems to drag its broken wings
Over the earth now.

And what is that laughter in the leafage,
And what is that dry chuckling sound?
With seven-league strides, O my soul,
Whither are you bound?"

Otakar Březina, who also signed the manifesto of the
modernists, was born in 1868. He can safely be described
as one of the greatest artistic intellects in modern Europe,
and is one of those rare personalities in which thinker
and artist are about evenly balanced. He has written
comparatively little, but his five small volumes of poems
form a quintessential record of a unique spiritual development, from the melancholy broodings of *The Secret
Distances* (1895) to the dithyrambic optimism of *The*

Hands (1901). Březina's poetry, perplexingly rich in imagery, profound and often transcendental in subject-matter, probes into the mystery of life, not merely in its relation to earth, but to the whole universe. Here, again, the Czech instinct for freedom and tolerance, which in Machar is expressed in clear-cut irony, in Sova by passionate invective, is found in Březina's poems, especially in his last volume, in the form of humanitarian mysticism, which is inspired by a fervid belief in the ultimate perfectibility of mankind and the advent of world-wide brotherhood. I here quote two poems, the first of which illustrates Březina's earlier attitude towards the problem of evil:

LEGEND OF SECRET GUILT

" Flash of my coming hours illumined this moment in dreams
And bloomed in my festive halls with every lustre ablaze,
My coming springtides and hidden graces rippled in tuneful streams,
I was dazed by lips, with breath that beguiles, with laughter that gleams,
And eyes, where awaited me muteness of rapture, glowed there with yearning gaze.
But vainly I strode where quivered, in rhythms that dumbfound,
Life's chant. The shadow of One before me and after me wended,
Flitting from hall unto hall, bright blaze at its coming was drowned.
Mirrors grew dim, yearning trembled, and music's conquering sound,
As if thrust into lowliest octaves of silent anguish, was ended.
O my soul, whence came it? And how many centuries has it passed
Haply through souls of my forefathers, ere unto me it came?
On how many marriage-tables as a requiem-cloth was it cast?
On how many rose-hued smiles came its chill and earthen blast?
And in how many lamps did it blanch amid salt and essence of flame?"

Dawning of the West (1896).

216

CZECHOSLOVAKIA

The second, entitled "Responses," shows how Březina has developed in his later years towards an optimistic affirmation of life:

" We are curse-laden: even amid our yearnings' loftiest flight
  We by burden of earth are vanquished, plunged into our blood's
      dim night—
  ' Ye are potent and deathless; and in your souls where secrets
      abound,
  Suns and spring-tides and vintages numberless are found.'
  In silence of cosmos, in midst of stars that are flecked with blood
      as they wane,
  We are cut off in solitude, as by watch-fires of foes in a chain.
  ' Armour of heavily armed is your burden; unto contest ye
  Are summoned, that ye therein may set all earth-born creatures
      free.'
  Upon the riven breast of the vanquished we strive to kneel,
  And even when we yearn to love, no love we feel, no love we
      feel.
  ' Hardened are ye like fruit, unripened; but in the blaze
  Of a secret summer ye ripen, your brethren's embraces to
      praise.'
  Gladness is sunshine beheld in a dream: on awakening it is
      dulled;
  Sorrow has thousands of eyes, and never in slumber is utterly
      lulled.
  ' With myriads in secret brotherhood ye are tied
  And only in gladness of myriads will gladness of yours abide.'
  To floating islands upon a furrow of fragrance we float. . . .
  We float and the islands float onward, and keep us ever
      remote. . . .
  ' Blindfold are ye with deceit that your kingly glances wield:
  Islands of radiance that bloom in your souls, before you they
      have revealed.' "

                                                    The Hands (1901).

Březina's prose essays are as characteristic in style as his poems, whose ideas they elaborate and amplify. They were published in 1903 under the title of *Music of the Springs,* and the following extracts give an idea of the style and subject-matter:

CONTEMPORARY EUROPEAN LITERATURE

" The soul never builds only for itself. In the spots where it constructs, space is filled with myriads of hands, uplifted from all ages, which meet in the pressure of an eternal brotherly sign, and pass on their labour one to the other. It is a fervid and overwhelming activity, from which memory returns mute and terrified, set grievously aquiver by beating of hammers, dazzled by white, furnace-like abysses, by clatter of implements in secret workshops, by behests soaring amid the glow, feverish with breath of myriads, by processions of those arriving and departing, and by the songs of them who are already building on high. In those regions there is nothing that accords with the attenuated earthly standards of selfishness and the circumspection, which locks up its hives, that they may yield no sweetness for the lips of brethren."

" Like all sublime endeavour of man, art also is accompanied by jealousy of hidden powers, hostile to the spirit. Even star-laden glances of beauty hinder man by their radiance, and can hypnotise the weak into slumber, amid which his labour sinks from his hands. He who creates has need of a struggle, a movement of the spirit, the surging of a spring that thrusts itself upward from the depths. It is needful that by toil he should develop girth and a strongly arched breast, which bestows depth and calm upon the rhythm of his breathing for his ascent and amid perils. So the hands of geniuses, goldenly tanned by eternal sun, had to be hardened by toil, in order to possess the power of always mowing a complete circle of the horizon with one sweep of the scythe, and to govern time like a waggon, seized by the rim of the wheel, and held back until their brethren had finished loading the sheaves."

" For even the labour of earth, the coarsest and the humblest, in which man and beast advance side by side amid the loop of a single sweltering breath, possesses its lineament of pathos, its sheen of grievous glory, ecstasy of self-oblivion, its entrancement at the gust which mingles the spiritual breath of myriads; its brow throbs with a gigantic pulse like the resonance of anvils upon which worlds are being shattered and moulded, and it has its own dream of omnipotence. Even from the uncouthest of features, jaded with toil, glitters, as from twisted prison-bars, the radiance of the soul, which was present at the construction of planets, and now suffers in captivity."

CZECHOSLOVAKIA

" Lo, the hand whose omnipotence you marvel at, before whose labour you wax in superhuman exaltation, in brother-hood of higher beings, this hand has passed in humility through a myriad centuries of transformation; through the ages it has learnt to struggle with soil, stone, timber, and metals, and to weld them imperiously in their essence, before their amazing structure was developed and their sinews were fashioned. Scourged by fire, it was rendered sensitive as the hands of the sightless, and, become spiritual, it is now extended over the earth, and like the upraised signs of a script for the sightless it reads its annals from nodes of rocks and from motion of glaciers, and uplifts itself to the script of golden points on the vaultage of the heavens. The gesture of reapers and sowers has given it that litheness, which in art seizes on the movement of trees in the wind, the frosty quivering of waters, the flight of birds, of radiances, of thoughts, and of stars. The concentrated power of multitudes which is quickened amid it gives it a magical sway over multitudes; and with kindly movement it even appeases the tempest of rhythms and the perilous surging of spirits."

Perilous Harvests.

" The mighty would tremble if they beheld the chart of our planet as it reveals itself to ecstatic glances of love. It would be a vain task to seek thereon the frontiers of king-doms and circuits of languages; from the heights, from which can be seen the architecture of continents and the coherence of islands in green mirrors of oceans, the white stones, set down as boundary marks of fields and vineyards, are no longer visible. The whole expanse of the earth, with its tropical bloom of rapture and perception, would be revealed to them as one of the smallest of spiritual cities, from which paths lead to all visible and invisible realms of the universe, to each dizzy spiritual metropolis, whose image cannot be dreamt by dream of man. The highest glaciers of human thought, still glowing between heaven and earth, when night has already blotted out the region whence they simmered over, tower up in their golden chillness to the stars of another firmament, like a number of points on a triangle from which it is possible to measure only a trifling segment of the dazzling expanses of spiritual realms. And yet merely the aspect of these azure distances, where all stars of the visible cosmos tremble like a golden morning cloud, which is merging with the sun, strengthens our vision and teaches it to gauge the height and weight of terrestrial things. Before the aspect of these promised and inaccessible kingdoms, the children of the earth nestle together in a feeling of inner brotherhood, which gives them hopes in common, and will give them one harvest of earth in common, riches of fields and gardens."

" Among those multitudes condemned to toil and hunger, there perish, perhaps, silenced singers who could have set their brethren's hearts astir with rapture of immortality, and in gardens of dream, where all echoes still recall the victorious chant of spirits at the creation of worlds, they could have plucked roses, for the paths of lovers and conquerors. In subterranean darknesses there are perhaps eyes growing blind, which were created that they might behold the most secret smiles of beauty and the signs given us by dwellers upon sister earths; perhaps the hands of betrayed princes are being maimed, which alone could have dared to open the treasure houses of their kindred, the secret granaries of age-long harvests, closed up by jealous years, and amid assuagement of fervour to hearken to some of the magical words from earth's monologue, when in her workshops she sets element beside element, and prepares the faery of her springtides for the marriage festivals of queens."

Aims.

There is one other poet, born during the sixties of last century, to whom attention must be drawn. This is P. Bezruč, an elusive personality, the author of a single volume of verses entitled *Silesian Songs,* which intone a fierce requiem for the " Seventy Thousand," the Czechs of Teschen and the surrounding district. By his unstudied but powerful art, Bezruč has elevated this localised theme of racial injustice to a plane upon which the appeal of its pathos becomes universal. On the strength of a mere handful of poems, the name Bezruč has become a household word, even beyond the frontiers of Czech speech. Yet their literary quality is far above the level reached by the versified rhetoric of the average socialist poet. Bezruč has poignantly felt the racial and social oppression of his people, and it is this emotional impulse which has enabled him to identify himself with the individuals whose destinies he portrays. This is the secret of his effectiveness. The outstanding features of his verse are so marked that they recognisably survive the process of translation. Here are two typical examples:

OSTRAVA

" A hundred years mutely I dwelt in the pit,
 A hundred years coal I hewed,
In a hundred years my shoulders were knit
 Stiff as if iron-thewed.

Coal-dust upon my eyes is smeared,
 The red from my lips has escaped,
And from my hair, from eyebrows, from beard,
 Coal clings icicle-shaped.

Bread with coal is my labour's prize,
 From toil unto toil I go.
Palaces by the Danube arise;
 From my blood and sweat they grow.

A hundred years I was mute in the mine,
 Who'll requite me those hundred years?
When my hammer made them a threatening sign
 They each began with their jeers.

I should keep my wits, in the mine I should stay,
 For my masters still I should moil—
I swung the hammer,—blood flowed straightway
 On Polská Ostrava's soil.

All ye in Silesia, all ye, I say,
 Whether Peter your name be or Paul,
Your breasts ye must gird with steely array
 And thousands to battle must call;

All ye in Silesia, all ye, I say,
 Ye lords of the mines below;
The mines flare and reek, and there comes a day,
 A day when we'll take what we owe."

Silesian Songs (1909).

I am the First of the Těšín People . . .

" I am the first of the Těšín people,
Firſt bard of the Bezkyds who uttered his ſtrains.
Of the foreigners' plough and his mines they are bondsmen.
Watery, milky, the sap in their veins.
Each of them has a God in the heavens,
Greater the one in their native land.
In the church they pay Him on high their tribute,
To the other with blood and a toil-seared hand.

He, He upon high, gave thee bread for thy life's sake,
Gave flowers to the butterfly, glades to the doe;
Thou, thou who were bred on the Bezkyd mountains,
To Him the broad lands beneath Lysá doſt owe.
He gave thee the mountains and gave thee the foreſts,
The fragrance borne by the breeze from the dale;
At a swoop the other has taken all from thee,
Speed unto Him in yon church, and wail.

Honour God and thy maſters, my son from the Bezkyds,
And this shall yield fair fruit unto thee.
Thou art chased from thy foreſts by guardian angels,
So humbly to them thou bendeſt the knee:
' Thou thief from Krásná! Is this thy timber?
Thou shalt sink down meekly, and earth shalt thou kiss!
Quit thy lord's foreſts and get thee to Frýdek!'
Thou upon high, what sayſt Thou to this?

But thine ugly speech is a bane to thy maſters,
To those guardian angels it is a bane.
Have done with it, thou shalt fare the better,
Thy son shall be firſt thereby to gain.
Thus it is. The Lord wills it. Night sank o'er my people,
We shall perish before the night be passed.
In this night I have prayed to the Demon of Vengeance,
The firſt of the Bezkyd bards and the laſt."

Silesian Songs (1909).

CZECHOSLOVAKIA

V

I turn to the Czech novel. As I have suggested, Czech prose developed more slowly than Czech poetry, and although during the nineteenth century there were several Czech novelists, such as Jirásek, who effectively evoked the past, it is not until the close of the century that we find anything like a European standard being reached in this respect. The Czech author who most deserves recognition outside his own country as a writer of novels and short stories seems to me to be Fráňa Šrámek (b. 1877). He has probably been influenced by Russian and Scandinavian writers, but he maintains a well-marked individuality. There is a curiously buoyant and whimsical cadence about much of his writing which renders it peculiarly distinctive, and, indeed, constitutes its chief charm. He is pre-eminently lyrical, and all his work is pervaded by this characteristic. His graphic and fanciful diction reproduces visual impressions with the utmost sensitiveness, and imparts a delicate romanticism to even quite realistic themes. His novel *The Silvery Wind* resembles in certain respects Joyce's *Portrait of the Artist,* and, in spite of a rather loose construction, it contains striking delineations of contemporary life. In his latest novel, *The Body,* his artistic methods are exhibited in what is probably the zenith of their development. Among the prose-writers of the younger generation, Šrámek's influence is manifest. The nineties had introduced an epoch of realism into the progress of the Czech novel, and one contemporary exponent of this tendency, K. Čapek-Chod (1860-1927), deserves to be mentioned. I should also point out that Karel Čapek, who is better

223

known here as a dramatist, has also written novels and short stories, some of which show remarkable insight into character. And this reference to Čapek leads me to Czech drama. The theatre was an important factor in promoting the national revival, but the plays themselves were rarely more than skilful imitations or adaptations of foreign pieces. As with the novel, the progress to a European standard has been slow, but there are signs, in the plays of Čapek and a few other dramatists, that it is being attained, and since the establishment of the Czechoslovak Republic the dramatic activity in Prague has been specially noteworthy.

VI

The effect of the War upon Czech literature was a complex one. In the first place, there were the War books, which were inspired by the actual experiences of their authors on the battle fronts in Albania, Russia, and elsewhere, and particularly among the legionaries in Siberia. This literature is very voluminous, and I can here mention only a few of those whose names are identified with it. Rudolf Medek and Josef Kopta have both written novels which have great documentary value as records of the epic events which they describe. Other ex-legionaries who have produced works of artistic value are František Langer, now also a successful dramatist, and František Kubka. Medek and Kubka have also written poems illustrating various aspects of the vicissitudes through which they passed during the long campaign. Life in the Austrian army prompted many writers, such as the famous poet S. K. Neumann, who described his military service in Albania, and more especially Jaroslav Hašek, who created in *Švejk, the Good Soldier,* a comic and already proverbial figure. Hašek was a great natural humorišt, and his three volumes about the exploits of Švejk, although uneven in quality, contain much firšt-rate satire.

Then, of course, the ethical and social problems, created or accentuated by War conditions, were also treated by a number of writers. The plays of the Čapek brothers may be assigned to this category. And nearly all the younger generation of Czech poets reveal a štrong social tendency in their work. It is probably only a passing phase, and in any case it produces the impression of being rather incoherent and experimental. Altogether, it seems likely that contemporary Czech literature will be richer in good prose than in good poetry.

VII

So far, I have said nothing about Slovak literature. As a matter of fač, it is a comparatively modern growth, and whereas modern Czech literature is a produč of revival, modern Slovak literature is a new creation. The use of the Sloval dialeč as a literary language is a comparatively new development, and it should be noticed that, although Kollár and Šafařík, who took so prominent a part in the Czech revival, were ačually Slovaks, they wrote only in Czech. The Slovak literary movement has a rather complicated political background, into the details of which it is not possible to enter here. The conditions under which the Slovaks lived before the War were not conducive to successful literary ačivity, but, nevertheless, they produced a few authors of significance, notably

Svetozar Hurban-Vajanský (1847-1916) and the poet who wrote under the name of Hviezdoslav (1849-1921). The latter's activities as a translator are somewhat analogous to those of Vrchlický among the Czechs. The younger generation is still in a formative stage, and its achievements so far may be regarded as promise rather than fulfilment.

PAUL SELVER.

HOLLAND

My task is not a very easy one. I have to deal with a subject incompletely known to most Englishmen. Dutch painting has always been appreciated in England, both that of the seventeenth century and the school of 1870, the Hague School, to which Maris belonged. And modern Dutch architecture is also fairly well known. But with Dutch literature—ancient as well as modern—the situation is quite different. Why? The reason can easily be found. It is the language, the Dutch language, which prevents foreigners from estimating it at its right value.

But my task becomes still more difficult. For I have not merely to write on modern Dutch literature in general, but chiefly on the influence of the Great War on Dutch literature—that is to say, on a subject which is only incompletely known to my readers. We can easily understand the difficulty, if we think of Holland's geographical position. It lies between the three most important countries of Europe, open to their influences. Moreover, every girl or boy in Holland who receives a better education than that of the elementary school knows his three modern languages (French, English, and German) so well that he can easily read and understand them. And in most literary periodicals, in papers, even, foreign books are reviewed on the same lines as our own. No translations, but the foreign books themselves! How would it be possible, then, to decide what part of the change in the literature is due directly to the War, and what to literary contact with the surrounding countries?

There was a literary revival in Holland about 1880, in poetry as well as in prose. The poetry sought the help and support of the English romantic poets, especially of Keats and Shelley, who since 1860 had met with a greater appreciation in their own country than they had had during the first half of the nineteenth century. They found the source of their inspiration especially in the imagination.

The prose, however, was closely connected with the French realists, who said that literature was merely the right description of reality. Imagination and reality, two principles which were the antithesis of each other, and which could only unite in one literary movement if there were a strong tie to bind them. This tie was the new and strong sense of beauty, or rather, the worship of beauty. Both repeated Keats' words: " Beauty is truth, truth beauty," but emphasised different halves of the sentence, poetry that beauty is truth, prose that truth is beauty. Both, however, had a passion for beauty—one of the poets (Jacques Perk) even worshipped Beauty in an imitation of the Lord's Prayer:

> " Beauty, Thou, whose name be hallowed,
> Thy will be done, Thy kingdom come."

But if we penetrate below the surface we find this one powerful movement divided into two separate lines—one romantic, one realistic.

First of all, the romantic; chiefly, though not wholly poetry. The man who was most conscious of the new movement was Willem Kloos, poet and critic, and at the same time an eminent propagandiſt of the new poetic sense. The beſt representative, however, is Herman Gorter, who, by his allegoric poem " May," illuſtrated what this movement wanted and what was its weak point. It will, therefore, be necessary, firſt of all, to say a few words about this poem.

May, one of the twelve ſiſters who ſtand on the moon hand in hand, descends to earth and wanders on the beach of Holland. She meets Balder, the god who has become blind, and who since then has been roaming the earth in loneliness. And when May has once seen him, her only desire is to reclaim, to be reunited with him. At laſt she finds him, confesses her love for him, but Balder refuses her.

> "It never can be that I liſten to another,
> I, Balder, for I am blind and never see
> Anything but myself, nor you, my child——"

And May dies of grief.

Now May is meant to represent the beauty of the earth in its fulleſt glory, the beauty which everyone of us can see with his own eyes, can hear with his own ears—in short, can observe with his own senses. But this is not the real Beauty; it is only the form in which Beauty reveals itself. Abſtraċt Beauty, the idea of Beauty, free of all temporary revelation, Gorter means to find in his heart only. It is Balder who is the prophet of this Beauty. And Balder is blind; he can see nothing but his own soul; he refuses any conneċtion with the world around him.

Such was the poet of 1880, a pure individualiſt who did not maintain sufficient conneċtion with the surrounding world, and who, therefore, perished in the observation of his own soul, in the exploitation of his own emotions, merely for the purpose of beauty.

One of these poets, however, Albert Verwey, understood at last that beauty was not everything in life. He understood that being a poet did not necessarily mean abstaining from social and cultural life, but that a higher literary attitude was possible, not based on a merely poetical constitution, but on a poetical *personality*. It was around him and his periodical *De Beweging* ("The Movement") that the greater part of the younger generation gathered.

These younger poets were not merely poets in the sense of creatures infatuated with beauty, but they were first of all *personalities,* men of wide, deep, and brilliant knowledge, but who, on the other hand, had learned from the previous generation how to express their inner feelings in forms of beauty. I cannot speak about all these poets. It would take, at least, as many hours as there were persons. For these poets did not constitute a strong literary unity; they differed greatly one from another, and they were only possible because of the great revival of beauty which had gone before, because they were the crown of that revival. I may, however, mention a few names: P. C. Boutens, Henriette Roland Holst, P. N. van Eyck, Geerten, Gossaert, A. Roland Holst, J. H. Leopold, J. C. Bloem, M. Nyhoff, J. W. F. Werumeus Buning. Most of these poets were in full strength in 1914, when the War broke out.

So much for the poetry. And now the prose. I have already told how in prose the doctrine was taught: beauty is the right description of reality. The man who propagated this opinion in Holland was Lodewijk van Deyssel. The beſt writer, however, was Jac. van Looy, painter and author.

At firſt these authors gave their attention to every detail of their piſtures. An old tree trunk, a simple flower, could be an objeſt of beauty equally with a charaſter, was as well worth describing. And they were surely right in that. Whether an author can produce beauty does not so much depend on the objeſt he describes as on the sense of beauty with which he looks at it. And we have already seen how very ſtrong this feeling for beauty was during the firſt years after 1880.

But later on the author's eye is no longer so completely occupied with what it sees at firſt sight, and man—not his outer appearance, but his inner being, his aſtions—asks more and more for his attention. We get the psychological novel. This novel remains a realiſtic one; the author's purpose continues to be the observation of reality, as before. But a new element is added—psychological analysis—and by that new element the aſtions of the persons described become more and more important; we get novels inſtead of piſtures. Two of the beſt authors are here—J. de Meeſter and H. Robbers.

And in ſtill later years a second type of novel takes its place beside this psychological one. In these novels the authors no longer paint their surroundings, the reality in which they live; they paint themselves, their own ideas, their own thoughts, their own beliefs, their own personality. They are no longer free in describing the persons and things they want, but they are only able to describe those persons and things with which they feel themselves intimately conneſted. An example of this kind of litera-

ture is Ina Boudier-Bakker's *Poverty,* which describes a
family, all with different characters, but yet of one
general type—that is to say, the type which bends under
the burden of a feeling of poverty, the personal feeling
of the authoress herself.

With this kind of novel we have moved from the
realistic to the romantic, from the objective to the individual.

The authors I have hitherto mentioned were in full
strength in 1914, when the Great War broke out, and it
seems desirable to discuss, first of all, the influence of the
War on this generation before passing over to the younger
authors, whose ideas were chiefly formed during the War
or shortly after.

Robbers, the writer of *The Tale of a Household,* has
written a few pages on this subject. He tells us how complete was the astonishment that such a thing as this War—
a combination of perfidiousness and cruelty—was possible
in this civilised world, how everybody took it as a bad
dream which would be over in a short time, but how war
lasted on and on from month to month, from year to year,
how people grew sick of war and sick of reading papers
about it, and sick of hearing of new cruelties, and how at
last they tried to avoid, as much as possible, contact with
this bad world outside, how they withdrew into the few
happy hours of family life or other pleasures which were
kept intact from this world of bloodshed, poverty, cold,
and hunger, how they retired into the illusion of their
work, even of writing novels.

Couperus might here be taken as an example. He
wrote historical novels on the period of the Roman
emperors during this modern war. But perhaps Couperus

is not a very fair example. For this is the attitude which is characteristic of Couperus' deepest personality. His attitude towards life is: to avoid hard reality, to save himself in his illusions, to try to be happy in his illusions. There are other examples, however. First of all, Robbers himself. And also van Looy, who during the first years of the War wrote his best book, *Jaapje,* recollections of his own youth, a very monotonous youth, in an orphanage at Haarlem. A wonderful book this, a book of perfect beauty, and typically Dutch too. But I must not discuss it at present; we have to go on with our subject—the influence of the War on the grown-up generation. For, I am glad to say, there was a deeper influence. Robbers expresses it like this: We all became more earnest and began to think more deeply, many of us became more simple and human through the suffering, saw better what was essential in life. And just because, once again—and now so very distinctly—it had become clear to us what very poor fellows we all were; just because of that, we felt more sympathy with each other. It seemed as if hate and jealousy were reigning. But in the meantime, also, brotherly love was wandering about and pity was weeping.

This is the feeling which is dominant in the latest novel of C. and M. Scharten-Antink, *The Youth of Francesco Campana,* which in a very short time became popular. Francesco Campana is the grandson of an old Italian peasant, who has taught him that Love is the ruling principle of the world. God is Love. But when Francesco grows up, doubt begins its work in his heart. What he sees is the contrary. The insects which God has created have a perfect mechanism for the killing of other insects.

And men are no better; they are more inclined to harm their fellow-creatures than to love them. It is not Love that reigns in the world, but Hate and Egoism.

But in later years, when he grows older, he finds an explanation in his belief in an invisible world, behind the visible one. Hate and Egoism are the ruling power in the visible world, but they are only a semblance. And in the essential world, the invisible world, Love is the only reigning principle!

The War breaks out, an outburst of hate which overwhelms everybody. Nobody is strong enough to withdraw from the suggestion of war.

Francesco has to become a soldier. He, the fervent seeker after Love, a servant of Hate! Still, he goes. For even among the soldiers, the servants of Hate, there is Love. Through their bloodshed and cruelty a new, unexpected Love reveals itself. And Francesco serves " the brotherhood of the damned" till he is drowned in a submarine.

This book illustrates in an effective way what I have already said about the influence of war. If Francesco had acted consistently with his dualistic theories, he ought to have refused to join the army and rather have died a martyr for his kingdom of Love. But the excitement and the suggestion of war carry them all away, even Francesco. Francesco is astonished that such an outburst of Hate is still possible in this civilised world to which he himself belongs, but, nevertheless, he is not strong enough to resist, and his principle of Love goes no further than this outburst of Hate allows it to go.

This is not so much an objection to the book itself, for the fascination of war is beautifully described and very impressive. It is more an objection to the behaviour of Francesco himself. And at the same time it is a characteristic of the generation to which Francesco belonged.

For, of all the books that have been written in Holland during the last five years, this is by far the most popular. I know that several conditions and qualities contribute to such a popularity, but the chief of all is this: that the ideas which are proclaimed in the book are also alive among its readers, that a book like this expresses the thoughts that live among men.

Before I come to speak of the influence of the War on the younger generation—that is to say, the generation that was formed during and after the War—I must make two remarks. First of all, it is impossible to define the influence of the War apart from other influences. The only thing we can do is to consider the development of their ideas in general, and to say that this development is partly due to the influence of the War.

And, secondly, I have to restrict myself principally to the generation in Holland itself, and leave out the important group of young Flemish authors such as Wies Moens, although they write in a language which is very closely connected with the language of Holland, which is also part of the Dutch language. The War influenced each of these two countries in a totally different way. In Holland we find the influence of the French. For Flanders, which for years, for centuries even, had to defend its language against the Walloons, French is the natural enemy, and it is therefore almost impossible for French civilisation to impose its influence consciously. On the other hand, during the War, when Flanders was occupied by the Germans, the Flemish intellectuals were in constant contact with German cultured life. A stronger influence from the German side may therefore be expected.

But there is still another, even more important, reason why Flanders and Holland should differ so much. Flanders was part of a country which actually took part in the War; Holland remained neutral.

We sometimes find the idea that the War affected neutral countries less than the countries which were at war themselves. This idea is definitely wrong. It affected them in a different way, that is all. The combatant countries had to act; they were so full of action that there was hardly any time left to think of the problem of war. With us, the greater part of our people, all our best men from eighteen to thirty, were on the frontiers, ready to fight—waiting. They saw the action going on on both sides, and looked on, and could think.

There is a little poem, written in war-time by an older poet (Adema van Scheltema), which expresses this attitude :

> " We, too, who stood bewildered,
> Listening after this hour of judgment,
> We, too, were wounded,
> Were marked by this fire.
>
> We, too, who did not fight,
> Lost something during the battle.
> We lost our past,
> Like a withered uselessness.
>
> Behind us the years are lying,
> So far away, useless and long.
> And what the future will bring,
> That seems so bitter and fright'ning.

HOLLAND

When we wish to consider the development of the younger generation, we can do that best by taking one separate section of society as an example, and by observing the change of thought amongst the members of that group. I will take the student class, and I do that deliberately, for the student class is a group of great variability. Every five years there is a new generation of students. And for this reason the power of tradition in the student class is not so strong as in the outside world. Moreover, the students' world is the world of the young people who stand on the threshold of life and who feel all the deeper because they are young.

And I think I am entitled to do so, because there is at present in Holland a strong connection between students and authors. By far the greater part of our authors have had an academic education, have led a student's life. They are especially discussed and appreciated in students' circles.

This has not always been so. Van Eeden, the author of *Little Johannes,* said in 1886 (the year in which *Little Johannes* was published) that all the permanent, real knowledge he had acquired he had learned outside the students' world. But the student class he calls "full of half-barbarous and backward manners." The students had no interest in the great movement of the world at that time.

But soon after that a revolution took place in the students' life. They developed social feelings, and consequently political and social differences penetrated the students' circle also. Their class was divided into parties.

But since 1914 the students have been far less certain about their political and social principles. The principles have become problems. There is a great, unrest and un-certainty. To be at ease is said to be unsafe. There is the feeling that " we lost our past like a withered uselessness." The old world has collapsed, and our task is to build a new one on the ruins of the old.

This is felt to be a difficult task, almost an impossible one. For we mostly find no fervent desire and no strong will to build up that new world, but long and sad com-plaints about the uncertainty, even the hopelessness, of building. It sometimes seems as if the support of the powerful tradition has fallen away, and yet the young generation is too weak to walk on its own legs.

> " Behind us the years are lying,
> So far away, useless and long,
> And what the future will bring
> That seems so bitter and fright'ning."

And the secretary of one of the students' clubs ex-presses this feeling in the following way : " The new style of life will not have been attained until we have proceeded further than thinking and trying, and the lives of the young students have too much intellectual ballast to feel totally free."

When we wish to consider this same development in literature, we receive great help from a beautiful anthology of modern poetry called *New Sounds* (*Nieuwe Geluiden*), by Dirk Coster. For the new literary life is not restricted to one circle or class, it grows up every-where. And the poetry which reveals this new life is pub-lished in all kinds of small and out-of-the-way periodicals. After the style of the German anthology, *Menschheits-dämmerung,* Coster has collected the best of these poems in his book, and written a beautiful introduction to them.

HOLLAND

He especially considers the versification of modern poetry, and finds that the generation of Bloem, van Eyck, and Gossaert were perfect masters of rhyme and rhythm. Sometimes we find a really astonishing feeling for poetical construction even in their first poems. Gossaert describes how he rides through the dunes towards the beach. And in a small poem of only three short stanzas ("Thalassa") are rendered the rest of the night, the calm step of the horse, a sudden unrest, the unexpected canter of the horse, the tiresome climb of the dune, the sudden halt on the dune top, the immense feeling of the wide sea in front.

But now, during war-time, this remarkable versification declines, the poetical construction collapses. Rhyme and metre have become *quantité négligeable*. And we get the immediate, the direct pouring out of the poet's feelings in free verses. A poem becomes an abundance of feelings poured out from the poet's heart.

These free verses did not have a very long life, however. The danger that they would become an utterance without a strong passion as driving power—that is to say, that they should become rhetorical—was too great. And so—only ten years later—this sudden, strong stream of emotion was forced again into dykes. A generation with strong powers of poetical construction has already taken its place.

Still, a change occurred in the meantime. This stream of passionate feeling broke down several barriers, and brought about a connecting link between feelings and words, between emotion and expression, where this seemed impossible before, and has created new poetical possibilities.

It is a very remarkable change, a revolution such as we had never seen before. So ſtrong that the poetical media which we had already possessed for centuries, and which we thought we could not do without, suddenly gave way. And at the same time so rapidly that some of the less important poets (like Verhoeven) went through all three ſtates successively, and wrote poems in all three manners.

Coſter gives the following explanation for this remarkable change. Before the War we were all romantic—that is to say, we had the inclination to isolate ourselves from the world. Since the War, when the old world collapsed, a new principle, just the opposite, broke through. We no longer isolated ourselves from the world; we surrendered to the world. And this surrendering to life was represented in poetry by free verse, and, later on, by the new poetic ſtyle.

This explanation, no doubt, is a profound and brilliant one. It enables us to underſtand a very prominent faċt in modern literature, the reason why we find the new symptoms less in prose than in poetry.

For, if I had to discuss the new ſtyle in prose only, I should hardly know what to mention. Perhaps one or two names, like R. Houwink, and even he only gave short visions in prose, no novels.

For poetry, however, we have quite a number of representatives, of whom H. Marsman, J. Slauwerhoff, and H. van Elro are the principal ones.

Why is that? If we think of Coſter's explanation, we can easily underſtand. A surrendering to life is only a short aċt, the deed of a single moment! And that is for me the principal charaċteriſtic of many modern poems.

HOLLAND

I often get the feeling that the poet is diving in the stream of the world around him, trying to grasp the essentials of life in one short and deep emotion, trying to express it in one line, a few words, a short and abrupt poem. And this is not an attitude suitable for longer works like novels.

This example illustrates the importance of Coster's explanation. There are, however, some objections to be made. First of all, Coster does not devote sufficient attention to foreign influences. And the poetry of other countries has certainly influenced the development in Holland to an important extent. We cannot, for instance, talk about free verse without mentioning the name of Walt Whitman, whose *Leaves of Grass* has been translated and was even more widely read in the original. But here again we are checked by the difficulty which I have already mentioned: it is impossible to make out which part of the change in literature is due to foreign influences and which part is direct development.

And, secondly, the collapse of the *old* world is not only due to the influence of the War. Especially not in literature. Literature has never been, and never will be, an even movement; it proceeds by means of undulations. Literature is not made by single persons who succeed each other unobserved; it is made by generations.

And here we have a new generation which had to create its own new literature.

It is remarkable to see how little the former generation interests them. They are nearly all alive still, and at work, but the interest of the younger people is not so much in them (though they are writing more and better) as in the rising generation.

And also the young authors themselves are only partly interested in their immediate predecessors. They are particularly interested in each other. They criticise each other, they write introductions to each other's works, they praise each other.

Some people say that they talk and write too much about each other. They are weighed down under the burden of their theories, but their production has been meagre up to the present.

This is the same objection which we have already heard made against the young generation in general. It also exists in literature. What we miss in present-day literature are the great personalities, the heroic figures, to carry those new theories on the shoulders of a new and powerful production.

These great figures have not come as yet. But we can understand that. Holland is a small country in the midst of three large countries. It has its culminating points, even in literature, and one of these was in 1880.

But it is a law of Nature that there must be retrogression as well. A people, and especially a small and cosmopolitan people like the Dutch, cannot always live at its highest point.

It certainly is not at its literary zenith now. But it has been; and I venture to say that in the future it most surely will reach this point again.

J. HAANTJES.

BIBLIOGRAPHIES

Note.—The bibliographies have been enlarged, in most cases, from material supplied by the respective contributors. In the absence in Japan of Professor del Re, the Italian bibliography has been compiled by the editors. An attempt has been made to record as many translations of contemporary literature as could be found. The list is inevitably incomplete, but it is hoped it will be found useful. Omission of any particular author from the bibliographies does not necessarily imply condemnation, but merely that for the purposes of this volume his work is irrelevant.

ENGLAND

H. P. Collins: *Modern Poetry.* Cape 1925.

Holbrook Jackson: *The Eighteen Nineties* (new edn.). Cape 1927.

J. M. Kennedy: *English Literature, 1880-1905.* Swift 1912.

Edwin Muir: *Transition.* Hogarth Press 1926.

Sherard Vines: *Movements in Modern English Poetry and Prose.* Milford 1927.

Harold Williams: *Modern English Writers* (1890-1914). Sidgwick and Jackson 1918.

Orlo Williams: *Contemporary Criticism of Literature.* Leonard Parsons 1924.

Scrutinies, edited by Edgell Rickword. Wishart 1928.

Lascelles Abercrombie: *Essay towards a Theory of Art.* Secker 1922.

Edmund Blunden:
The Waggoner. Sidgwick and Jackson 1920.
The Shepherd. Cobden-Sanderson 1922.
English Poems. Cobden-Sanderson 1925.
Poems. (Benn's Sixpenny Series) 1925.

Roy Campbell: *The Flaming Terrapin.* Cape 1924.

Norman Douglas: *South Wind.* Secker 1917.

T. S. Eliot:
Poems, 1909-1925. Faber and Gwyer 1925.
The Sacred Wood. Methuen 1920.
Homage to John Dryden. Hogarth Press 1924.

E. M. Forster:
Howard's End. Arnold 1910.
A Passage to India. Arnold 1924.
Aspects of the Novel. Arnold 1927.

Halcott Glover:
Wat Tyler and Other Plays. Kegan Paul 1925.
Three Comedies. Routledge 1928.

BIBLIOGRAPHIES

Robert Graves :
Poems, 1914-26. Heinemann 1927.
Poetic Unreason. Cecil Palmer 1925.
On English Poetry. Heinemann 1922.
Poems. (Benn's Sixpenny Series.)

T. E. Hulme : *Speculations.* Kegan Paul 1924.

Stephen Hudson :
Richard Kurt. Secker 1919.
Elinor Colhouse. Secker 1921.
Prince Hempseed. Secker 1923.
Tony. Constable 1924.
Myrtle. Constable 1925.
Richard Myrtle and I. Constable 1926.

Aldous Huxley :
Antic Hay. Chatto and Windus 1923.
Crome Yellow. Chatto and Windus 1921.
Those Barren Leaves. Chatto and Windus 1925.

James Joyce :
Dubliners. Grant Richards 1914.
Exiles (play). Grant Richards 1914.
A Portrait of the Artist as a Young Man. Egoist Press 1916
and Cape 1924.
Ulysses. Shakespeare and Co., Paris 1922.

D. H. Lawrence :
The White Peacock. Heinemann 1911.
Sons and Lovers. Duckworth 1913.
The Prussian Officer. Duckworth 1914.
Aaron's Rod. Secker 1922.
England, My England. Secker 1924.
The Plumed Serpent. Secker 1926.
Studies in Classic American Literature. Secker 1924.
Psychoanalysis and the Unconscious. Secker 1923.
Fantasia of the Unconscious. Secker 1923.

P. Wyndham Lewis :
Blast. 1914.
The Enemy. 1927.
Tarr. Egoist Press 1918.
The Caliph's Design. Egoist Press 1919.
Time and Western Man. Chatto and Windus 1927.

CONTEMPORARY EUROPEAN LITERATURE

Katherine Mansfield.
  Bliss. Constable 1920.
  The Garden Party. Constable 1922.
  The Dove's Nest. Constable 1923.
  Something Childish. Constable 1924.
  Journal. Constable 1927.

J. M. Murry :
  The Evolution of an Intellectual. Collins 1920.
  The Problem of Style. Milford 1922.

Wilfred Owen : *Poems.* Chatto and Windus 1920.

Herbert Read :
  Reason and Romanticism. Faber and Gwyer 1926.
  English Prose Style. Bell 1928.

I. A. Richards : *Principles of Literary Criticism.* Kegan Paul 1925.

Edgell Rickword : *Behind the Eyes.* Sidgwick and Jackson 1921.

Isaac Rosenberg : *Poems.* Edited by L. Binyon and Gordon
  Bottomley. Heinemann 1922.

Siegfried Sassoon :
  The Old Huntsman. Heinemann 1917.
  Counter-Attack. Heinemann 1918.
  War Poems. Heinemann 1919.
  Satirical Poems. Heinemann 1926.
  Poems. (Benn's Sixpenny Series.)

Edith Sitwell :
  Bucolic Comedies. Duckworth 1923.
  The Sleeping Beauty. Duckworth 1924.
  Troy Park. Duckworth 1925.
  Rustic Elegies. Duckworth 1927.
  Poetry and Criticism. Hogarth Press 1925.
  Poems. (Benn's Sixpenny Series.)

Sacheverell Sitwell :
  The Hundred and One Harlequins. Grant Richards 1922.
  The Thirteenth Cæsar. Grant Richards 1924.
  The Cyder Feast. Duckworth 1927.
  All Summer in a Day. Duckworth 1926.

G. Lytton Strachey :
  Eminent Victorians. Chatto and Windus 1918.
  Queen Victoria. Chatto and Windus 1921.

BIBLIOGRAPHIES

Virginia Woolf :
    The Voyage Out. Duckworth 1915.
    Night and Day. Duckworth 1919.
    Monday or Tuesday. Hogarth Press 1925.
    Jacob's Room. Hogarth Press 1922.
    Mrs. Dalloway. Hogarth Press 1925.
    To the Lighthouse. Hogarth Press 1927.
    The Common Reader (criticism). Hogarth Press 1925.

FRANCE

André Billy : *La Littérature française contemporaine*. Colin 1927.

F. W. Chandler : *The Contemporary Drama of France*. Boston 1920.

René Lalou : *Histoire de la littérature française contemporaine*. Crès 1922; Eng. trans. *Contemporary French Literature*. Cape 1925.

Eugène Montfort (ed.) : *Vingt-cinq ans de littérature française*, 2 vols.; illustrated. Librairie de France.

Daniel Mornet : *Histoire de la littérature et de la pensée française contemporaines*. Larousse 1927.

John Palmer : *Studies in the Contemporary Theatre*. Secker 1927.

Albert Schinz : *French Literature of the Great War*. N.Y. 1920.

Marcel Achard : *Voulez-vous jouer avec moâ*. N.R.F.

Alain (pseud. of E. Chartier) :
Les Propos d'Alain. N.R.F. 1906.
Mars, ou la guerre jugée. 1920.
Système des Beaux Arts.
Souvenirs concernant Jules Lagneau. 1925.
Eléments d'une doctrine radicale. 1925.

Guillaume Apollinaire :
Les Idées et les âges, 2 vols. 1927.
Propos sur le Bonheur. 1928.
Alcools: Poèmes, 1898-1913. Paris 1913.
Calligrammes: Poemes. 1913-1916. L'Hérésiarque et Cie. 1922.
Le Poète assassiné. 1927.

Henri Barbusse : *Le Feu*. Flammarion 1916.

Jean Jacques Bernard :
La Maison epargnée. 1920.
Le feu qui reprend mal. 1921.
Martine. 1923.

BIBLIOGRAPHIES

Jean Jacques Bernard (*continued*):
L'Invitation au voyage. 1924.
Le Printemps des autres. 1924.
L'Âme en peine. 1926.

Jean Richard Bloch:
Lévy. N.R.F. 1912.
Et Compagnie. 1918.
Carnaval est mort. 1920.
La Nuit Kurde. 1925.
Le Dernier Empereur. 1926.

André Chamson:
Roux le Bandit. 1923.
L'Homme contre l'histoire. 1925.
Les Hommes de la route. 1927.

Paul Claudel:
Art Poétique. 2nd edn. 1907.
Morceaux Choisies. 1925.

Jean Cocteau:
Poesie. 1916-1923.
Lettre à Jacques Maritain. 1926.
Orphée. 1927.

Roland Dorgelès: *Les Croix de Bois.* Albin Michel 1919.

Georges Duhamel:
Vie des martyrs. 1917.
Civilisation. 1918.
Confession de minuit. 1920.
Essai sur le roman. 1925.
Essai sur une renaissance dramatique. 1926.
(and Charles Vildrac), *Notes sur la technique poetique.* 1910.

Ramon Fernandez: *Messages.* N.R.F. 1926.

Paul Fort:
Anthologie des ballades françaises: 1897-1920. Mercure.
Louis XI., curieux homme. Flammarion 1921.
La Ronde autour du monde. Flammarion 1922.

André Gide:
Les Nourritures terrestres. N.R.F. 1897.
Saul. N.R.F. 1902.
Prétextes. N.R.F. 1903.
Le Retour de l'Enfant Prodigue. N.R.F. 1907.
La Porte étroite. Mercure 1909.
Les Caves du Vatican. N.R.F. 1913.

CONTEMPORARY EUROPEAN LITERATURE

André Gide (*continued*):
La Symphonie pastorale. 1919.
Dostoievsky. 1923.
Corydon. 1924.
Les Faux Monnayeurs. N.R.F. 1926.
Journal des Faux Monnayeurs. N.R.F. 1927.

Jean Giraudoux:
Simon le pathetique. Grasset 1918.
Suzanne et le Pacifique. E. Paul 1921.
Siegfried et le Limousin. Grasset 1922.
Bella. 1926.

Remy de Gourmont:
Le Chemin de Valours: Nouvelles dissociations d'idées. 1902.
Un Cœur Virginale. 1907.
Epilogues. 1903 onwards.
Les Idées du jour. 1918.
Lettres d'un satyre. 1913.
Une Nuit au Luxembourg. 1906.
Le Problème du style. 1902.
Promenades littéraires. 1904 onwards.
Promenades philosophiques. 1905.

Fernand Gregh:
La Maison de l'enfance. 1896.
Les clartés humaines. 1904.
Couleur de la vie. Flammarion 1923.

Pierre Hamp (pseud. of Bourillon):
Le Rail. N.R.F. 1912.
L'Enquête. N.R.F. 1913.
Les Métiers blessés. N.R.F. 1919.
Le Lin. N.R.F. 1924.
Théâtre. 1927-1928.

Jacques Maritain:
Art et Scholastique. 1920.
Reflexions sur l'intelligence et sur sa vie propre. 1924.
Réponse à Jean Cocteau. 1926.

Roger Martin du Gard:
Jean Barois. N.R.F. 1913.
Les Thibault, 4 vols. N.R.F. 1922 onwards.

François Mauriac:
Le baiser au lepreux. Grasset 1922.
Génétrix, 1923.

BIBLIOGRAPHIES

François Mauriac (*continued*):
  Le Désert de l'amour. 1925.
  Thérèse Desqueyroux. 1927.
  Destins. 1928.

Charles Maurras :
  Le Chemin de Paradis. Boccard 1895.
  L'Avenir de l'intelligence. 2nd edn. 1922.
  Athènes antique. Boccard 1918.
  Poètes. 1923.

Eugène Montfort :
  La Turque. Flammarion 1906.
  La chanson de Naples. Flammarion 1921.
  César Casteldor. Calmann Levy 1927.

Henry Montherlant :
  Le Songe. Grasset 1922.
  Les Bestiaires. Grasset 1926.

Paul Morand : *Ouvert la Nuit.* N.R.F. 1922.

Jean-Victor Pellerin : *Têtes de Rechange.* 1926.

Marcel Proust : *A la Recherche du temps perdu.* N.R.F. 1913-1927.

Raymond Radiguet :
  Le Diable au Corps. 1923.
  Le Bal du Comte d'Orgel. 1924.
  Les joues en feu. 1925.

Jacques Rivière :
  Etudes. 1911.
  (and Alain Fournier) *Correspondence:* 1905-14. 2 vols. 1926.
  (and Paul Claudel) *Correspondence:* 1907-1914. N.R.F. 1926.

Jules Romains (pseud. of Louis Farigoule) :
  La Vie unanime. N.R.F. 1908.
  Mort de quelqu'un. N.R.F. 1911.
  Odes et prières. N.R.F. 1911.
  Les Copains. N.R.F. 1919.
  Europe. N.R.F. 1919.
  Cromedeyre le vieil. N.R.F. 1920.
  Lucienne. 1922.
  M. le Trouhadec saisi par la débauche. 1922.
  Le Vin blanc de La Villette. 1922.
  Knock. 1924.
  Le Mariage de le Trouhadec. 1925.
  Le Dictateur. 1926.

CONTEMPORARY EUROPEAN LITERATURE

Jerome and Jean Tharaud :
Dingley l'illuſtre écrivain. E. Paul 1902.
La maîtresse servante. Plon 1910.
L'Ombre de la Croix. 1917.
Un Royaume de Dieu. Plon 1920.
Quand Israël est roi. 1921.
L'An prochain à Jerusalem. 1924.

Albert Thibaudet :
Le Bergsonisme (Trente ans de vie française). 4th edn. 1913.
Les Idées de Charles Maurras. 1920.
Paul Valéry. 1923.
Étranger, ou études de littérature anglaise. Genève 1925.
Le Liseur de romans. 1925.
La République des Camarades. 1927.

Paul Valéry :
La Soirée avec M. Teſte. N.R.F. 1896.
La Jeune Parque. 1917.
Introduction à la méthode de Leonard de Vinci. N.R.F. 1920.
Eupalinos et l'Ame de la Danse. N.R.F. 1923.
Poésies. N.R.F. 1923.
Variété. N.R.F. 1924.
Monsieur Teſte. N.R.F. 1927.
Charmes. N.R.F. 1927.

TRANSLATIONS

G. Apollinaire : *The Poet Assassinated.* N.Y., Broom 1924.

H. Barbusse :
We Others. Dent 1918.
Chains. Cape 1925.
Under Fire. Dent 1926.

J. J. Bernard: *Glamour. Martine* (in *Eight European Plays*). Brentano 1927.

Henri Brémond : *Prayer and Poetry.* Burns Oates 1927.

B. Cendrars : *Sutters Gold.* 1928.

P. Claudel :
The Eaſt I Know. Milford 1914.
The Tidings brought to Mary. Chatto and Windus 1916.
The Hoſtage. Oxford 1917.

BIBLIOGRAPHIES

P. Claudel (*continued*):
  Tête d'Or. Yale U.P. 1919.
  Three Poems of the War. Milford 1919.
  The City. Milford 1920.

J. Cocteau: *The Grand Ecart.* Putnams 1925.
  Thomas the Impostor. Appleton 1925.
  A Call to Order (includes *Cock and Harlequin, Professional Secrets,* and other critical *Essays.* Faber and Gwyer 1926.

R. Dorgelès:
  Wooden Crosses. Heinemann 1920.
  Saint Magloire. Collins 1923.

G. Duhamel:
  The New Book of Martyrs. Heinemann 1918.
  Civilization (1914-18). 1919.
  Stories and Sketches. Boston 1926.

R. Fernandez: *Messages.* Cape 1927.

A. Gide:
  Oscar Wilde. 1905.
  Prometheus Illbound. Chatto and Windus 1919.
  Strait is the Gate. 1924.
  Dostoievsky. Dent 1925.
  The Counterfeiters. Knopf 1927.

J. Giraudoux:
  Suzanne and the Pacific. Putnams 1923.
  Bella. Knopf 1927.
  My Friend from Limousin. Harper, N.Y. 1923.

R. de Gourmont:
  A Night in the Luxembourg (tr. Arthur Ransome). 1912.
  Decadence and Other Essays on the Culture of Ideas. 1922.
  Natural Philosophy of Love. Routledge 1926.
  A Virgin Heart (tr. Aldous Huxley). 1926.
  Book of Masks. J. W. Luce, Boston 1921.
  Horses of Diomedes. J. W. Luce, Boston 1922.
  Philosophic Nights in Paris. J. W. Luce, Boston 1920.
  Very Woman (Sixtine). Brentano 1922.

P. Hamp: *People.* Cape 1922.

J. de Lacretelle:
  Silbermann. Benn 1923.
  Marie Bonifas. Putnams 1927.

CONTEMPORARY EUROPEAN LITERATURE

J. Maritain : *The Philosophy of Art.* St Dominic's Press, Ditchling 1923.

F. Mauriac :
>*The Kiss to the Leper.* Heinemann 1923.
>*Thérèse.* 1928.

A. Maurois :
>*The Silence of Colonel Bramble.* Lane 1921.
>*Ariel.* Lane 1924.
>*Captains and Kings.* Lane 1925.
>*Mape.* Lane 1926.
>*Bernard Quesnay.* Cape 1927.
>*Disraëli.* Lane 1927.

C. Mauron : *Nature of Beauty in Art and Literature.* Hogarth Essays 1927.

P. Mille :
>*Two Little Parisians.* Lane 1913.
>*Under the Tricolour.* Lane 1915.
>*Barnavaux.* 1915.
>*Louise and Barnavaux.* Lane 1916.
>*The Monarch.* Blès 1925.

H. de Montherlant : *The Bull Fight.* 1928.

P. Morand :
>*Green Shoots.* 1923.
>*Open All Night.* 1923.
>*Closed All Night.* 1924.
>*Lewis and Irene.* 1925.
>*Europe at Love.* 1926.
>*East India and Company.* N.Y. 1927.
>*Earth Girdled.* 1928.

M. Proust :
>*Swann's Way.* 1922.
>*Within a Budding Grove.* 1924.
>*The Guermantes Way.* 1925.

J. Romains :
>*The Death of a Nobody.* 1914.
>*Doctor Knock.* Benn 1925.

J. and J. Tharaud : *The Shadow of the Cross.* 1918.

P. Valéry :
>*Le Serpent* (Intro. by T. S. Eliot). 1924.
>*Variety.* 1927.

GERMANY

Albert Soergel: *Dichtung und Dichter der Zeit—Im Banne des Expressionismus*. R. Voigtländer, Leipzig 1925.

Robert Riemann: *Von Goethe zum Expressionismus*. Dieterich'sche Verlagsbuchhandlung, Leipzig 1922.

Oskar Walzel:
Die deutsche Dichtung seit Goethes Tod. Askanischer Verlag, Berlin 1920.
Deutsche Dichtung der Gegenwart. Quelle und Meyer, Leipzig 1925.

Wolfgang Stammler: *Deutsche Literatur vom Naturalismus bis zur Gegenwart*. F. Hirt, Breslau, 2nd. ed. 1927.

Kasimir Edschmid: *Ueber Expressionismus in der Literatur*. E. Reisz, Berlin 1919.

F. J. Schneider: *Der expressive Mensch und die deutsche Lyrik der Gegenwart*. J. B. Metzler, Stuttgart 1927.

W. Knevels: *Expressionismus und Religion*. J. C. B. Mohr, Tübingen 1927.

Bernhard Diebold: *Anarchie im Drama*. Frankfurter Verlags-Anstalt, Frankfurt a.M. 3rd. ed. 1925.

Hanne Back: *Thomas Mann*. Phaidon-Verlag, Vienna 1925.

Richard Specht: *Franz Werfel*. Zsolnay, Vienna 1926.

Wilhelm Worringer: *Nach-Expressionismus*. Klinkhardt und Biermann, Leipzig 1926.

Fritz Strich:
Stefan George. Zeitschrift für Deutschkunde. Heft 7. 1925.
Rainer Maria Rilke. Zeitschrift für Deutschkunde. Heft 5. 1926.
Thomas Mann und die bürgerliche Zivilisation. Die Neue Rundschau. June, 1925.

Kurt Pinthus: *Menschheitsdämmerung*. E. Rowohlt, Berlin 1920.

Albert Sergel: *Saat und Ernte*. Bong, Berlin 1924.

Willi R. Fehse and Klaus Mann: *Anthologie jüngster Lyrik*. Gebrüder Enoch, Hamburg 1927.

CONTEMPORARY EUROPEAN LITERATURE

Fanny Johnson: *The German Mind*. Chapman and Dodd 1922.

H. W. Hewett-Thayer: *The Modern German Novel*. The laſt two chapters, *The Novel of the Great War* and *The War Unheeded*. Marshall Jones Coy., Boſton 1924.

G. P. Gooch: *Germany*. Benn 1925.

C. H. Herford: *The Mind of Poſt-War Germany*. The *Bulletin of the John Rylands Library*, Vol. 10, No. 2. July, 1926.

Albert Soergel: *German Literature*—article in *Encyclopædia Britannica*, 13th ed.

B. Deutsch and A. Yarmolinsky: *Modern German Poetry*. Lane 1923.

Maurice Muret: *La Littérature allemande pendant la Guerre*. Payot, Paris 1920.

Paul Colin: *Allemagne* (1918-21). Rieder, Paris 1923.

Camille Poupeye: *Les Dramaturges exotiques*. The article *Le Théâtre expressioniſte*. La Renaissance d'Occident, Brussels 1924.

Geneviève Bianquis: *La Poésie autrichienne de Hofmannſthal à Rilke*. Les Presses Universitaires de France, Paris 1926.

TRANSLATIONS

Stefan George: *Seleƈtions*, tr. by Cyril Scott. Elkin Mathews 1910.

Hugo von Hofmannſthal: *Lyrical Poems*, tr. C. W. Stork. Milford 1918.

Georg Kaiser:
From Morn to Midnight. Henderson 1920.
Gas. 1924.
Fire in the Opera House (in *Eight European Plays*). Brentano 1927.

Heinrich Mann:
Mère Marie. Paris 1927.
Liliane et Paul. Paris 1927.

Thomas Mann:
Bashan and I. Collins 1923.
Buddenbrooks, 2 vols. Secker 1924.
The Magic Mountain, 2 vols. Secker 1927.

BIBLIOGRAPHIES

Arthur Schnitzler:
Anatol. Paraphrased by Granville Barker. Sidgwick and Jackson 1911.
The Green Cockatoo and Other Plays. Gay and Hancock 1913.
Casanova's Homecoming. Brentano 1922.
Fräulein Else. Philpot 1925.
Professor Bernhardi. Faber and Gwyer 1927.
Beatrice; A Novel and Other Stories. T. Werner Laurie 1927.

Ernst Toller:
Masses and Man. Nonesuch Press 1923.
The Machine Wreckers. Benn 1923.
The Swallow Book. Milford 1924.
Brokenbrow. Nonesuch Press 1926.

Hermann Ungar: *Enfants et meutriers*. Paris 1927.

F. von Unruh: *Way of Sacrifice*. Knopf 1928.

Clara Viebig: *Daughters of Hecuba*. Allen and Unwin 1922.

Jacob Wassermann:
The World's Illusion, 2 vols. 1921.
The Goose Man. Stanley Paul 1923.

Frank Wedekind: *Tragedies of Sex*. Frank Henderson 1923. (Includes *Frühlings Erwachen, Erdgeist, Die Büchse der Pandora, Tod und Teufel*.)

Franz Werfel: *The Death of a Poor Man*. Benn 1927.

Stefan Zweig:
The Burning Secret. Allen and Unwin 1921.
Jeremiah. Seltzer, N.Y. 1922.
Passion and Pain. Chapman and Hall 1924.
Conflicts. Allen and Unwin 1928.

SPAIN

Rafael Altamira y Crevea : *Historia de España y de la Civilización española*. Barcelona 1909-1914.

Azorín : *Los Quinteros y otras paginas*. 1925.

Aubrey F. Bell : *Contemporary Spanish Literature*. Knopf 1926.

C. E. Chapman : *A History of Spain (founded on Altamira)*. Macmillan, N.Y. 1918.

La Gaceta Literaria (a fortnightly periodical directed by E. Gimenez Caballero). Canarias 31, Madrid.

Ramón Menéndez Pidal : *L'Epopeé Castellane à travers la littérature espagnole* (tr. Henri Mérimée). Paris 1910.

C. Pitollet : *Vicente Blasco Ibañez, Les Romans et le roman de sa vie*. Paris 1921.

Revista de Occidente (a monthly periodical directed by J. Ortega y Gasset). Avenida de Pi y Margall 7, Madrid.

Salvador de Madariaga : *The Genius of Spain and Other Essays on Contemporary Literature*. Oxford 1923.

W. Starkie : *Jacinto Benavente*. Milford 1924.

J. B. Trend : *A Picture of Modern Spain: Men and Music*. Constable 1921.

Azorín (pseud. of José Martínez Ruíz) :
   La Ruta de Don Quijote. 1905.
   Castilla. 1912.
   Las Confesiones de un Pequeño Filósofo. (1904).
   Clásicos y Modernos. 1913.
   Al Margen de los Clásicos. 1915.
   Lecturas Españolas. Colección Española Nelson, London.
   Un Pueblecito: Riofrío de Avila. 1916.
   Don Juan. 1922.
   Doña Ines. 1925.
   Old Spain: Comedia. 1926.

BIBLIOGRAPHIES

Pío Baroja :
  La Lucha por la Vida:
    La Busca; Mala Hierba; Aurora Roja. 1904.
  Camino de Perfección. 1902.
  El Arbol de la Ciencia. 1911.
  La Ciudad de la Niebla. Colección Española Nelson, London.
  Memorias de un Hombre de Acción, especially *El Escuadrón
    del Brigante* and *Los Recursos de la Venganza.*

Jacinto Benavente : *Teatro.* Introduction by Gregorio Martínez
  Sierra. Colección Española Nelson, London. His most recent
  work is *La Noche Iluminada.* 1927.

José Bergamín : *El Cohete y la Estrella.* Biblioteca de Indice,
  No. 2.*

Vicente Blasco Ibáñez :
  It is difficult to give a selection of the works of this popular
  author. By far the best novels, in our opinion, are his early
  and little known works of a strongly regional Valencian
  character :
    La Barraca. 1898.
    Entre Naranjos. 1900.
    Cañas y Barro. 1902.

E. Giménez Caballero: *Los Toros, las Castañuelas y la Virgén.*

Américo Castro : *El Pensamiento de Cervantes.* 1925.

Enrique Diez-Canedo : *Algunos Versos.* 1924.

Juan Ramón Jiménez :
  Poesías Escogidas. 1899-1917. New York, Madrid 1917.
  Segunda Antologia Poética. 1898-1918. Madrid, Barcelona
    1920.
  Poesías, en verso. 1917-1923. Madrid 1923.
  Platero y Yo. Edited with notes, exercises and vocabulary by
    Gertrude M. Walsh. Heath's Modern Language Series,
    London.

Manuel Linares Rivas :
  El Caballero lobo. 1919.
  La Mala Ley. 1922.

Antonio Machado : *Poesías Completas.* (Ed. Residencia de
  Estudiantes.)

---

* The publications of the *Biblioteca de Índice* are to be recom-
mended to those who wish to acquaint themselves with some of
the youngest and most original writers in Spain.

CONTEMPORARY EUROPEAN LITERATURE

Ramiro de Maeztu :
Authority, Liberty and Function in the Light of the War.
G. Allen and Unwin 1916.
Don Quijote, Don Juan y la Celestina. Ensayos de simpatía.
1926.

Eduardo Marquina :
En Flandes se ha puesto el Sol. 1912.
Las Hijas del Cid. Leyenda trágica en cinco actos. 1912.
El Pavo Real. 1922.

Enrique de Mesa : *Cancionero Castellano.* (Introductory essay by Ramón Pérez de Ayala.) 1917.

Gabriel Miró :
Nuestro Padre San Daniel. 1921.
El Obispo Leproso. Segunda parte de Nuestro Padre San Daniel. 1926.

Eugenio d'Ors :
Esparragueras. 1921.
El Nuevo Glosario. 1921.
El Molino de Viento. Essays. Valencia 1925.

José Ortega y Gasset : *Meditaciones del Quijote.* 1921.

Ramón Pérez de Ayala :
Prometeo. Luz de Domingo. La Caída de los Limones.
Novelas poemáticos de la vida española. 1916.
Belarmino y Apolonio. 1921.
Tigre Juan.
El Curandero de su Honra: Segunda Parte de Tigre Juan.
(Complete Works, Vols. 18 and 19, 1926.)

Serafín and Joaquín Álvarez Quintero :
Teatro Completo. Madrid, 1923, etc.

Pedro Salinas : *Presagios.* Biblioteca de Índice. No 7.

Ramón Gómez de la Serna :
El Rastro. 1915.
Greguerías. 1917.
Pombo. 1918.

Gregorio Martínez Sierra : *Canción de Cuna.* Edited with notes and vocabulary by Rachel Alcock. Clarendon Press, Oxford 1923.

Ramón María Tenreiro : *La Esclava del Señor.* 1927.

Claudio de la Torre : *En la Vida del Señor Alegre.*

BIBLIOGRAPHIES

Miguel de Unamuno :
Vida de Don Quijote y Sancho según Miguel de Cervantes Saavedra explicada y comentada por M de Unamuno. 1905.
Niebla. Madrid, Buenos Aires 1914.
Del Sentimiento Trágico de la Vida. 1913.

Don Ramón María del Valle-Inclán :
Sonata de Primavera—Sonata de Estío—Sonata de Otoño—Sonata de Invierno. Memorias del Marqués de Bradomín. Las Publica Don. R. del Valle-Inclán. 4 vols. Madrid 1902-7; *La Guerra Carlista* (3 novels) : *Los Cruzados de la Causa* (1908), *El Resplandor de la Hoguera* (1909), *Gerifaltes de antaño* (1909).
Águila de Blasón: comedia bárbara dividida en cinco jornadas. Barcelona 1907.
Romance de Lobas: tragedia pastoril. 1912.
Voces de Gesta: comedia bárbara dividida en cinco jornadas. 1908.
La Pipa de Kif, versos. 1919.
Luces de Bohemia.
Tirano Banderas. 1927.
There is also a uniform edition of the complete works.

TRANSLATIONS

Azorin : *Don Juan,* tr. by C. A. Phillips. Constable 1923.

Pio Baroja :
Cæsar or Nothing, tr. by Louis How. Cape 1922.
The Lord of Labraz, tr. by Aubrey F. G. Bell. Knopf 1926.

Jacinto Benavente : *Plays,* tr. by J. G. Underhill. 3 vols. Scribner 1920-1923.
Include : *His Widow's Husband, La Malquerida, Evil Doers of Good, Bonds of Interest, No Smoking, Princess Bébé, The Governor's Wife, Autumn Roses, The Prince who Learnt Everything out of Books, Saturday Night, In the Clouds, The Truth, School of Princesses, A Lady, Magic of an Hour, Field of Ermine.*

Vicente Blasco Ibáñez :
The Shadow of the Cathedral. 1909.
Blood and Sand. Simpkin 1913.
The Matador. Nelson 1918.

Vicente Blasco Ibáñez (*continued*):
The Four Horsemen of the Apocalypse. Chatto 1919.
Sonnica. Long 1919.
The Cabin (La Barraca). Hurst and Blackett 1919.
Woman Triumphant. Constable 1921.
The Mayflower. Fisher Unwin 1922.
The Enemies of Woman. Fisher Unwin 1922.
The Torrent (Entre Naranjos). Fisher Unwin 1923.
La Bodega. Fisher Unwin 1923.
The Dead Command. Fisher Unwin 1923.
In the Land of Art. Fisher Unwin 1924.
The Mob. Butterworth 1927.

Gabriel Miró: *Figures of the Passion of Our Lord,* tr. C. J. Hogarth. Guy Chapman 1924.

Ramón Pérez de Ayala:
Appolonius et Bellarmin. Paris 1923.
La Chute de la Maison Limon. Paris 1927.

S. and J. Alvarez Quintero: *Four Plays,* tr. Helen and Harley Granville-Barker. Sidgwick and Jackson 1927.

Ramón Gómez de la Serna:
Echantillons. Paris 1923.
Cirque. Paris 1927.

G. Martínez Sierra: *Plays,* tr. J. G. Underhill and Helen and Harley Granville-Barker. Chatto 1923.
Include: *The Cradle Song, The Lover, Love Magic, Poor John, Madame Pepita, The Kingdom of God, Two Shepherds, Wife to a Famous Man, The Romantic Young Lady.*

Miguel de Unamuno:
The Tragic Sense of Life in Men and in Peoples, tr. J. E. Crawford Flitch. Introduction by Salvador de Madariaga. Macmillan 1921.
Life of Don Quijote and Sancho according to Miguel de Cervantes Saavedra, expounded with Comment by M. de Unamuno. Knopf 1927.

R. M. de Valle-Inclán:
The Pleasant Memories of the Marquis of Bradomin.
Four Sonatas. Constable 1925.
Divines Paroles. Paris 1927.

ITALY

H. W. Carr : *The Philosophy of Benedetto Croce.* 1917.

B. Crémieux : *Panorama de la littérature Italienne.* Paris 1928.

Angelo Crespi : *Contemporary Thought of Italy.* 1926.

Benedetto Croce : *La Letteratura della Nuova Italia.* Laterza, Bari 1914.

Francesco Flora : *Dal Romanticismo al Futurismo.* 1921.

C. H. Herford : *Gabriele D'Annunzio.* 1920.

L. MacClintock : *The Contemporary Drama of Italy.* Boston 1920.

Giovanni Papini and Pietro Pancrazi : *Poeti d'oggi* (1900-1920). 1920.

R. Piccoli : *Benedetto Croce.* 1922.

G. Prezzolini :
Tutta la guerra: Antologia del popolo italiano sul fronte e nel paese. 1920.
La Coltura Italiana. 1923.

Luigi Russo : *I Narratori.* 1923.

W. Starkie : *Luigi Pirandello.* 1926.

Luigi Tonelli : *Il Teatro Italiano.* 1924.

Karl Vossler : *Die neuesten Richtungen der italienischen Literatur.* Marburg 1925.

G. A. Borgese :
Rubé.
Tempo di edificare. 1923.
La vita e il libro, 3 vols. 1910-13.

Riccardo Bacchelli : *Il Diavolo al Pontelungo.* 1927.

Roberto Bracco : *Teatro,* 7 vols. 1905-10.

Emilio Cecchi : *Osteria del Cattivo Tempo.* 1927.

Luigi Chiarelli : *La Maschera e il volto.* Milano 1924.

Carlo Linati :
I doni della terra. Milano 1915.
Sulle Orme di Renzo.

CONTEMPORARY EUROPEAN LITERATURE

F. T. Marinetti :
>*Le Roi Bombance.* Paris 1905.
>*Mafarka le Futuriste.* Paris 1910.
>*Le Futurisme.* 1911.
>*Catalogue of Works by the Italian Futurist Painters.* Sackville
>Gallery. March 1912.
>*I Manifesti del Futurismo,* 4 vols. 1920.

Fausto Maria Martini :
>*Ridi, Pagliaccio.* Zanichelli, Bologna 1919.
>*La Porta del Paradiso.* Mondadori, Rome 1920.

Ercole Luigi Morselli : *Orione. Glauco.* Treves, Milano 1919.

Alfredo Panzini :
>*La Lanterna di Diogene.* Milano 1907.
>*Io cerco Moglie.* Milano 1920.
>*Donne, madonne e bimbi.* Milano 1921.
>*Diario sentimentale.* 1923.

Rosso di San Secondo :
>*La mia esistenza d'acquario.* Carro, Roma 1919.
>*Le donne senza amore.* Carro, Roma 1920.
>*Primavera.* Carro, Roma 1920.
>*L'ospite desiderato.* Treves, Milano 1921.

Renato Serra :
>*Le Lettere* 1920.
>*Esame di Coscienza di un letterato.* 1919. With English
>introduction. Oxford 1922.
>(*Complete Works in Course of Publication.*)

Scipio Slataper : *Il mio Carso.* Firenze, La Voce.

Ardengo Soffici :
>*Giornale de Bordo.* Firenze 1921.
>*Lemmonio Boreo.* Firenze 1921.
>*Primi principe de una estetica futurista.* Firenze 1920.
>*Kobilek.* Firenze.
>*Six Essays on Modern Art,* ed. G. R. Vincent. Oxford 1922.

TRANSLATIONS
G. D'Annunzio :
>*The Triumph of Death.* 1895.
>*The Virgin of the Rocks.* 1899.
>*The Child of Pleasure.* 1898.

BIBLIOGRAPHIES

G. D'Annunzio (*continued*):
The Romances of the Rose. N.Y. 1898.
Episcopo and Company. Boston 1896.
The Flame of Life. 1900.
The Dead City, tr. Arthur Symons. 1900.
Gioconda, tr. Arthur Symons. 1901.
Francesca di Rimini, tr. Arthur Symons. 1902.
The Honey Suckle. 1915.
Tales of my Native Town. 1920.

G. A. Borgese. *Rubé.* Lane 1923.

Luigi Chiarelli: *The Mask and the Face* (adapted by C. B.
Fernald). French 1927.

Benedetto Croce:
*What is Living and What is Dead of the Philosophy of
Hegel.* 1915.
Æsthetic. 2nd ed. (The first is incomplete.) 1922.
Philosophy of the Spirit. 1909-21.
The Essence of Æsthetic. 1921.
The Poetry of Dante. 1922.
Gœthe. 1923.
Ariosto, Shakespeare, and Corneille. 1921.
European Literature in the Nineteenth Century. 1924.
An Autobiography. 1927.

Grazia Deledda:
Ashes. N.Y. 1908.
After the Divorce. N.Y. 1905.
Nostalgia. 1905.

Giovanni Gentile:
The Theory of Mind as Pure Act. 1922.
The Reform of Education. Intro. by Croce. 1923.

Alfredo Panzini: *Wanted a Wife.* Brentano. 1923.

Giovanni Papini:
The Story of Christ. 1923.
Four-and-Twenty Minds. 1923.
A Man-Finished. 1924.

Luigi Pirandello:
Six Characters in Search of an Author.
Henry IV.
Right you Are if you Think So. 1923.
Each in his Own Way, and Two Other Plays. 1925.

Luigi Pirandello (*continued*):
    Shoot (Si gira). With bibliography by C. K. Scott Moncrieff.
      1923.
    The late Mattia Pascal. 1926.

Rosso di San Secondo:
    Passion de Fantoches, tr. Alfred Mortier. Paris 1926.
    The Stairs (in *Eight European Plays*). Brentano 1927.

Giovanni Verga:
    Maestro di Gesualdo, tr. D. H. Lawrence. 1923.
    Little Novels of Sicily, tr. D. H. Lawrence. 1925.

RUSSIA

Prince D. S. Mirsky: *Contemporary Russian Literature, 1881-1925.*
Routledge.

O. M. Sayler: *The Russian Theatre.* 1923.

C. Stanislavsky: *My Life in Art.* 1924.

A. Tairov: *Das entfesselte Theater.* Potsdam 1927.

Leo Trotsky: *Literature and Revolution.* Allen and Unwin.

B. Deutsch and A. Yarmolinsky: *Modern Russian Poetry.* N.Y.
1921.

M. Aldanov: *Saint Helena.* 1924.

M. P. Artsybashev:
The Millionaire. 1915.
Breaking Point. 1915.
Sanine. 1915.
Tales of the Revolution. 1917.
War: a Play. N.Y. 1916.
Jealousy. Enemies. The Law of the Savage. N.Y. 1923.

Leonid Andreyev:
Anathema. 1923.
Katerina. 1924.
The Seven that were Hanged. 1909.
The Life of Man. 1915.
He who gets Slapped. 1922.

Isaac Babel:
The Letter. Calendar of Modern Letters, April, 1927.
Cavalerie Rouge. Paris 1928.

Alexander Blok:
The Twelve, tr. Bechhofer. Chatto and Windus 1920.
The Twelve, tr. Deutsch and Yarmolinsky. Huebsch, N.Y.

Ivan Bunin:
The Gentleman from San Francisco. Hogarth Press 1922.
The Village. Secker 1923.
The Dreams of Chang. Knopf 1923.
Mitya's Love. N.Y. 1926.

267

CONTEMPORARY EUROPEAN LITERATURE

K. Chukovsky: *Reminiscences of Leonid Andreyev.* The Dial, November, 1923.

Ilya Erenburg: *Julio Jurenito.* Paris. Renaissance du Livre. 1925.

S. Esenin:
La Confession d'un Voyou. Povolotsky, Paris 1924.
Requiem. Paris 1927.

N. Evreinov:
The Theatre of the Soul. 1915.
A Merry Death and The Beautiful Despot, tr. C. E. Bechhofer in Five Russian Plays. Routledge 1916.
The Theatre in Life. 1927.

Maxim Gorky:
My Childhood. Werner Laurie 1915.
In the World. Werner Laurie 1917.
My Universities.
Fragments from my Diary. Philip Allan 1924.
Reminiscences of Tolstoy. Hogarth Press.
The Lower Depths. 1923.
Decadence (The Artamonovs' Business). 1927.

Z. Hippius: *The Green Ring.* 1920.

Vs. Ivanov: *The Child (Nation and Athenæum),* 1925.

Boris Pilnyak:
Tales of the Wilderness. Routledge 1924.
Bielonkonskoie. Paris 1924.
L'Année Nue. N.R.F., Paris 1926.

Alexei M. Remizov:
The Clock. Chatto and Windus 1924.
The Fifth Pestilence. Wishart 1927.
Sur le champ d'azur. Paris 1925.
Pierrot. Paris 1925.

Lydia Seifulina: *Virineya.* N.R.F., Paris 1927.

L. Shestov:
Anton Tchekhov and Other Essays. 1916.
All Things are Possible. Secker 1920.
La Nuit de Gethsémani. Paris 1923.
Dostojewski und Nietzsche. Köln 1924.
Les Revelations de la Mort. Dostoïevsky-Tolstoi. Intro. by Boris Schloezer. Paris 1923.

V. Shklovsky: *Un Voyage Sentimental.* Paris, Kra 1926.

BIBLIOGRAPHIES

A. Tolstoy :
L'Amour, livre d'or. Paris 1922.
Ibicus. Editions Montaigne. Paris 1926.

Sergeyev-Tsensky : *Transfiguration.* N.Y. 1926.

V. Veresayev : *The Deadlock.* Faber and Gwyer 1927.

Zamyatin : *The Cave.* Slavonic Review, No. 4. 1923.

Flying Osip, ed. Alexander Chramoff. Fisher Unwin 1925.
> Contains stories by Kasatkin, Shishkov, Pilnyak, Seifulina, Ivanov, Arosev, Kolosov, Semenov, and Zozulya.

"*transition.*" Shakespeare and Co. Paris 1927-8.
> Contains translations of plays, poems, and stories by Blok, Esenin, Fedin, Ivanov, Lidin, Pilnyak, Romanov, and Seifulina.

SCANDINAVIA

Ejnar Skovrup : *Hovedtræk af Nordisk Digtning i Nytiden*, 2 vols. Copenhagen 1920-21.

Richard Steffen : *Oversikt av svenska litteraturen*, vol 5 (1900-20). Stockholm 1920.

Fredrik Böök : *Resa kring svenska Parnassen*. Stockholm 1926.

Hans Ahlmann : *Det danske Parnas*, 1900-20. Copenhagen, 1920.

C. Rimestad : *Fra Stuckenberg til Seedorff: Den lyriske Renaessance i Danmark*, 2 vols. Copenhagen 1924.

Harald Nielsen : *Af Tidens Træk*. Copenhagen 1909.

Jorgen Bukdahl :
Norsk National Kunst. Copenhagen 1924.
Det skjulte Norge. Copenhagen 1926.

Illet Gröndahl and Ola Raknes : *Chapters in Norwegian Literature*. Gyldendal, London 1923.

The Oxford Book of Scandinavian Verse. 1925, ed. E. W. Gosse.

O. Friis : *A Book of Danish Verse*. N.Y. 1922.

C. W. Stork : *Anthology of Swedish Lyrics, 1750-1915*. N.Y. 1917.

F. A. Judd : *Under the Swedish Colours*. 1911.

Carl Gad : *Johan Bojer, the Man and his Works*. 1920.

H. A. Larsen : *Knut Hamsun*. Gyldendal, London 1923.

J. Wiehr : *Knut Hamsun*. Northampton, Mass. 1922.

TRANSLATIONS

SWEDEN

Sigfrid Siwertz : *Downstream*. Gyldendal, London 1922.

Sweden's Best Stories, ed. H. A. Larsen. American-Scandinavian Foundation 1928.

BIBLIOGRAPHIES

DENMARK

Herman Bang: *Denied a Country*. Knopf 1927.
Holger Drachmann:
 The Cruise of the Wild Duck. 1893.
 Byron in Homespun. Harrap 1920.
Jens Peter Jacobsen:
 Marie Grubbe. Scandinavian Classics. N.Y. 1917.
 Niels Lyhne. Scandinavian Classics. N.Y. 1919.
 Poems, tr. P. Selver. Blackwell, Oxford 1920.
Johannes V. Jensen:
 The Long Journey. Gyldendal 1922.
 The Cimbrians. Gyldendal 1923.
 Chriſtopher Columbus. Gyldendal 1924.
Martin Andersen Nexö:
 Ditte: Girl Alive. Heinemann 1920.
 Ditte: Daughter of Man. Heinemann 1922.
 Ditte: Towards the Stars. Heinemann 1923.
 Pelle the Conqueror. Sidgwick and Jackson, 4 vols. 1913-1916.
Johan Anker-Larsen:
 The Philosopher's Stone. Gyldendal 1924.
 Martha and Mary. Knopf 1926.
Henrik Pontoppidan:
 The Promised Land. Dent 1896.
 Emanuel. Dent 1896.

NORWAY

Hjalmar Bergman: *God's Orchid*. Gyldendal 1924.
Johan Bojer:
 The Power of a Lie. Heinemann 1908.
 The Great Hunger. Hodder and Stoughton 1918.
 The Face of the World. Hodder and Stoughton 1919.
 Our Kingdom. Hodder and Stoughton 1920.
 Life. Gyldendal 1922.
 The Laſt of the Viķings. Century 1923.
 The Prisoner who Sang. Hodder and Stoughton 1924.
 A Pilgrimage. Fisher Unwin 1925.
 The Emigrants. Hodder and Stoughton 1926.
Laurids Bruun:
 Van Zanten's Happy Days. Gyldendal 1920.
 The Promised Isle. Gyldendal 1921.

271

CONTEMPORARY EUROPEAN LITERATURE

Knut Hamsun:
: *Hunger*, tr. George Egerton (1899). Duckworth 1921.
Shallow Soil. Duckworth 1914.
Growth of the Soil. Gyldendal 1920.
Pan. Gyldendal 1920.
Mothwise. Gyldendal 1921.
Wanderers. Gyldendal 1923.
Victoria. Gyldendal 1923.
Children of the Age. Gyldendal 1924.
In the Grip of Life. Gyldendal 1924.
Segelfors Town, 2 vols. Gyldendal 1925.
Benoni. Knopf 1926.
Rosa. Knopf 1926.
Mysteries. Knopf 1927.

Sigrid Undset:
: *Jenny*. Gyldendal 1920.
The Garland. Gyldendal 1922.
The Mistress of Husaby, 2 vols. Gyldendal 1925.
The Cross. Knopf 1927.

Norway's Best Stories, ed. H. A. Larsen. American-Scandinavian Foundation 1928.

CZECHOSLOVAKIA

F. Chudoba : *A Short Survey of Czech Literature.* Kegan Paul 1924.

H. Jelínek :
Histoire de la littérature tchèque. Paris, Mercure de France 1902.
Études tchécoslovaques. Bossard, Paris 1927.

Count Francis Lutzow : *A History of Bohemian Literature.* 2nd ed. W. Heinemann 1907.

Paul Selver : *Otakar Březina: a Study in Czech Literature.* Basil Blackwell, Oxford 1921.

TRANSLATIONS

Comenius (Komenský) :
The Great Didactic. Black 1896.
The Labyrinth of the World and the Paradise of the Heart. 2nd ed. (The Temple Classics). J. M. Dent and Co. 1905.

Josef Čapek : *The Land of Many Names: a Play in Three Acts and a Transformation.* G. Allen and Unwin 1926.

Karel Čapek :
Letters from England. Geoffrey Bles 1925.
R.U.R. Oxford University Press 1922.
Krakatit. Geoffrey Bles 1925.
The Absolute at Large. Macmillan 1927.
The Macropulos Secret. Holden 1927.

Brothers Čapek : " *And so ad infinitum* " (*The Life of the Insects*). Oxford University Press 1923. Second impression 1924.

Czech Folk Tales, ed. Dr. J. Baudiš. George Allen and Unwin 1917.

Czechoslovak Stories. Duffield and Co., New York 1920.

Svatopluk Čech : *Songs of the Slave.* The Poet Lore Co., Boston, 1919.

CONTEMPORARY EUROPEAN LITERATURE

Alois Jirásek : *The Lantern*. In the review *Poet Lore*, Boston, 1926.

J. S. Machar :
Magdalen. Kennerley, New York 1916.
The Jail: Experiences in 1916. Blackwell, Oxford 1921.

T. G. Masaryk : *The Spirit of Russia: Studies in History, Literature, and Philosophy*. George Allen and Unwin 1919.

Božena Němcová : *The Grandmother: a Story of Country Life in Bohemia*. A. C. McClurg and Co., Chicago. 1892.

Selected Czech Tales (The World's Classics). Oxford University Press 1925.

Paul Selver :
Anthology of Modern Slavonic Literature in Prose and Verse. Kegan Paul 1919.
Modern Czech Poetry: Selected Texts with Translations and an Introduction. Kegan Paul 1920.

Karolina Světlá : *Maria Felicia, the Last Mistress of Hlohov: a Story of Bohemian Love*. McClurg and Co., Chicago 1900.

HOLLAND

Dirk Coster: *Nieuwe geluiden.* 1918-1923. Arnhem 1924.

Herman Robbers: *De Nederlandsche literatuur na 1880.* Amsterdam 1922.

A. Verwey: *Inleiding tot de nieuwe Nederlandsche dichtkunst.* 1880-1900. Amsterdam 1905.

J. C. Bloem. Poetry: *Het verlangen.*

Ina Boudier-Bakker. Prose: *Machten; Grenzen; Het beloofde land; Wat komen zal; Kinderen; Armoede; Het spiegeltje; De straat.* Drama: *Het hoogste recht.*

P. C. Boutens. Poetry: *Verzen; Praeludien; Stemmen; Vergeten Liedjes; Carmina; Lentemaan; Liederen van Isoude; Zomerwolken; Beatrijs.*

J. W. F. Werumeus Buning. Poetry: *In memoriam. Dood en leven.*

Dirk Coster. Prose: *Marginalia.* Criticism: *Nieuwe geluiden; Proza.*

Louis Couperus. Prose: *Eline Vere* (Eline Vere); *Noodlot* (Foot steps of Fate); *Extaze* (Ecstasy); *Majesteit* (Majesty); *Wereldvrede; Hoogetroeven; Metamorfoze; Psyche* (Psyche); *Fidessa; De stille kracht* (The Hidden Force); *Langs lijnen van geleidelijkheid* (The Law Inevitable); *De boeken der kleine zielen* (The Books of Small Souls); *Dionyzos; De berg van licht; Van oude menschen, de dingen, de voorbijgaan* (Old People and the Things that Pass); *Van en over mijzelf en anderen; Korte arabesken* (Eighteen Tales); *Antiek toerisme* (The Tour); *Antieke verhalen; Herakles; De ongelukkige; Van en over alles en iedereen; De komedianten; Iskander; Het zwevende schaakbord; Proza; Oostwaarts* (Eastward); *Nippon* (Nippon).

Lodewijk van Deyssel. Prose: *Een liefde; De kleine republiek; Verzamelde opstellen.* Criticism: *Verzamelde opstellen.*

275

CONTEMPORARY EUROPEAN LITERATURE

Frederik van Eeden. Poetry: *Ellen, en lied van de smart; Van de passielooze lelie; Het lied van schijn en wezen; Dante en Beatrice.* Prose: *De kleine Johannes I., II., and III.* (Little Johannes); *Johannes Viator; Van de koele meren des doods* (Depths of Deliverance); *De nachtbruid.* Drama: *De Gebroeders, Tragedie van recht; Lioba, Drama van trouw.* Criticism: *Studies.*

P. N. van Eyck. Poetry: *De getooide doolhof; Getijden; De sterren; Uitzichten; Het ronde perk; Lichtende golven; Inkeer; Voorbereiding.* Prose: *Opgang.*

Herman Gorter. Poetry: *Mei; Verzen; Een klein heldendicht; Pan.*

Geerten Gossaert. Poetry: *Experimenten.*

A. Roland Holst. Poetry: *Verzen; De belijdenis van de stilte; Voorbij de wegen; De wilde kim* (With strong War impressions). Prose: *De afspraak.*

Henriette Roland Holst. Poetry: *Sonnetten en terzinen; De nieuwe geboort; Opwaartsche Wegen; De vrouw in het woud; Het feest der gedachtenis; Versonken grenzen.* Drama: *De opstandelingen; Thomas More; Het offer; De kinderen; De arbeid.*

R. Houwink. Prose: *Maria.* Poetry (pseud. H. van Elro): *Hesperiden; Madonna in tenebris.*

Willem Kloos. Poetry: *Okeanos; Verzen; Nieuwe Verzen.* Criticism: *Nieuwere literatuurgeschiedenis.*

J. H. Leopold. Poetry: *Verzen I. and II.*

Jac. van Looy. Prose: *Proza; Gekken; Reisen; Feesten; Jaapje; Jaap; De wonderlijke avonturen van Lebedews.*

H. Marsman. Poetry: *Verzen; Penthesileia; Paradise Regained.*

J. de Meester. Prose: *Een huwelijk; Deemoed; Allerlei menschen; Over het leed van den hartstocht; Geertje; De zonde in het deftige dorp; Carmen.*

Wies Moens. Poetry: *De boodschap; De tocht; Opgangen; Landing.* Prose: *Celbrieven.*

M. Nijhoff. Poetry: *De Wandelaar; Vormen.*

Jacques Perk. Poetry: *Mathilde, een sonnettenkrans; Iris.*

BIBLIOGRAPHIES

H. Robbers. Prose : *De roman van Bernard Bandt; De bruidstijd van Annie de Boogh; De roman van een gezin* (The Fortunes of a Household); *Helena Servaes; Sint Elmsvuur; Op hooge golven.*

C. S. Adama van Scheltema. Poetry : *Van zon en zomer; Zwervers verzen; Eenzame liedjes; Levende steden; Uit stilte en strijd. Zingende stemmen; De keerende kudde; De tors.*

C. Scharten and M. Scharten-Antink. Prose : *Een huis vol menschen* (A House full of People); *De vreemde heerschers; t'Geluk hangt als een druiventros; De jeugd van Francesco Campana.*

F. J. Slauwerhoff. Poetry : *Archipel; Clair-Obscur.*

B. Verhoeven. Poetry : *De pelgrim* (selections).

Albert Verwey. Poetry : *Persephone; Demeter; Van de liefde, die vriendschap heet; Cor Cordium; Van het leven; Aarde; De nieuwe tuin; Het brandende braambosch; Dagen en daden; De kristaltwijg; Uit de lage landen bij de zee; Het blank heelal; De maker; De legende van de ruimte.* Criticism : *Stille toernooien; Luide toernooien; Proza.*

TRANSLATIONS

Louis Couperus :
> *The Books of the Small Souls.* Heinemann 1914-1918.
> *The Law Inevitable.* Thornton Butterworth 1921.
> *The Hidden Force.* Cape 1922.
> *Eighteen Tales.* F. V. White 1924.
> *The Comedian.* Cape 1926. Etc., etc.

F. W. van Eeden :
> *Little Johannes.* 1895.
> *The Deeps of Deliverance.* 1902.

H. Robbers : *The Fortunes of a Household.* Allen and Unwin. 1924.

C. and M. Scharten : *A House full of People.* Cape 1923.

INDEX

INDEX

INDEX

INDEX

INDEX

284

INDEX

INDEX

INDEX

INDEX

INDEX

INDEX

WITHDRAWN

JUN 2 7 2024

DAVID O. McKAY LIBRARY
BYU-IDAHO